W9-AHM-737

BY MARGUERITE YOURCENAR

NOVELS AND SHORT STORIES

Alexis ou le traité du vain combat, 1929;
in English, *Alexis*, 1984
La nouvelle Eurydice, 1931
Denier du rêve, 1934; revised edition, 1959;
in English, *A Coin in Nine Hands*, 1982
Nouvelles orientales, 1938; revised edition, 1963, 1978;
in English, *Oriental Tales*, 1985
Le coup de grâce, 1939; in English, *Coup de Grâce*, 1957
Mémoires d'Hadrien, 1951; in English, *Memoirs of Hadrian*, 1954
L'oeuvre au noir, 1968; in English, *The Abyss*, 1976
Comme l'eau qui coule, 1982;
in English, *Two Lives and a Dream*, 1987

POEMS AND PROSE POEMS

Feux, 1936; in English, *Fires*, 1981
Les charités d'Alcippe, 1956
Blues et gospels, 1984; photographs by Jerry Wilson

DRAMA

Théâtre I, 1971
Théâtre II, 1971

ESSAYS AND AUTOBIOGRAPHY

Pindare, 1932
Les songes et les sorts, 1938
Sous bénéfice d'inventaire, 1962;
in English, *The Dark Brain of Piranesi*, 1984
*Discours de réception de Marguerite Yourcenar
à l'Académie Royale belge*, 1971
Le labyrinthe du monde I: Souvenirs pieux, 1974;
in English, *Dear Departed*, 1991
Le labyrinthe du monde II: Archives du nord, 1977;
in English, *How Many Years*, 1995
Le labyrinthe du monde III: Quoi? L'éternité, 1988
Mishima ou la vision du vide, 1980;
in English, *Mishima: A Vision of the Void*, 1986
*Discours de réception à l'Académie Française
de Mme M. Yourcenar*, 1981
Le temps, ce grand sculpteur, 1983;
in English, *That Mighty Sculptor, Time*, 1992

How Many Years

HOW MANY YEARS

Marguerite Yourcenar

Translated from the French

by Maria Louise Ascher

Farrar Straus Giroux

New York

English translation copyright © 1995 by Maria Louise Ascher
Originally published in French under the title Archives du Nord
© 1977 Editions Gallimard, Paris
All rights reserved
Published simultaneously in Canada by HarperCollinsCanadaLtd
Printed in the United States of America
First American edition, 1995

Library of Congress Cataloging-in-Publication Data
Yourcenar, Marguerite.
[Archives du Nord.   English]
How many years / Marguerite Yourcenar; translated from the French
by Maria Louise Ascher.
p.   cm.
Second volume of the author's autobiography, the first of which
has the title: Dear departed.
1. Yourcenar, Marguerite—Family.   2. Authors, French—20th
century—Family relationships.   3. Cleenewerck de Crayencour family.
4. Nord (France: Dept.)—Biography.   I. Ascher, Maria Louise.
II. Title.
PQ2649.08Z51413   1995   848'.91209—dc20   95–3572   CIP

Rubens and Isabella Brant and State Portrait of Helena Fourment are
reproduced with the permission of the Alte Pinakothek, Munich. Helena
Fourment with Fur Cloak is reproduced with the permission of the Kunst-
historisches Museum, Vienna. The photo of the portrait of Charles-
Augustin Cleenewerck is courtesy of M. Georges de Crayencour. All other
illustrations are courtesy of the Petite Plaisance Trust, whose assistance is
gratefully acknowledged.

Excerpt from "Blowin' in the Wind," by Bob Dylan, copyright © 1962 by
Warner Brothers Music; copyright renewed in 1990 by Special Writer
Music. All rights reserved. Used by permission.

Contents

Illustrations

Genealogical Chart

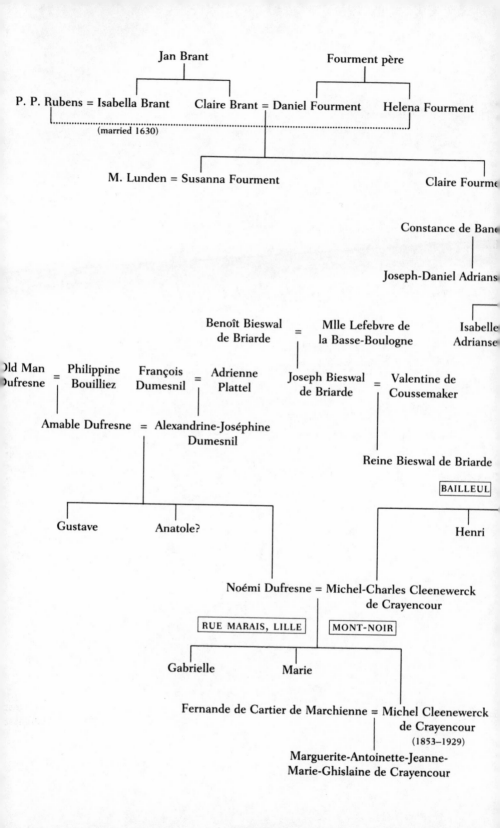

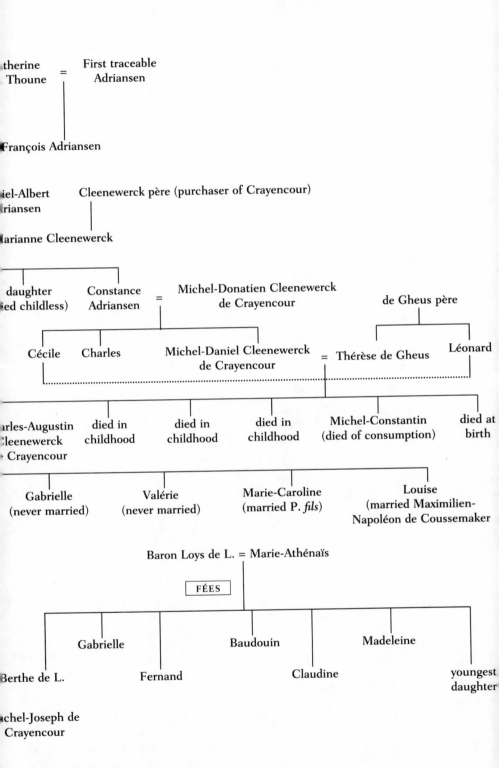

PART I

High-hearted son of Tydeus, why ask of my generation?
As is the generation of leaves, so is that of humanity.

—HOMER, Iliad, 6:145–46,
trans. Richmond Lattimore

THE MISTS

OF TIME

In an earlier volume, meant to be seen with this one as the two panels of a diptych, I tried to evoke a married couple of the Belle Epoque, my father and mother; then to pass beyond them into time's upper reaches, toward maternal fore-bears living in nineteenth-century Belgium, and eventually, with ever more frequent gaps and increasingly sketchy portraits, toward rococo Liège and even the Middle Ages. Once or twice, through an effort of the imagination, and temporarily abandon-ing that tightrope—the history of a family—which sustained me amid the past, I attempted to raise myself as far as Roman or rather pre-Roman times. In this book I would like to reverse the itinerary: to depart at the outset from remote, uncharted regions and arrive at last—narrowing proportionately the field of vision but defining and delineating the human personalities all the more clearly—at nineteenth-century Lille, at the proper but somewhat disjointed household of a wealthy bourgeois gentleman and his solid bourgeois wife, living under the Second Empire; and finally, at that eternally unconventional man who was my father, and at a little girl learning about life, between 1903 and 1912, on a hillside in French Flanders. If the necessary time and energy are granted me, perhaps I'll continue to 1914, to 1939, to the moment the pen falls from my hand. We shall see.

It is that family, or rather those families, whose intertwinings constitute my paternal line; but I'm going to try to keep my distance from them, to return them to their place, which is negligible, in the limitless expanse of time. Let's move beyond those long-dead people, those human dust motes, to a period when their existence still lay far in the future. And let's do the same with the settings: let's leave behind that place de la Gare, that citadel of Lille and belfry of Bailleul, that street with its "aristocratic air," that château and its grounds as they appear on old postcards depicting the landmarks and curiosities of the region. Let's take off, as it were, from the *département* of Nord—from the corner of it that once formed part of the Spanish Netherlands, and, in the even more rarefied altitudes of the past, part of the duchy of Burgundy, the *comté* of Flanders, the kingdom of Neustria, and Belgian Gaul. Let's fly over it at a time when it was still uninhabited and unnamed.

"Before the birth of the world . . ." intones Racine's L'Intimé pompously, in his comical legal argument. "Counsel, please! Let's proceed to the Flood!" exclaims the judge, stifling a yawn. And it's indeed a flood that concerns us here. Not the mythical flood that engulfed the whole world, not even some local inundation whose traces can be found in the folklore of the frightened inhabitants, but those immemorial high tides that throughout the centuries have alternately covered and exposed the North Sea coast, from Cape Gris-Nez to the isles of Zeeland. The earliest of those encroachments occurred well before the first humans appeared. The long rows of dunes slanting toward the east were submerged once again in prehistoric times, and yet again toward the close of the Roman era. As you cross the plain that extends from Arras to Ypres and that continues, oblivious to our boundary lines, toward Ghent and Bruges, you feel as if you're traveling over ground that the sea receded from only yesterday and might well return to tomorrow. Near Lille, Anzin, and Lens, beneath the humus that has been scraped raw by mining, are sunken layers of fossil forests, the geological residue of another, even more ancient cycle of climate changes and seasons. From Malo-les-Bains to L'Ecluse stretch the undulating dunes built by the sea and the wind, defiled nowadays by coquettish villas, lucrative casinos, small shops dealing in luxury goods or junk, not to mention military installations—all the clutter that in ten thousand years will be indistinguishable from the organic and inorganic debris the ocean has slowly pulverized into sand.

Mountains that elsewhere would be called hills—Mont Cassel, giving way in the north to the fourfold wave of the "Flanders Mountains" (Mont-des-Cats, Mont Kemmel, Mont-Rouge, and Mont-Noir, the last of which I know more intimately than the others because I spent my childhood on its slopes)—form humps on the low, flat land. Their sandstones, their fine sands, their clays are themselves sediments that little by little became terra firma. Fresh intrusions of seawater then eroded the terrain around them to the level we see today: their modest peaks are the evidence. They date from a time when the bed of the Thames extended toward Holland, when the umbilical cord between the Continent and what would eventually become England had not yet been cut. From other points of view, too, these hills are evidence. The plain that surrounds them was relentlessly deforested by the monks and villeins of the Middle Ages; highlands, more difficult to convert into arable land, tend to keep their trees longer. Mont Cassel, though, was denuded at an early date to make room for the entrenchments where one tribe took refuge from the attacks of its neighbors and, later, from Caesar's soldiers. War scoured its base at nearly regular intervals, as the tides of the sea had earlier. The other hills retained more of their forests, in which exiles and outlaws sought refuge from time to time. Mont-Noir in particular owes its name to the somber pines that covered its flanks prior to the futile holocausts of 1914, when artillery shells changed its appearance even more radically than they did in destroying the château built in 1824 by my great-great-grandfather. The trees gradually grew back, but as always in such cases, other species took over like relief troops: the black pines, so similar to those visible in the background of German Renaissance landscape paintings, no longer predominate. It would be useless to try to imagine the deforestations—and reforestations, if any—that will take place in centuries to come.

But we're moving too quickly: unable to stop ourselves, we're rushing down the slope that leads back to the present. Let's look instead at that world still unencumbered by humans, at those miles of forest alternating with open country that extend nearly uninterrupted from Portugal to Norway, from the coastal dunes to the steppes of what will someday be Russia. Let's re-create within us that green ocean—not static, like most of our representations of the past, but billowing and changing in the course of the hours, days, and seasons that flow away untallied by our calendars and clocks. Let's watch the deciduous trees turn color in the autumn and, in the spring, see the pines flourish their brand-new needles still encased in thin brown sheaths. Let's bathe in the almost virginal silence that is innocent of the sounds of human tools and voices, a silence broken only by the singing of birds or by their warning calls when some enemy, a weasel or a squirrel, approaches; by the droning of countless mosquitoes, at once predators and prey; by the growling of a bear searching the crevice of a tree trunk for a honeycomb, despite the attacks of fiercely buzzing bees; or perhaps by the dying gasps of a stag being torn to pieces by a lynx.

The Mists of Time

In the marshes brimming with water, a mallard dives; a swan, taking flight to return to the sky, fills the air with the sound of sails catching the wind; snakes glide silently over the moss or rustle through the dry leaves; the stiff grasses that crown the dunes sway in the breeze coming off a sea which has not yet been fouled by soot from any smokestack or oil from any engine, and on which no ship has ever embarked. From time to time, far in the distance, a whale sends up its mighty spout; dolphins leap joyfully, just as I remember seeing them from the bow of a boat laden with women and children, with hastily gathered assortments of household utensils and eiderdown quilts—a boat on which I found myself along with members of my family in September 1914, returning to uninvaded France by way of England; and the child of eleven was already vaguely aware that the blitheness of those creatures belonged to a world both purer and more divine than the one in which men inflict suffering on men.

We're tumbling back into human anecdote again. Let's regain our control. Let's revolve along with the earth, which, as always, speeds along in its orbit unaware of itself, that fair planet in the heavens. The sun warms the thin living crust, causes buds to bloom and carrion to decay, draws from the soil a mist that it afterward dissipates. Then great banks of fog mute all colors, muffle all noises, blanket the rolling plains and the ocean's waves in a single dense layer of gray. The rain, in turn, drives the fogbanks away, splashing on billions of leaves, refreshing the earth, nourishing the roots; the wind bends the saplings, topples old trees, sweeps over everything with an immense murmur. At last, only the silence reigns once more—only the stillness of the snow, its surface flawless except for the prints of hooves, paws, or talons, or the stars made by birds as they alight. On nights when the moon is full, its beams play over the landscape without there being any need for a poet or painter to gaze on them, without any prophet to foresee that one day clumsily caparisoned insects will venture through the dusty air of this dead sphere. And when the moonlight does not overpower them, the stars shimmer, in more or less the same positions they occupy today, but not yet linked together by the human imagination into squares, polygons, and triangles, and not yet bearing the names of gods and monsters that are of no concern to them.

But already on the scene, to some extent every-where: man. Man still widely scattered, furtive, sometimes dis-placed by the latest encroachments of the nearby glaciers, which have left few traces on this land without caves or crags. The king predator who hews down wild creatures and murders trees; the trapper who sets snares in which birds are strangled and stakes on which fur-bearing animals are impaled; the tracker who watches for the great seasonal migrations so that he can store up dried meat for the winter; the builder who strips branches and tree trunks of their bark; wolf-man, fox-man, beaver-man, uniting within him every type of animal ingenuity; the one of whom it is said, in rabbinical tradition, that the earth refused God a handful of mud to give him form; and of whom Arab accounts say that the animals trembled when they first saw this naked worm. Man with his powers that, however we assess them, constitute an anomaly in the larger sum of things; with his formidable gift of being able to go deeper into good or evil than any other living species that we know of; with his horrible and sublime ability to choose.

Comic strips and popular-science books depict this Adam

without glory, rendering him as a hairy brute brandishing a club: we are far from Judeo-Christian legend, in which the original man wanders in peace through the sylvan shade of a lovely garden, and even farther, if possible, from Michelangelo's Adam, coming to life in all his perfection at the touch of God's finger. Certainly he was brutish, that man who chipped and polished stones, for the same brute lives on within us; but that fierce Prometheus discovered fire, the cooking of food, and the resin-soaked stick that illuminates the night. He and his fellows were more skilled than we are at distinguishing plants that are edible from those that are deadly and those that, instead of providing nourishment, bring on strange dreams. They noticed that the sun sets further to the north in summer, that certain heavenly bodies revolve about the zenith or move regularly through the zodiac, and that others, in contrast, come and go, with capricious movements that are repeated after a certain number of lunar cycles or seasons; they made use of this knowledge in their nocturnal or diurnal journeys. Those brutes doubtless invented song, the companion of toil, pleasure, and pain right up to the present day, when humans have almost completely forgotten how to sing. Contemplating the forceful rhythms they imparted to their cave paintings, we can almost hear them chanting their prayers and incantations. Analysis of soil from their burial sites shows that they placed their dead on carpets of flowers arranged in complex designs, perhaps not very different from the ones that old women used to lay out along the routes of processions when I was a child. Those prehistoric Pisanellos and Degas felt the strange compulsion of the artist, which consists in superimposing on the teeming features of the real world a multitude of figures born of the artist's own mind, eye, and hands.

In the mere century during which our ethnologists have been at work, we have begun to realize that there is such a thing as primitive mystical lore, primitive wisdom, and that the shaman ventures along paths analogous to the ones which Homer's Odysseus or Dante took through the night. It is because of our arrogance, which continually refuses to endow men of the past with perceptions similar to ours, that we scorn to see in those cave paintings anything more than the products of a utilitarian magic; the relations between humans and animals, on the one hand, and between humans and their art, on the other, are more complex and go much further. The same disparaging formulas could have been used—in fact, were used—when cathedrals were seen as the result of a vast bargaining with God, or as a form of obligatory labor imposed by a bunch of greedy and tyrannical priests. Let's leave such simplifications to Monsieur Homais. Nothing prevents us from assuming that the prehistoric sorcerer, gazing at the image of a bison pierced with arrows, felt at certain moments the same anguish and the same fervor that any Christian feels before the sacrificed Lamb.

And next, separated from us by at most three hundred generations: the clever, skillful, adapted humans of the Neolithic, followed closely by the technocrats of the age of copper and iron; artisans dexterously performing the gestures that humans have made and repeated right up to the generation preceding our own; builders of huts perched on pilings and of dry-stone walls; hollowers of tree trunks that would become canoes or coffins; mass producers of pots and baskets; villagers whose back yards contained dogs, beehives, and grindstones; herders whose pact with their domesticated animals was continually violated by slaughter; those for whom the horse and the wheel were discoveries of last night or tomorrow morning. Hunger, defeat, a taste for adventure, the same east and west winds that would blow fifty centuries later beginning with the barbaric invasions doubtless drove them here, as their predecessors and successors were driven, or will be driven someday. A slender line made from the debris of many peoples formed periodically along these shores, just as nowadays on the same dunes, after a storm, one sees a fringe of algae, shells, and bits of wood that have been tossed up by the sea. Those people resemble us: put face to face with them, we would recognize in their features our own characteristics, ranging from stupidity to genius, from ugliness to beauty. Tollund Man, who lived during the Iron Age in Denmark and who was found mummified with a rope around his neck in a bog—where, it seems, right-thinking citizens of those days threw their real or alleged traitors, their deserters, and their effeminates as offerings to some goddess—has a face as intelligent as can be. In his agony, he must have passed judgment from a great height on those who judged him.

Then, all of a sudden, voices speaking a language of which we can still hear traces—isolated vocables, sounds, roots; mouths pronouncing more or less as we do the word "dune," the word "bran," the word "bit," the word "mill." Brawlers, braggarts, quarrelers, seekers of fortune, swashbucklers, and decapitators: such were the Celts, with their woolen cowls, their smocks much like the ones our peasants wore not long ago, their sportsman's shorts and their loose-fitting trousers, a fashion that would return with the *sans-culottes* of the Revolution. The Celts, also known as the Gauls (writers in antiquity used the two terms interchangeably), pulled in opposite directions by the chauvinism of scholars, fraternal enemies of the Teutons with whom they have carried on family feuds for twenty-five centuries. Tall youths, gaudily dressed and shabby, who were fond of beautiful bracelets, beautiful horses, beautiful women, and beautiful page boys, and who traded their prisoners of war for jars of Italian or Greek wine. According to ancient legend, those fiery-tempered men, in the course of one of their first treks across the low-lying coasts of the North Sea, advanced fully armed to confront the great incoming tides which threatened their encampment. That handful of men defying the cresting sea reminds me of the sieges that my childhood friends and I used to play at with feverish excitement on those same beaches, under that same gray sky, holding out to the bitter end in our forts of sand insidiously invaded by the water, waving our twopenny flags, totems of various nationalities, which in a few weeks would be ennobled by the bloody prestige of the Great War. Our schoolbooks continually reminded us that those spirited Gauls feared nothing, except that the sky might fall. More courageous or more despairing than they were, we have acquired the habit, since 1945, of expecting the sky to fall on us.

History is always written from the starting point of today. Histories of France that date from the early twentieth century, books whose first illustration invariably shows mustachioed warriors accompanied by a white-robed Druid, give the impression that the Celts were bands of primitives who, though no doubt sublime, were defeated in advance, propelled willy-nilly along the path of progress by the somewhat harsh attentions of a great civilizing force. Vercingetorix, who was strangled, and Eponine, executed at the mouth of her underground refuge, were reckoned up with the profits and losses. The student toiling over the *Commentaries* was a bit surprised that this victory over some worthy savages should have covered Caesar's bald head with so many laurels. The fifty thousand men assembled by the Morini of Thérouanne, the twenty thousand men called to arms by the Menapii of Cassel—even in the obscure backwater of Gaul, these reveal the nature of the duel between a military machine analogous to the ones we wield today and that vast and more vulnerable but also more adaptable world, which likewise possessed its millenarian traditions but which remained approximately at the stage that Greece and Rome had reached in the days of Hercules and Evander. Those roadless territories into which the legions forced their way were the home not of a handful of grimy natives but of a prolific people that, in the foregoing centuries, had more than once spilled over onto Rome and the Mediterranean Orient. We sense that, like a stream beneath a lovely stone arch, something is flowing throughout the four centuries of Roman domination: a Middle Ages of prehistory, which will join imperceptibly with our own Middle Ages. We recognize those turreted keeps in the forest, with their stakes and heavy beams, and those villages of mud huts coiffed with thatch. The Gallo-Roman auxiliaries stationed in distant frontier garrisons are the sons of Gaulish mercenaries seeking their fortunes in Ptolemaic Egypt and of Galatians flooding into Asia Minor. Beneath the oaks, hermits will replace the Druids preparing for eternal migrations. Legends of many a beautiful woman who was banished to the forest, where she and her newborn child were nourished by a doe, flowed from the lips of the old women of protohistory; people spoke in low tones of babies eaten by the ogre or stolen by water fairies, of the women who weave Death, and of journeys to the Otherworld.

But all is there: the shapes visible by the light of the villages set ablaze by Caesar (and that skilled tactician would soon put an end to such straw-fed fires, because the flames and the smoke betrayed the position of his troops to the enemy) are the distant faces of the ancestors of the Bieswals, the Dufresnes, the Baert de Neuvilles, the Cleenewercks, and the Crayencours from whom I am descended. I catch a glimpse of those who have said yes: the clever ones who know that the conquest will bring a tenfold increase in exports to Rome, for the people there are fond of smoked hams and of geese that are sent to them preserved or alive, waddling along under the eye of a little herder who is taking his time; they prize the fine woolens woven in Atrebatian workshops; they like the well-tanned leathers for their belts and saddles. I hear, as well, the yes of enlightened minds who prefer the Roman academies of rhetoric to the Druids' schools and who diligently set about learning the Latin alphabet; there is the yes of the large landowners eager to exchange their Celtic names for the triple appellation of the Roman citizen, envisioning for their children, if not for themselves, positions in the Senate or the military tribunes; and the yes of the political experts already weighing the advantages of the *pax romana*, which will in effect give this country—where the horrors of war are almost perpetually alive in people's memories—its only three centuries of security.

Those who have said no are fewer in number: they are the precursors of the villagers massacred in the Middle Ages by French men-at-arms, of those banished and tortured during the Reformation, such as a certain Martin Cleenewerck, who may or may not have been one of my relations, beheaded near Bailleul on Mont des Corbeaux (Crow Mountain). They prefigure the émigrés of 1793, loyal to the Bourbons just as their ancestors a century earlier had been loyal to the Hapsburgs; the timid, liberal bourgeois of the nineteenth century, who, like one of my great-uncles, hid their republican sympathies as if they were vices; the troublemakers like my ancestor Bieswal, who in the seventeenth century refused to have his coat of arms entered in D'Hozier, because it seemed to him that this process of registration was just another of the king's ruses for extorting a few gold coins from his subjects. Faces of eternal partisans, forest renegades, Gueux, restive parliamentarians, and outlaws. In Caesar's time, these people will take refuge in Britannia with Commius, their Atrebatian leader, beginning—or perhaps continuing—the incessant shuttling of exiles between the Belgian coast and what will one day be England. At a later date, they will be supporters of the movement led by Claudius Civilis, the Batavian rebel whose network will extend just as far. Those insurgents appear in our mind's eye much as they appeared to

Rembrandt: gathered in some underground room lit by a flickering lantern, slightly intoxicated perhaps, swearing an oath that they will destroy Rome or—what will be easier—destroy themselves in the attempt, raising high their fine glass chalices (imported from the Rhineland, manufactured in Alexandria, studded with barbaric jewels) and partaking together of their coarse luxury and their danger.

Already we can discern some of the characteristics of this wary and intractable people: the inability to unite except in the heat of the moment, a trait bestowed on them by the malicious Celtic fairies; the refusal to bend beneath any authority whatsoever, which explains in part the entire history of Flanders. But these attributes are often countered by others: a deep attachment to money and physical comfort that leads to an acceptance of any status quo, a fondness for fine-sounding words and earthy jests, a ravenous sensual hunger, a robust love of life that is bequeathed from generation to generation and that constitutes the only inalienable patrimony. Mark Antony, stationed here at the head of his legions in the intolerable winter rain while his commander in chief returned to Italy to take care of politics, must, like everyone else, have taken advantage of the comely, voluptuous girls whose bacchantic ardor elicited surprise and even a little alarm among English officers in 1914. In that land of carnal festivals, rape (as one of those soldiers would say) was unnecessary.

W_e can know a people well only through its gods. Those of the Celts are difficult to see from so far away. We catch vague glimpses of Teutates; Belenus; the Gaulish or Germanic mother-goddesses, a species of benevolent Fates; the moon god, guider of souls, who was assimilated to Mercury; Nehelenna, another benevolent mother-goddess, to whom travelers prayed in the seaports of Zeeland—anxiously when setting sail and gratefully when disembarking—and who must have been invoked as well farther to the south of those coasts; and finally Epona, queen of draft horses and of the ponies that preserve her name, mounted sedately on her sidesaddle with her feet resting on a small, narrow plank. But the images we have of these deities are Greco-Roman, or else crudely made. The religious artifacts which were found at Bavay, and before which my ancestors almost certainly prayed, are indistinguishable from those unearthed at sites throughout the empire: the Gaulish artisan revealed himself only here and there, and only through his clumsiness. When we think of the highly distinctive genius that was already apparent in the Celts' earliest coins, despite the techniques they adopted from Greece, and when we consider their talent for imparting movement to animal forms or extending and intertwining plant motifs—a skill that would reappear in the artists and illuminators of the Christian era— we have no doubt that those people could also have drawn their gods if they had wanted to. Perhaps they preferred them half-invisible, barely emerged from the stone yet sinking back into it, participating in the vague chaos of the unformed earth, the clouds, and the wind. Some of this ancestral refusal might explain the rage of the iconoclasts who would come along centuries later. "We ought not to give the Good Lord a face," a farmer once said to me in a church in Flanders, gazing with displeasure at some image of the Eternal Father.

In this region which Caesar, and Saint Jerome long after him, treated as a forgotten backwater, traces of the Druids are exceedingly rare; and they have become rarer still in almost all countries ever since it was discovered that the noble upright stones of Carnac and the monoliths of Stonehenge, the work of some prehistoric Le Corbusier, antedate those gatherers of mistletoe. Those priests who established themselves in sacred spots more ancient than they were remind us of the way Protestants used cathedrals after denuding them, or of the way Christians christianized the temples of Rome. In any case, the town of the Carnutes—that is to say, Chartres, their meeting place—was too close to Belgian Gaul for their influence not to have been felt here and there amid those lowlands and dunes. Just as the reverend fathers and abbots among my paternal forebears would one day go to Louvain, Paris, and even Rome to complete their studies, some of those young Menapii who had little taste for their tribesmen's violent way of life must have entered druidical seminaries on the isle of Britannia, as was customary among Celts from the Continent. They learned by heart the Druids' vast cosmogonic and genealogical poems, in which the knowledge of the Celts was stored; their teachers revealed to them the principles of metempsychosis, a notion that appeals to the mind precisely because it appears to be just as absurd as, but no more so than, the other realities of organic life (deglutition, digestion, copulation, parturition), whose strangeness is hidden from us by habit alone and which constitute the most beautiful of metaphors for our relationship to all things. They were taught the various properties of plants and the correct way to conduct trials by ordeal (whether or not the outcomes were fixed in advance), since the Judgment of God was, initially, the Judgment of the Gods. On certain feast days, they witnessed the grand ceremonial burning of animals and humans in wicker cages, just as, under other pretexts that masked the same ferocity, men and women who were believed guilty and animals that were believed maleficent would be burned alive by the thousands throughout the Christian era, at least up to the end of the seventeenth century. It is possible, too, that the students were taught a bit of Greek, since those priests who seem to us to be buried in a venerable prehistory conducted their correspondence in that language. The Gaulish Druid Diviciacus, whom Caesar brought to Rome and who discussed philosophy with Cicero, seems the very prototype of the prelate who dines out.

One would like to know at precisely what date those people exchanged their primordial gods for a Savior from Palestine—at what moment some housewife (who preceded by centuries the Valentines, Reines, Joséphines, and Adriennes from whom I am descended) allowed a husband or son with ideas more advanced than hers to bring to the smelter the little lares of bronze whose metal, it seems, was then reused to make a stewpot or a frying pan. Unless, as different examples show, the draped and bearded gods were camouflaged as holy Apostles. Other renegades (for the convert is always a renegade from something), more respectful of lost causes, devoutly buried them in some corner of the cellar or garden; those are the gods which are unearthed today, covered with verdigris. In fact, that was not the first time a divinity adorned with the prestige of exoticism had made its way into these regions: Italian traders had brought figurines of Isis and Harpocrates in their bags of cheap goods, and veterans returning from their garrisons had carried back little images of Mithra. But those gods were more accommodating and did not demand exclusive loyalty. We might even suspect that pagans who were too set in their ways to renounce their worthy old religion persisted in those rural areas until the sixth century, or even the seventh. We would have to be able to distinguish those who were converted quite early, in the days when adherence to the new faith was still a heroic endeavor, from the herd that joined the movement after the state had already approved it from above.

The two most revolutionary moments in history are probably the point at which a Hindu ascetic realized that a man cleansed of all illusion became master of his own destiny and either left the world or remained there only to serve other living creatures, surpassing even the gods; and the point at which some more or less hellenized Jews came to see their rabbi as a god voluntarily engaged in human life and pain, condemned to death by both civil and religious authorities, and executed by the local police under the eye of an army ready to maintain order. Let's postpone the discussion of Buddhist wisdom, which I first encountered when I was about twenty. As for the second unprecedented event, the Passion of Christ, which flings a challenge at all human institutions, there are so few Christians nowadays who are imbued with it that we can scarcely believe it so deeply penetrated those Gallo-Roman converts. A few pure souls no doubt opened themselves to the sublime spirit of the Sermon on the Mount; in the course of my life, I have known two or three who did likewise. A fair number of troubled people became intoxicated with hopes of salvation beyond the grave, hopes that also existed in the days of the pagan cults. Most of them made, in their own fashion, the crude wager of Pascal: What was there to lose by converting? Despite the sacrifice of so many chickens and young bulls, Galliena Tacita could not get rid of her stomach pains, and Aurelianus Cauracus Galbo was omitted from the final list of promotions. The barbarians who were Rome's enemies—or, worse, its allies—swarmed not only along the ill-defined frontiers but also in the regions adjacent to Nemetacum (today's Arras) and Bagacum (now Bavay). Soon, from the cloistered recesses of a monastery in the Orient, Saint Jerome's voice would ring out—a cry of horror before the breach in the empire's western front: "The flood of Quadi, Vandals, Sarmatians, Alans, Gepidae, Heruli, Saxons, Burgundians, and Alemanni (oh, unfortunate country!) is sweeping down from the Rhine and the North Sea toward Aquitania: all Gaul is engulfed in fire and blood." The new god saved no one; the old gods wouldn't have saved anyone either. And neither would the goddess of Rome, sitting dejectedly in her curule chair.

Encumbered by the precious objects they were hauling with them, rich folk perished, murdered on the road along with their remaining handful of loyal servants; slaves took flight and passed all at once into the ranks of free men or were absorbed into the barbarian masses. Smoke billowed from piles of wreckage in which the usual number of unidentified bodies lay buried; women taken voluntarily or by force died of mistreatment, cold, and abandonment, or gave birth to the victors' offspring; the bones of villagers who had been killed while defending their fields and flocks slowly whitened in the rain, mingled with those of dead animals. Then people set about repairing and rebuilding. It wouldn't be the last time.

THE
NETWORK

Toward the beginning of the sixteenth century, a minor personage named Cleenewerck becomes visible, tiny from this distance like the figures that Bosch, Breughel, and Patinir inserted along the roads in the background of their landscape paintings to give a sense of scale. I know virtually nothing about this fellow, of whom I am a thirteenth-generation descendant. I picture him living comfortably on his plot of land (since those who are destitute rarely leave traces on the parchments of history) and imagine that, when his hour had come, he was buried in his parish churchyard to the accompaniment of a High Mass. It is known that he arranged good matches for his two sons, meaning that he found wives for them within the circle of patrician bourgeois and extremely minor nobility that he doubtless belonged to, without marrying them either too high or too low. It is known, as well, that he was from Caestre, a town located between Cassel and Bailleul which today is merely a featureless urban sprawl, but which at that time, in the rosy dawn of the Renaissance, was participating in the vigorous life of the little towns of Spanish Flanders. Caestre had its commandery of the order of Malta, its parish church or churches, its "justice" with its gallows tree erect on the horizon; and it doubtless still contained traces of the Roman encampment, or *castra*, that had given the area its name. That large town also had its Poetry Society, whose members would meet to dabble at composing ballads or rondeaux, to prepare, in honor of visiting notables, festive ceremonial "entries" embellished by compliments in verse, and to mount lavish stagings of dramas taken from biblical history, or of farces. Later, at Bailleul, one of my forebears would be the "young leading man" in the productions of the local Poetry Society. The Cleenewerck of about 1510 must have likewise participated in those pleasures of a bourgeoisie that still knew how to devise its own entertainments and whose descendants would later amuse themselves watching prefabricated shadows flicker across screens.

In those solid and obscure families, the names of the daughters-in-law sometimes clarify the situation or character of the group. The eldest of that Cleenewerck's sons, who like his father bore the name Nicolas, married a certain Marguerite de Bernast; I am descended from this couple. The younger son took as his wife Catherine Van Caestre, whose family apparently gave rise to the branch that settled in Tournai and that later produced the Jacqueline Van Caestre of Rubens: a gloomy-looking woman in her posthumous portrait, decked out in gold jewelry and rich brocade. From Jacqueline's husband, Michel de Cordes, who appears in a companion portrait and who served in an important capacity under the archdukes, descended, via a second marriage, a female ancestor of my father's first wife. A son of Nicolas *fils* married, in his turn, a Marguerite Van Caestre. I present these various facts to show at the outset the complicated network of names, bloodlines, and landed property woven by three dozen families that repeatedly intermarried over the course of three centuries.

Among the descendants of the first Nicolas, one married

Pierre de Vicq, a squire; another, Catherine Damman, from an old family of magistrates; another, Jacques Van der Walle, treasurer of the city of Dunkirk, scion of a vast *gens* whose name translates into French as "De Gaulle"; another, Philippe de Bourgogne, squire; another, Jacques de Bavelaere de Bierenhof, "noble man"; yet another, Jeannette Fauconnier; another, Jean Van Belle; and another, Pradelles Van Palmaert—whose names I distributed liberally to the secondary characters in my novel *The Abyss*. My ancestor Michel, the first to bear this name, which subsequently became obligatory within the family for every eldest son, married a certain Marguerite de Warneys in 1601; their offspring Mathieu, bailiff of Caestre, married Pauline Laureyns de Godsvelde, daughter of one Josine Van Dickele; the Michel who was born of this union, bailiff of Caestre in his turn, married Marianne Le Gay de Robecque, dame of Forestel, daughter of a royal counselor and a woman of the Bayenghem family (dame of Wirquin, whose father was a lieutenant in the bailiwick of Saint-Omer). Let's stop there. These strangers offer us nothing more than the poetry of Flemish names, punctuated here and there with a few French ones; enumerating them makes me feel as if I am passing my hand over the flatlands, hollows, and hills of a province that often changed masters, but where the stability of human groups, at least until the upheavals of the two great wars of this century, astounds an observer from 1977.

Who were those Cleenewercks? Their surname, which they didn't add to until the early eighteenth century, can mean either "little work" (in the sense of "odd jobs") or, more picturesquely, "works little." The English surname Doolittle, given by Bernard Shaw to the dustman-turned-philosopher in his play *Pygmalion*, is an almost exact equivalent of it; there is none in French. Thus, I can imagine that around the time family names came into use—that is, in the twelfth or thirteenth century—

my forebears were laboriously cultivating a little farm, devoting themselves assiduously to some sort of handicraft or humble trade, perhaps even that of peddler, trudging from village to village like the exquisite little fabric seller in Charles d'Orléans' poem ("Little mercer! Little basket! / Pennies are my wage; / Hardly the riches of Venice!"), balancing their load of wares with a hitch of their shoulder, and sometimes menaced by watchdogs. Or, if I prefer, I can picture to myself handsome young fellows downing tankards of ale under a shady bower and determined not to exert themselves unduly.

At the time we make contact with them, the Cleenewercks seem to have been established in the class of *Heeren*, which was quite large in Flanders. These were minor noblemen possessing small fiefs that were encroaching little by little on the ancient feudal demesnes and spreading like an oil stain over the peasants' tiny farms. Modern historians see the *Heeren* as upstart tradesmen, which was true in certain cities in what was to become Belgium—Antwerp, Ghent, and Bruges. It was true, as well, in Arras, where wine importers and leather curriers formed an age-old patriciate. But neither large-scale commerce nor banking developed to any great extent around Cassel. Among my forebears I can find only a single wealthy trader—Daniel Fourment, who was something of a merchant prince—and he belonged to the business circles of Antwerp. I would prefer to find that the easy circumstances of the Cleenewercks grew little by little, beginning with purchases of land and with loans perhaps negotiated by straw men, just as those of the nobleman Montluc, elsewhere in France, were arranged by Jews serving as middlemen. The administration of property owned by the Church or by great lords was, at that time, yet another means to enrichment, sometimes even honestly. One must also keep in mind the bonds issued by cities, the shares in rural manufactures or the speculations in great fairs, the construction of townhouses—in short, the myriad aspects of the capitalism that was already rampant among the upper middle class during the Renaissance.

In the Middle Ages, Bailleul, where my forebears would settle in the next century, had had a countinghouse in London together with eighteen other cities in the Flemish merchant guild: its cloth had sailed as far as Novgorod. It may be that those Cleenewercks of long ago profited from the regional cultivation of flax or from the linen weaving in some workshop employing the rural proletariat; they may thus have furnished fine and coarse fabrics for the garments worn by rich and poor, for the sheets on which people slept and made love, and finally for shrouds. In our day of synthetic linens, flax growing has become rare. I remember that a few years ago, on the outskirts of some Andalusian village, I walked through one of those fields which are as blue as the sky and sea—a delightful experience that seems more dream than reality from this distance. It did not displease me that the unpoetic Cleenewercks should have earned their first écus from flax plants in bloom, then from flax retted in the canals of Flanders, the gluey brown chrysalis of snow-white linen.

Everyone in that milieu had a coat of arms, sometimes granted by a count of Flanders or a duke of Burgundy; later, the kings of Spain were not stingy about bestowing letters patent and armorial bearings on those who had served as tools in the worthy cause—that is to say, their own. The assassin of Guillaume d'Orange acquired his posthumously. But on the whole, the majority of those coats of arms were the sort that one bestows on oneself—a practice that contemporary treatises on heraldry maintained was legal. It is a too-little-known fact that the power to grant coats of arms was regulated and tariffed only at a much later date, and that at the end of the Middle Ages, perhaps nowhere more than in Flanders, every family of even minor importance composed for itself a heraldic shield ornamented to its taste, with the same satisfaction that today's bank president takes in combining letters and symbols into a logo.

In the fifteenth century especially, a nostalgia for the fading medieval world seized everyone who had a spark of imagination, producing masterpieces of historical romanticism—tournaments, chivalric romances, miniatures of *The Heart by Love Enflamed*—and culminating a century later in the heroic follies of Don Quixote. It produced, as well, an enormous number of new coats of arms. Those of the handful of families that concern us here combined and recombined their colors and devices so often that one suspects these clans were linked by alliances older than those for which we have evidence. When I was a child, elderly relatives assured me that the martlets, which evoked migratory birds, symbolized pilgrimages and crusades; the stars, as I regretfully learned, were not the ones visible in the heavens but spurs won by warlike but hypothetical ancestors.

As for pilgrimages, those took place so often that every one of us surely has forebears who made their way to Rome or Compostela, partly out of piety, partly to see the country and, upon their return, tell tall tales about their adventures. And during the Crusades, the roads were thronged with so many foot soldiers, so many humble retainers, so many pious widows, and so many loose women straggling along in the train of their lords that we all can pride ourselves on having participated, through some ancestor, in one of those magnificent expeditions. Those people knew the rolling wheat fields that bordered the roads in Hungary, the wind and the wolves in the stony mountain passes of the Balkans, the mercantile bustle of the teeming ports of Provence, the ocean squalls that made the princes' oriflammes writhe like so many tongues of fire, the lavishly gilded city of Constantinople, streaming with sparkling gems and blinded eyes, and visits to the Holy Sites, which, when people have seen them once, even from afar, make them feel as if they have to some degree attained salvation, and which, if they return home, they will remember on their deathbed. And they had other experiences: brown-skinned girls, willing or forced; booty seized from the infidel Turks or the schismatic Greeks; bittersweet oranges and lemons, as unknown in their homeland as the fruits of Paradise; also buboes that mottle the skin with purple, dysenteries that deplete the body, solitary death agonies during which one can see and hear in the distance the travelers who wend their way along the road, singing, praying, and blaspheming, and during which all the sweetness and purity of the world seem to reside in an unobtainable sip of water. We are not the first to have seen the dust of Asia Minor in summer, its white-hot stones, the islands smelling of salt and aromatic herbs, the sky and the sea harshly blue. Everything has already been felt and experienced a thousand times; but often these experiences have not been put into words, or the words that expressed them have not existed, or if they have, they have been unintelligible to us and have failed to move us anew. Like clouds in the empty sky, we take shape and we dissipate against that background of oblivion.

Our family customs, based on a name transmitted from father to son, have given us the mistaken impression that we are linked to the past by a slender stem, onto which are grafted, in each generation, the wives' names—always viewed as secondary, unless they are of such brilliance as to be a source of vanity. In France especially, a land that chose the Salic law, to say that you are "descended from someone on the female side" has almost the effect of a pleasantry. Who (aside from a handful of people) knows the name of the maternal grandfather of his paternal great-grandmother? Nonetheless, the man who bore that name contributed as much to the amalgam that composes us as the ancestor of the same degree whose name we inherit. On the paternal side, which is the only one that concerns me here, I count four great-grandparents in 1850, sixteen great-great-great-grandparents around Year II of the Revolution, 512 forebears in the youth of Louis XIV, 4,096 during the reign of François I, approximately one million at the death of Saint Louis. These figures must be lowered somewhat if we take into account the crossing of bloodlines, since the same ancestor is frequently found at the point where several lineages intersect, like a knot at the meeting point of several strings. Still, it is indeed true that we inherit an entire province—an entire world. The angle at whose apex we are lodged gapes behind us toward infinity. Seen in this way, the science of genealogy, which is so often placed in the service of human vanity, leads first to humility—by making us conscious of the little that we are amid these multitudes—and then to vertigo.

I am speaking here only of the flesh. If we include the mass of transmitted elements that are less susceptible of analysis, we are the universal heirs of the entire earth. A Greek poet or sculptor, a Roman moralist whose native country was Spain, a painter born in an Apennine village to a Florentine notary and a tavern maid, an essayist from Périgord whose mother was Jewish, a Russian novelist or a Scandinavian playwright, a Hindu or Chinese sage, have perhaps formed us to a greater extent than those men and women of whom we may be one of the descendants—one of those seeds which perish fruitlessly by the billions in the recesses of the body or between a couple's sheets.

Thus, I shall not take the time to trace, generation by generation, the course of those Cleenewercks who slowly became Crayencours. The family, strictly speaking, interests me less than the *gens*, and the *gens* less than the group, the collection of beings who lived in the same places during the same periods of time. Concerning a dozen of those lineages which I know a bit more about, I would like to mention here some analogies, some recurrences, some parallel (or, on the contrary, divergent) courses, even to take advantage of the obscurity and mediocrity of most of those people, in order to discover laws hidden from us elsewhere by the overly splendid figures that dominate the foreground of history. Patience! It won't be long before we arrive at the individuals in our vicinity, whom we, rightly or wrongly, think we know almost everything about; it won't be long before we arrive at ourselves.

To begin with, we must dismiss all thought of most of the Spanish alliances which are legendary among so many families in northern France. Of those that I have examined closely, I have authenticated only two, and these are not related to me directly. Such marriages took place most frequently among the high aristocracy in attendance at the courts of Mechlin, Valladolid, Madrid, and Vienna. Neither should we put too much credence in the adulterous liaisons of captains of Aragon or Castile, or in the cruder games of soldiers serving under the duke of Alba or Alessandro Farnese: those armies contained just as many Teutons, Albanians, Hungarians, and Italians as they did men of *sangre azul*—and might have contained even more. The same goes for the Latin blood that naïve conceit attributes to every Frenchman, at least in those periods when the political weathervane turns toward the south: the soldiers of Rome who mounted guard against the barbarians at Caestre or Bavay were, more often than not, barbarians themselves. Other exotic filiations remain to be proved. On this point, the Bieswals had two contradictory legends: according to one, they descended from a gentleman glassmaker from Bohemia who had settled in France; according to the other, which my grandfather heard directly from Reine Bieswal de Briarde (his mother), the ancestor was a Swiss soldier who was serving under the French flag and who thus may conceivably have fought at Marignano or Cerignola, for the Bieswals were already tranquilly settled at Bailleul toward the end of the sixteenth century. The Van Elslandes claimed to be descended from a Hungarian reiter who preferred Flemish comforts to the marches and countermarches of the imperial armies; this has not been verified. One ancestor, Marguerite Franeta, stirs my imagination with the Italian, Spanish, or Portuguese sound of her name, but I know nothing of her family.

Other unions, in contrast, are clearly documented. In 1643 my ancestor François Adriansen married a woman whose name evokes sumptuous nudes in mythological or bourgeois settings: Claire Fourment, a native of Antwerp. A distant relative married a certain Guillaume Verdegans, supposedly a remote descendant of the gloomy Roger Mortimer, the regicide who figures in a play by Marlowe. Doubtless a legend, but it seems that those who were exiled during the War of the Roses did indeed sometimes settle in Flanders, and especially in Bruges, as did other exiles from England in the seventeenth century. It is not certain that they founded families there, however. One forebear was the daughter of a man who was burgomaster of the Freehold of Bruges in 1596; this was a quarter-century too late to assist, or to join in crushing, the Zeno of *The Abyss*. From time to time—just as a procession moving down a quiet street casts reflections from its torches on the windows of a sleeping house, and makes the panes rattle with the sound of its tambours and fifes—so history projects its light on a family that has almost no history of its own.

Town clerks' records, which are unfortunately incomplete, provide me with something else besides a marriage contract. In 1603 my ancestor Nicolas Cleenewerck, a magistrate of Cassel, had to pass sentence on his brother Josse, who had been convicted of murder and was being detained temporarily in the convent of Récollets. The fact that he was in a convent rather than a prison already gives the impression that he had been accorded preferential treatment. But our information goes no further. A novelist (which in this case I am not) could, if he wished, picture to himself a Corneillian before the fact—a magistrate who applied the law in all its severity without letting himself be swayed by fraternal love; or, on the contrary, a more tenderhearted judge helping the accused man escape; or perhaps a pre-Balzacian character who engineered the affair from the beginning, so that he could rid himself of a younger brother and thus seize the entire family fortune. These various speculative assumptions do not take us very far, given our ignorance of the motives and circumstances of the crime. At most, we can infer that this Josse was probably a hothead.

I have noted that few men of war are to be found in this family. The mother of Marie de Bayenghem was a Zannequin, a descendant of the generous fishmonger of Furnes who was torn to pieces at the head of his band of fellow villagers by French cavalrymen, beneath the walls of Cassel: those families who covered the interiors of the churches with their escutcheons were sometimes the descendants of insurgent beggars. Jean Maes, the father of another female ancestor, was killed by the duke of Lorraine himself while defending the banner of Charles the Bold at Murten; his son had fallen two years earlier at the battle of Wattendamme. François Adriansen, mentioned above, who was a volunteer in the armies of Philip IV of Spain and kept two horses with him at his own expense, took part in the defense of Louvain, in the sack of Aire, in the siege of Hesdin. His son, too, was a man of the sword. Five combatants, of whom three were killed: that's not many in such a country, over the course of five centuries.

Contrary to what one might think, there were few ecclesiastics. The reverend father François-Mathieu Bieswal gazes at me with his intelligent dark eyes. His face is finely molded and a bit soft-looking; he has beautiful hands, as did most churchmen in those days. The interior life of people can rarely be read on their faces; this one, the face of a man still young, gives above all the impression of self-control, of a sensuality and dreaminess held in check, and of that prudence which consists in remaining silent or in not saying all that one knows. But the reverend father did not lack energy. François-Mathieu was the treasurer of his order, and rector successively at Halle, Ypres, Dunkirk, and Bailleul; and when the school he had attended was burned by Louis XIV's troops, he had it rebuilt and forced the local authorities to pay the costs. Twice sent to Paris "to negotiate the desperate affairs of his region," he was reputed to be quite adroit. The intendant of the King of France had called together the rectors of the various secondary schools and seminaries of Flanders, enjoining them to cease all communication with the head of their order and to address themselves henceforth only to a French official in their province. That very evening François-Mathieu secretly sent a messenger onto imperial soil to convey this news to his superiors, who succeeded in persuading the King of France to issue a less severe edict. This priest who was so skilled in the affairs of his age died twenty years later in his ecclesiastical residence in Antwerp, having chosen to live out his days in those provinces still under Spanish rule; evidently he remained loyal to what must be called the old regime.

The nuns in the family were scarcely more numerous, and there are no images of any of them, those holy women perhaps considering it indecent to sit for a painter. There is only a single portrait whose subject is wearing a habit; furthermore, it is a picture of a young girl who died at sixteen and never took her vows. Twice, my great-great-aunt, the little Isabelle Adriansen, is depicted full length in the traditional attire of the canonesses with whom she was placed as an orphan: her voluminous dress of greenish velvet, stiff with pleats and adorned with flame-colored ribbons, confines her in a past even more outmoded than her own: one would think she had lived in the reign of Louis XIII rather than that of Louis the Well-Beloved. The delicate round face seems blurred with childhood; the lips have not yet learned to smile. Her unhealthy pallor and the rose she holds in her hand remind us of the infantas of Velázquez, which the excellent provincial painter who bequeathed us her ephemeral little form doubtless never saw.

Nor were there any martyrs. I have looked through the lists of those who were tortured and exiled during the Time of Troubles. They seem to contain names from nearly all the families of that violence-torn land. A few of these people are related to me, but there are none whom I can place exactly in the garden of genealogies, from which they have perhaps been carefully weeded out. Toward the end of the sixteenth century, several brothers of Jérôme de Bayenghem left Saint-Omer for England, and it is possible that their faith had something to do with their departure; they drop out of sight. On the whole, the Cleenewercks and their relatives and allies are in favor of order, both on the streets and in the Church. When curés are murdered, when English Protestants disembark on the dunes, ready to aid the exiled and accused who have taken refuge in the forests of Mont-des-Cats, and doubtless also in the nearby woods of Mont-Noir, the Cleenewercks are filled with worry and indignation. The rebels, in contrast—just like the Celts who emigrated with Commius the Atrebatian, the royalist Chouans during the Revolution, and the Resistants of our own era— direct their heroism toward defying the local enemy or the foreign tyrant, become expatriates if necessary, and return with the help of allies from abroad. The bourgeois who drink to the health of the duke of Alba insist on seeing these partisans as no more than scum: rogues and scoundrels, wayward boys and girls, defrocked monks and libertines, and stupid, easily conned peasants, mixed with a few nobles who have fallen into error or been won over by Elizabeth Tudor's money. The aldermen of Bailleul, who work in concert with the Brussels tribunal dealing with the Troubles, are sometimes embarrassed by ac-

Isabelle Adriansen

cusations that they lack zeal in punishing offenders. These Catholics who regularly attend Mass do not ask themselves if the wealth of the churches might itself be an offense to the plight of the poor, or if those cloisters filled with monks ready at the slightest pretext to jump the wall and run wild might perhaps be in need, if not of the Reformation, at least of reforms.

Around 1870 Edmond de Coussemaker, a cousin of one of my great-grandmothers, published a scholarly book in which that handful of heretics was still depicted as a contemptible rabble; he denied the courage of those who were martyred and the beauty of the psalms rising boldly on the night air after a sermon. The smell of fire-gutted farm buildings, once the hideouts of the rebels, does not shock him either. He is not the only one to hold his nose like this from afar. When confronted by excesses committed in the past by the party to which one belongs, the simplest response is always to denigrate the victims, on the one hand, and, on the other, to declare that the tortures were necessary to maintain order; moreover, that those tortures were much less frequent than people have supposed, and that they conformed with the thought of the age—an argument which, in the present case, does not take into account either Sébastien Castalion or Montaigne. This sort of apologetics is not unique to defenders of papist crimes here and Protestant crimes there: the fanatics and ideological profiteers of our own day are no different in the way they defend their lies.

Martin Cleenewerck, common councilman of Merris, near Bailleul, does not figure in my family archives, and even if he had had the right to do so, his name obviously would have been stricken out. Furthermore, it must be noted that his surname or sobriquet was not rare in Flanders: the Cleenewercks of Caestre, Bailleul, and Meteren might have been unaware of or hostile to those of Merris. For my part, I would be glad to assume that all these various Do-littles, living in an area twenty leagues in diameter, had a common ancestor. No matter: without necessarily sharing Martin's views on the Marian cult or the small number of the elect (even though a glance at the world proves him right on this point), I adopt this intrepid protester as a cousin.

On a hot day in June, along a road thick with dust but bordered by green hop-vines whose branches offer him alms in the form of a bit of shade, Martin makes his way on foot from his prison in Bailleul to Mont des Corbeaux, the site of his decapitation. He will doubtless find there the remains of quite a few of his co-religionists, who have already been broken and torn by iron. He himself is lucky: villein though he is, it is no doubt because of his status as a councilman that he has escaped the worst; he will not be treated like the rebellious Jacques Visaige, bourgeois of Bailleul, who was beaten in the four corners of the main square before being thrown, covered with wounds, into the fire burning in the center. Martin will be accorded a seemly death and, he hopes, will die at a single stroke. Besides, he has not been a party to any murder or defaced any statues. His crime has been to go from house to house, from farm to farm, soliciting contributions and thereby doing his part to raise the three million livres which those of his religion hoped to offer King Philip in exchange for freedom of worship. Martin, that simpleton, actually believed in this nonsense.

En route to his death, he doubtless still wears the large felt hat and the blue leggings that he wore on his rounds, the sign of solidarity with his confreres. He is thirsty. Along the road that leads to Mont des Corbeaux, peasants sometimes offer the condemned a glass of water, or even beer; but perhaps they will not do this for a heretic. Rivulets of sweat trickle from under his hat; drops of urine trace a furrow down his hose, symptoms of a bodily anguish that even a stouthearted man cannot completely master. Worst of all is that the state has confiscated his modicum of worldly goods, estimated to be worth 520 livres. His execution, according to the figures carefully inscribed on the official register, will cost the authorities ten livres and ten deniers: the state, as we have seen, will recoup that sum. An execution by fire would have been more expensive: for one heretic who was also something of a brigand, nineteen livres and thirteen sous was the rate recorded at that time, and moreover, the bookkeeper had crossed off the nineteen sous for the torch furnished by the executioner, arguing that the stake could just as well be set afire with the aid of a coal pan. It takes a bit longer with coals, that's all. Will Martin die consoled by his faith in the God of Calvin, sustained by his just wrath against the ineptitude of the judges? Or, on the contrary, will he be broken past the point of all resistance, so that he ceases to worry about what will become of his wife and children without flocks, fields, or barn? We shall never know. Let us leave him in the company of his guards, to continue along his road.

Those dozen or so families divide Bailleul among them. They hold the offices of "pensionary," in the sense in which Jean de Witt was grand pensionary of Holland; *"avoué,"* which means more or less mayor, town registrar—that is to say, a lawyer serving as head of the city council; "appeaser," which we should understand as a magistrate responsible for maintaining order via methods that can sometimes be fairly harsh; and "alderman," meaning a city councillor as well as a judge in civil and criminal matters. These gentlemen evidently prefer, like Caesar, to be first in a very small town rather than be relegated to the tenth or the hundredth rank in Rome. All of them are rich, especially the treasurer, who is expected to lend the city money if there is a deficit. The situation is scarcely different in Boulogne, Dunkirk, or Ypres, where the Adriansens are "noble aldermen." To find a father and son serving as counselors to the dukes of Burgundy, and thus occupying positions not merely on the city level but on that of a state, we have to go back to the end of the Middle Ages. Later, under the French regime, these gentlemen become counselors to the parliament yet continue to be identified with their provincial corner of the world. They acquire a somewhat weighty sense of assurance, an almost rustic inability to be other than what they are or to picture themselves elsewhere; but they also have a certain independence, or at least skepticism, with regard to the changing masters of the day, who are perpetually felt to be strangers, and a complete and fairly refreshing lack of ostentation. One really has to have lived in a small town to know the extent to which the workings of society are exposed in such a place, the extent to which the dramas and farces of life, both public and private, unfold there in all their rawness and vitality. What results is a curious mixture of rigid integrity and cynicism. These men, who feel that they are princes within the radius of their clock tower's shadow and as far as their rolling green lands extend, would be less than nothing in Saint-Simon's view—mere bits of dust, if by some chance he even had occasion to speak of them. In their eyes, in contrast, the lofty personages that dance attendance on the king at his morning levee would appear to be little more than menials.

One cannot be so deeply rooted in a piece of land without being subjected to the machinations of skillful opponents, which are known as politics, and the follies of the powerful, which are known as war. In 1582 Guillaume Van der Walle, ancestor of an ancestress, is dispatched to the siege of Tournai, to beg the prince of Parma to spare Bailleul; he dies during this mission, probably of some fever or other, and his petition is never heard: that same year Bailleul is three-fourths destroyed by the hardened soldiers of Alessandro Farnese; partly rebuilt by its inhabitants, it is sacked and burned again in 1589; famine follows on the heels of the war; the town loses two-thirds of its population to death and departure. In the meantime (that is, in 1585), Charles Bieswal signs a peace agreement between Bailleul and King Philip II; he also signed, one year earlier, the parchments accompanying the wine jar filled with eight thousand livres that was sent to Farnese, so that this town stripped of all its resources could resume trade with the Protestant Low Countries. The seventeenth century is no better: Flanders suffers the effects of the Thirty Years War. Bailleul burns yet again in 1657, set aflame by the soldiers of Condé. After these fiery ills comes the plague; another Charles Bieswal (son of the above-mentioned), treasurer, alderman, and *avoué* of Bailleul, dies in 1647 of this scourge, along with two of the children he has had with Jacquemine de Coussemaker; she herself will die by the light of the flames of 1681, set this time by French troops.

In 1671 Nicolas Bieswal, chief alderman, and Jean Cleenewerck, *avoué* of Bailleul, wait at the head of the entire municipal magistrature for the arrival of the King of France, who is coming to take possession of his newly won prize. Nicolas Bieswal, in his severe brown coat and conservative wig, looks quite distinguished: that hard mouth and eagle's beak of a nose are the features of a man who will not be dislodged from his positions. We have no portrait of Jean Cleenewerck. The faces of the two magistrates are not brightened by any hint of a smile. It might seem that these Flemings would have reason to smile, now that they could do so at the expense of the Spanish regime; but old allegiances, themselves stemming from an ancient loyalty to the house of Burgundy, ally them to the Hapsburgs. Charles V, who ordered the liquidation of the defenders of Thérouanne and had the city razed as methodically as any modern virtuoso of technological warfare, does not seem to have inspired outrage among the good people of the neighboring localities: no one thought it a bitter irony that an exception was made for an especially venerated figure of Christ, which was duly deposited in a church in Saint-Omer. The effigy of the man who assured his disciples that the meek would inherit the earth witnessed other ironies as well. The atrocities of the duke of Alba had not caused these people of order any unease at all; far from it. Their memories of Alessandro Farnese's reiters had more or less faded, but their memories of Condé's soldiers were still searingly vivid. These shrewd politicians have the strong sense that despite the bells pealing in honor of Louis' joyous entry into the town, the disasters and disappointments have not ended. Above all, they sense that their age-old privileges in a nearly free city will be nibbled away by the king's provincial administrators.

They are right on both counts. The warlike ballet continues: the Treaty of Nijmegen definitively cedes this patch of ground to France, but the regiments marching by to the spirited airs of Lully, the pillaging, and the burning continue until the Treaty of Utrecht—in other words, for thirty-five years. They make the peasants of Flanders, even more than poor folk elsewhere, into those wretched animals that La Bruyère described during this period, when (according to a nineteenth-century poet) the setting sun of the Great King, "in all its beauty, gilded life with its rays." At a time when the gentle Fénelon, responding to an officer plagued by scruples, is content to advise him to moderate the depradations of his troops as best he can (such pillaging is considered an essential supplement to a soldier's rations), the payments in kind collected by owners of fiefs must have become ever scantier, and the farmers' thin gruel must have become even thinner. In town, the patriciate reacted against the encroachments of the French provincial powers by buying back the hereditary civic offices that had been put up for sale by the new government; it was a heavy financial burden, but at least one could remain among one's fellows. In an earlier chapter I mentioned the order to register family coats of arms in D'Hozier—a new decree, which applied, moreover, to all of France and which was designed to add a bit of revenue to the king's coffers. The Bieswals, among others, refused to comply: perhaps they didn't have much faith that the French regime would last. The king's intendant did his best to ridicule those poor devils who were too short of money to pay what they owed; nothing made any difference. Other, more docile families, such as the Cleenewercks, complied with the order, against their pocketbooks and against their will. This was also the period in which the king, who needed cash, offered for sale five hundred letters patent of nobility, at six hundred livres each. Only one man from Flanders saluted and obeyed, so to speak.

The earth recovered rapidly in the days when mankind was not yet capable of destroying and polluting on a large scale. For their part, human beings close ranks and set to work again with an insectlike zeal that one scarcely knows whether to call admirable or stupid—though the second adjective seems more apt than the first, since humanity has never learned a single lesson from experience. Despite the fact that a few thousand rascals in uniform were blown to bits at the orders of Villeroy, Malbrouck, and Frederick II, thus lightening the world, whose surface (as Pangloss would have said) they encumbered, the eighteenth century was one of those golden moments when life was especially good. But the Flanders of antiquity has gotten into step: its ancient bronze color has yielded to French gray. The old patriciate is turning into a "nobility of the gown"; entertainments that take place in private, away from the life in the streets, are ever more frequently supplanting the lavish public festivals of the recent past. Bailleul passes into the rank of those respectable provincial backwaters, always dear to the hearts of French novelists, where more or less titled magistrates and minor nobles who prefer the conveniences of the city to the discomforts of their country estates play backgammon by the light of two silver candlesticks. The life of the masses persists above all in the suburb of L'Ambacht, where the tavern-keepers offer lower prices than those found in the city, where brewers brew, where weavers weave in their homes, and where lacemakers bent over their little cushions perform a painstaking dance with their ten fingers. L'Ambacht also furnishes that array of disreputable (or just slightly vulgar) pleasures, that small ferment of lawlessness, which is essential to any agreeable town. In 1700 a father and son, well-born people, are murdered there at the inn. The guilty parties are hanged, a Mass is said for the victims at Saint-Vaast, and Nicolas Bieswal records carefully in his notebook the three livres that are owed him for the banner and the pall used at first-class funerals. This minor tax is, for the treasurer, one means of reimbursing himself, at least in part, for the money he has lent to the town.

It is around this time that certain of these gentlemen begin lengthening their family names, if they have not already done so, and the name they add to their own is, as if by chance, a French one. The Cleenewercks take the name Cleenewerck de Crayencour, from a small viscontial fief belonging to the court of Cassel; the Bieswals of the branch to which I belong henceforth use the name Bieswal de Briarde; the Baerts call themselves Baert de Neuville. The use of French, the language of culture and the emblem of a certain social rank, was common long before the conquest by Louis XIV; the letters that were exchanged in the sixteenth century between Bailleul and the regent of the Low Countries were almost always written in that language. But in the eighteenth century Flemish still reigns in legal documents, financial records, and epitaphs. Poetry societies, fading away almost everywhere, even in the Belgian provinces, are regarded with suspicion by the French authorities, who rightly believe that they are loyal to the former government; but their members doubtless compose, in both languages, just as many bad poems as they did formerly. The marriage contracts and estate inventories, which itemize silver platters and holy-water basins, gold crosses and women's diamonds, are silent when it comes to books. Still, here and there weighty volumes in French, in Latin, and more rarely in Dutch reveal their rows

of sheepskin spines, tooled and gilded. Nicolas Bieswal ornaments his ex libris with his coat of arms, which has become
illegal but which he nevertheless tranquilly displays. Michel-
Donatien de Crayencour has his engraved in Paris, and surrounds his escutcheon with cupids frolicking in a kind of rococo
glory.

It is likewise during the period of reattachment to France
that the oldest surviving family portraits were painted; their
predecessors, with two or three exceptions, no doubt disappeared in the recurring bonfires of war. The men have been or
will be described in their respective places, but for the sake of
convenience I will group a few of the women here. Constance
de Bane, grandmother of one of my female forebears, supports
in her lovely hands the cloud of muslin that veils her ample
bosom at the lowest possible point; her face, which is rather
plain as well as quite young, her lively eyes, and her wide,
smiling mouth bespeak a proud and singular nature. I picture
her as a hospitable mistress of the house who leads her guests
in the eating and drinking and who laughs at their risqué jokes
without giving Daniel-Albert Adriansen, her husband, much
cause to fear the whims of this honest woman. Isabelle du
Chambge, a distant relative, is dressed up as Hebe; a blue velvet
ribbon, à la Nattier, adorns her attractive neck, which is slightly
tanned by the sun; the large vermeil pitcher she holds in her
hand has been one of the accessories of Flemish painting since
Rubens, whether the scene is an Olympian banquet (as is the
case here), a wedding in Cana, or a family celebration. Isabelle
de la Basse-Boulogne has one of those names that Molière could
have appropriated for one of his provincial marquises; but from
a distance of five generations, this ancestor has the almost un-
settling and bewitching power of beauty. Her portrait seems to
commemorate a masked ball or some torchlit village festival:
resting on her lap are the bow and quiver that we associate with

Love, but her indifference and her pallor are lunar. Slim and erect in her dress of Louis XV's court, she seems related less to the softly rounded women of the *Embarkation for Cythera* than to the nymphs of Primaticcio: the somewhat outmoded technique of a provincial painter has pulled her further back in time. As for the things that lie hidden behind this face—the images that formed in those large, clear, slightly oblique eyes —let us not search for them. We know only that she married a Bieswal de Briarde and died at the age of forty-six.

One tradition assures me that my ancestor Hyacinthe de Gheus and his wife, Caroline d'Ailly, chose to be interred in the chancel of the cathedral of Ypres, as close as possible to the flagstone which, lying in the center of the pavement and engraved with nothing but a date, marks the sepulcher of Bishop Jansen, known as Jansenius. By means of this anonymity, the church wardens managed to reconcile both their respect for the censures of Rome and the consideration that was due a venerated prelate. Actually, human vanity has always viewed the precincts of a chancel as a desirable place to decompose: Hyacinthe de Gheus perhaps did not think any further than this. It has been pointed out that in this region the Jesuits alone dispensed knowledge to a family's sons: their students, with the exception of a few incorrigibles, came away from their hands with little taste for Jansenist notions. From the drama of the Expulsion to the somber farce of the Convulsionaries, the posthumous adventure of the bishop of Ypres takes place mostly in Paris, even if the excommunications come from Rome. All the same, for a great many pious Christians living in Flanders and elsewhere, the austerity of the Jansenists, their scorn for their century, their complete and almost bitter refusal to compromise seemed the living and persecuted image of the Christianity of the heroic age. A confidential letter sent from Brussels by Antoine Arnauld to Jean Racine recommends to the poet (or rather to the king's historiographer) another of my forebears, this one on the maternal side: Louis de Cartier, "a true Christian," who feared that his fine mansion in Liège and his country house near Aix-la-Chapelle would fall prey to the depradations of French soldiers, and who could have benefited from a surreptitious word of warning conveyed by Racine to the marshal of Luxembourg. This friend of Arnauld's was, moreover, an exemplary Catholic, a dutiful son of the Church who was praised to the skies by the curé of his parish. Nevertheless, like so many others, he expressed Jansenist views in the privacy of his own home.

In 1929 I sold to a Paris antiquarian a Christ with thin arms that had been left to me by my father, and whose tall silver body he had allowed to grow black with tarnish in the recesses of a wardrobe. This victim could hardly be distinguished from the ebony to which he was nailed. "You've been cheated, my dear," said my stepbrother when I told him the price I had settled for. But to me, the tradition (actually mistaken) which associates these seventeenth-century Flemish Christs with Jansenism made this large knickknack, at once conventional and lugubrious, one of those objects that can't be gotten rid of too quickly. I have mentioned elsewhere the extent to which predestination seems to cling to the facts such as we observe them in our limited universe; already vexing to our notions of justice, it becomes scandalous as soon as it is linked to the concept of a God-Providence who is supposed to be the epitome of goodness. How could I have accepted the idea of a god who did not die for all human beings when I had already rejected the idea of a god who died only for them? Neither pity nor love flowed from those chiseled wounds. That crucifix had never presided over any death agonies except those in which fear and trembling had overcome serenity.

But in this milieu, the austere advocates of Jansenism had never been more than a respected minority. The majority of the flock were the sort of people who were less rigorous toward the self. These included several types, from the dull skeptic who sleeps through the sermon, gently ridicules Saint Cunegonde and Saint Cucuphas, but dies anointed, confessed, and blessed (partly in conformity to custom and partly because "one never knows"), to the sensitive, self-indulgent Christian of the Counter-Reformation who is lulled into a pleasant daze by the music at Benedictions, who consumes a hearty meatless dinner every Friday, and who leaves sufficient money to his parish so that Masses will be said for him in perpetuity. "To tell one's rosary while cultivating one's orchard," as the Antwerp poet Plantin advised in a famous sonnet, represented for these small, well-provided communities the ideal harmony between piety and prudence.

I am not unaware that, here and there, a few saints could also have kneeled on the red velvet cushions of the prie-dieux. But they are scarcely visible from such a distance. The "devout daughters" who are often mentioned in family documents doubtless had none of the essential breadth or elevation of spirit. In 1739 Marie-Thérèse Bieswal, a woman of canonical age living in the annex of a Jesuit convent, bequeathed four hundred florins to the good fathers so that they could beautify their church, as well as two hundred florins to the poor. She charged her confessor, and no one else, with the responsibility of opening the drawers of her writing desk and burning the papers they contained. It is doubtful that these could have been the drafts of a learned treatise on prayer. One suspects, rather, that they were old love letters, or the correspondence of close women-friends that was filled with the gossip of their little circle.

Let's descend a bit further—that is, toward Hell. In 1659, halfway through that seventeenth century which is even more entitled than the Middle Ages to be called the golden age of demonology, Pierre Bieswal and Jean Cleenewerck, along with twenty-five of their colleagues, signed the official statements decreeing that a sorcerer be tortured and put to death. The man in question was a certain Thomas Looten, a native of the town of Meteren, not far from Mont-Noir. Thomas was accused of casting a spell on his neighbors' animals and of killing a child by means of poisoned plums. Banal crimes: even in those periods when Asmodeus, Beelzebub, Ashtaroth, and their king Lucifer himself ensure that their names are often on people's lips, they seem to be capable of only a handful of heinous crimes, always the same ones—the worst and the most varied of them in any case reserved for human beings. Even though the entire village came forward to testify against him, Thomas did not confess. It is often thought that witchcraft trials represented an orgy of superstition or cynicism on the part of the judges, and that death sentences were handed down at random in great numbers. In fact, legality (if not justice) was given its due. The preliminary examination lasted two months. Just as the spirits of the dead that are called up by spiritualists nowadays usually like to communicate through a medium, evil spirits, which were rarely seen by most people, preferred to commit their crimes through the agency of possessed individuals and witches, a fact that made the work of exorcists and torturers indispensable. Despite a brief, routine interrogation, which lasted seven hours but which the lout's constitution withstood, Thomas maintained his silence, and the trial would have come to a standstill had not the executioner of Dunkirk, by a fortunate coincidence, come to Bailleul on personal business. This officer of the law prided himself on having put to death, with his own hands, six hundred witches and sorcerers. He asked permission to visit the prisoner—a request that the magistrates of Bailleul immediately granted, since they were only too happy to turn the matter over to an expert.

This practitioner's examination of Thomas' body straightway revealed the telltale signs of an infernal pact: those notorious patches of insensitivity, nowadays held to be pathological, where technicians can insert pins at will without making the patient flinch or cry out. The rack was now unavoidable. After a few bones and veins had been broken, Thomas confessed all that was expected of him: he had attended a witches' Sabbath; he had conversed with the Fiend, doubtless after performing the customary ritual gesture of kissing his backside; he had learned from him the secrets of casting spells and poisoning plums. The devil who had been present at the Sabbath that night had a name: it was Harlequin.

Harlequin, Hellequin, Hielekin, Hölle-König, Hell-King: *"J'oïe le mesnie Hielekin, mainte kloquète sonnant"* ("I heard the cohorts of Harlequin, and the pealing of many a bell"). At the time the judges of Bailleul were interrogating Thomas, Harlequin was no longer anything but a traditional character from

Italian comedy, appearing onstage at country fairs to the delight of wide-eyed peasants, leaping about, cracking jokes, and twirling his long bat. But in olden times his tights, with their pattern of red and yellow diamonds, had been a costume adorned with flames, and his black mask had been that of the Prince of Darkness. Vilified by preachers who railed against the indecencies of the theater, Harlequin, in the Europe of pagan times, had imitated the King of the Wood and the remote figure of the Horseman Thracian; amid yelping and neighing, over hill and dale, through moors and marshes, he had led the Infernal Horsemen on their galloping ride, during which a single night lasts a hundred years. Since the science of folklore had not yet come into being, no one, either in the pulpit or in the theater pit, recognized the god beneath his disguise as a buffoon, but Thomas Looten's fatal encounter with the Harlequin of antiquity on a Sabbath night says a great deal about the survival of myths in the imagination of humble villagers. The case of this devils' accomplice was settled. Pierre Bieswal and Jean Cleenewerck affixed their signatures to the verdict of death by fire. A stake was erected in the main square, which was already thronged with people. But the aides who had been sent to take delivery of the principal party concerned found him lying huddled in a corner of his prison cell, his neck broken. The disappointed public was cleared from the square. Harlequin had killed his henchman in a rage after hearing his name revealed —unless, on the contrary, he did it out of pity (if pity can enter the soul of a devil), so as to deliver the man from a worse death. A compassionate jailer, or one who had been bribed by the rascal's family, had perhaps played the role of the Devil, and it would be nice to think that the order had come to him from Pierre Bieswal or Jean Cleenewerck. But magistrates rarely interfere in the course of justice.

A fair number of the victims of *The Hammer of Witches*

and other treatises written by overexcited demonologists and read assiduously by judges were undoubtedly poor, inoffensive wretches who had aroused the antipathy of their neighbors by their odd appearance or behavior, their fits of temper, their taste for solitude, or some other characteristic that people look on with disapproval. Thomas Looten very likely fell into this category. But one must also take into consideration those who were drawn to the Sabbath, in fact or in dream, by their genuinely evil natures, by their vague resentment born of some misfortune or mistreatment they had suffered, some preference that had been disparaged, or some unsatisfied need. After days spent hoeing the turnip fields or digging in the peat bogs, the shabby rustics find, in the small tattered group squatting in a thicket around a pile of glowing embers, the equivalent of our neo-primitive dances, of our music made of crashes and shouts, perhaps of the hallucinatory substances we drink and smoke. There they satisfy their instinctual urge to mass together like larvae. They experience the warmth and the promiscuity of bodies; nudity, which is forbidden elsewhere; the slight shudder and the low snicker at things that are ignoble or illicit. Not only is the firelight that plays over these wretches an omen of death on the gallows, which is always ready for them, but those flickering gleams come from deep within their selves, if not also from another world.

Whoever believes in God can, and almost must, believe in the Devil; whoever prays to the saints and the angels has every chance of hearing infernal harmonics as well. Better still, nothing in human reason and logic prevents us from assuming that interferences, exchanges, could take place here and there between the solitary islands that we are and other, half-visible formations, willful impulses only partly personified, awakened, or established in us, capable of guiding us or of causing our destruction. The hypothesis remains to be proved in a universe in which the only forces that we perceive are indifferent to human beings. But the appetite of theologians and judges for so-called occult phenomena has falsified the problem: the monstrous image of the Fiend incarnate has blinded them to the fact that evil is never more harmful than when it appears in banal human guise, without supernatural allure of any sort, and is especially so when it is completely unnoticed or even respected. The signatures of Pierre and Jean on parchments that condemn an ignorant and possibly innocent man to torture and suffering are no less hideous than Thomas' poisoned plums; the regiments of the Great Condé devastated Flemish farms, killed livestock, and delivered up the people to plague and famine more effectively than all the devils of Harlequin's cohorts could ever have done.

Pierre Bieswal and Jean Cleenewerck would seem to have every excuse, since in those days any magistrate would have thought and acted as they did. But to act and think like everyone else is never a recommendation; nor is it always an excuse. In every age there are people who do not think like everyone else—that is, who do not think like those who do not think. Montaigne would have wanted to give witches potions of hellebore, instead of shirts of boiling pitch and pyres of flaming straw; Agrippa of Nettesheim, himself suspect for having explored the world of magic with the eye of a humanist who searches everywhere for laws, joined forces with a village curé to defend an old woman accused of witchcraft by her neighbors and claimed by an inquisitor. Théophraste Renaudot, some ten years prior to the sentence signed by my ancestors, had noted that the alleged demonic possession of the nuns of Loudun was merely hysterical theatrics, and one of the bishops involved in that affair was of the same opinion.

When the judge in Racine's play *The Litigants* offers his future daughter-in-law the opportunity to attend a torture session as entertainment, the charming Isabelle responds just as she would in our own day, when the same diversion could, unfortunately, be offered her.

> *"Ah, sir! How can watching men suffer be pleasing to you?"*
> *"Oh well, it's a good way to help pass an hour or two."*

A typical bit of dialogue, in which we sense that Racine is on Isabelle's side. Pierre Bieswal and Jean Cleenewerck, in contrast, thought like everyone else—that is, they bore a closer resemblance to Judge Dandin than to Montaigne. We already suspected as much.

I would like to have as an ancestor the imaginary Simon Adriansen of *The Abyss*, a cuckold who felt no resentment and who died in a sort of ecstasy of pity and forgiveness with bleak Münster in the background—a city torn repeatedly by rebellion and suppression. In reality, the earliest Adriansen forebear whose traces I have found lived nearly three-quarters of a century after that just and greathearted man, and not, like him, at Flessingue, but at Nieuwpoort, where in 1606 at Saint Martin's Church he married a certain Catherine Van Thoune. This is all we know of him; nothing indicates whether he was born in that small seaport ringed by dunes or whether he came from somewhere else. The family later settled in Ypres.

The name, which means "son of Adrian," is fairly common in the Netherlands. Despite the large number of people who went by it, there are no records that allow me to claim any kinship whatever with Brother Cornélius Adriansen, a Franciscan who lived in the mid-sixteenth century and who was banished from Bruges for having shown a bit too much tenderness in applying the lash to some charming penitents. Still, I had occasion to think of his little group of eagerly consenting flagellants when I chose the same setting, at once dangerous and sensual, for another secret group, that of the "Angels," which led to Zeno's doom. Neither can I, in the absence of any proof, include among my family a certain Henri Adriansen, a sorcerer who went to the stake in Dunkirk in 1597 at the age of eighty, along with his daughter Guillemine; or, likewise in Dunkirk, the pirate François Adriansen, who on his small ship the *Black Dog* was a sea wolf in the service of Philip IV and returned to terra firma to live out his days. If all these people belonged to what I call the same "network," the lines that connected them have become invisible. But all of them breathed the same air, ate the same bread, felt on their upturned faces the same rain and the same sea breezes that my authentic Adriansen forebears did. They are my relations by virtue of the fact that they existed.

The François Adriansen who was incontestably my ancestor was christened at Nieuwpoort in the same church where his father and mother had been married; I referred above to his career as an officer in the service of Spain. This is less relevant here than his marriage to Claire Fourment, which brings us to the borders of the mythological world of Rubens.

The Fourments were long established in Antwerp as merchants in rare hangings and Oriental rugs, exotic treasures so highly prized that we can see them displaying their almost cabalistic designs at the feet of Van Eyck's Virgins, or, hung between two pillars, forming screens in the cold interiors of churches. The fashion would endure, for the same Shirvans and Sennas would figure in the indoor spaces of seventeenth-century Holland, covering with their worn folds the tables over which Vermeer's women are bending. Fourment *père* lived on the place de la Vieille-Bourse (Old Stock Exchange Square) in a house called At the Golden Stag, doubtless because of a statue perched on its ridgepiece, since it was the custom in Flanders in those days to ornament the rooftops with real or fantastic animals, busts of emperors, and Madonnas gilded with fine gold. His son Daniel, a doctor of law, had bought from the King of Spain, at a very high price, the fief of Wytyliet, which gave him power over high, low, and mid-level justice. It would be nice to think that he continued, nevertheless, if not to sell fabrics and carpets, at least to give them to his friends in exchange for money, as did Monsieur Jourdain's father in the Paris of those days.

Daniel Fourment married Claire Brant, one of the two daughters of Dr. Brant, a highly respected jurist and humanist; Rubens wed the other, Isabella, and the attic of the doctor's house served as the painter's first studio. Isabella Brant died young and was subsequently replaced in Rubens' affections by the blond Helena, the younger sister of that same Daniel, who thus twice became the brother-in-law of this great creator of forms. My distant forebear Claire Fourment, daughter of Daniel and Claire Brant, was therefore the niece of two of the most frequently painted and lavishly doted-on women of their century.

Rubens had a gift for happiness. But happiness had not come to him early in his life. He'd been born in Cologne, the offspring of a father who was banished from Antwerp for his Protestant affiliations, then condemned to death for adultery with a princess; and of a passionate mother, who saved the life of her faithless husband. Rubens' past was, for him, like the somber undercoats that he laid on his canvases, soon covered with glowing washes and veils of color. He quickly won renown and riches as an artist, was familiar from his youth with the easygoing little courts of Italy and the austere court of Spain, was given sensitive missions early in his diplomatic career, was ennobled by two kings, and spoke and read five languages, all the while being (as Charles V would have said) five times more of a man. Rubens' well-founded happiness stayed with him to the end and has continued posthumously in his worldwide fame. In this almost too-complete success, Isabella is the first feminine stage, since we know nothing about the beautiful Italian women the young artist may have met during the eight years he spent on the peninsula. The day after their marriage, Rubens painted a picture of himself with her in the doctor's garden, which was already colored by autumn. He is thirty-two years old. This robust man, richly dressed in black velvet and lace, has a calm, thoughtful air. In her brocades, beneath a grotesque high-crowned hat which is quite "the latest thing," the little bride of seventeen, displaying a virginal grace, rests her hand on that of the husband the doctor has chosen for her.

The portraits that followed show us, as if in close-up, Isabella as wife and mother. Her low bodice lifts up her breasts, which are pressed together like peaches in a basket; large eyes like those of a heifer brighten her face, which is transparently good but shines with little intelligence; the weak chin, slightly receding, bespeaks a docile and passive sensuality; consumption is already whitening and ruddying her delicate skin in the light filtered by her famous straw hat. Rubens did not—as Rembrandt would later do with his Saskia—sketch the young woman as she lay dying, ravaged by fever: the realm of slow death agonies was not for him.

Nonetheless, in a letter to a friend, the widower reveals that he fell prey to the melancholy he seems to have deliberately excluded from his work: "Since the only remedy for all our ills is forgetfulness, which comes with time, I must look to time as my sole refuge . . . I think traveling would help me . . . I don't claim to have attained stoicism . . . and I cannot believe that emotions so well suited to their object could be unbecoming to a worthy man, or that a person could be completely insensible to all the vicissitudes of life, *sed aliqua esse quae potius sunt extra*

Peter Paul Rubens, *Rubens and Isabella Brant in a Honeysuckle Bower*, 1609–10

vitia quam cum virtutibus, and these emotions take revenge within our soul." Ahead of his time, Rubens saw that the courage which too thoroughly represses grief poisons it, and us as well. He who wrote these lines was not merely a witless fellow with a paintbrush.

Four years later, having returned from missions and important works abroad, this courteous man renewed relations with his in-laws; around this time he painted a portrait of the elderly Dr. Brant, and the rosy cheeks of the learned fellow make us suspect that he was an expert in French wines as well as in Greek and Latin grammar. In the Fourment house, he again met the two Claires, the dead woman's sister and niece, the latter of whom was still quite young. In the intervening years, little Helena had crossed the threshold from childhood to adolescence. In December 1630, Rubens married the sixteen-year-old. That there was a difference of thirty-seven years in the newlyweds' ages did not surprise anyone in those days, and perhaps wouldn't have done so in any day, with the exception of our own. But this time the artist did not include himself in the portrait, alongside his wife. "I resolved to marry, finding that I was not yet ready for the austere life of a celibate, and thinking that if we ought to give highest honors to the mortification of the flesh, we can also, in giving thanks to heaven, seek out lawful pleasure." He adds that everyone had advised him to marry a noblewoman, naturally in her declining years, but that it would have been hard for him to "exchange the precious treasure of liberty for an old woman's caresses." Just as Antaeus regained his strength by touching the earth, Rubens, in making love to Helena, regained his youth.

During the ten years of life that remain to him, the artist confines himself more and more to his sumptuous mansion near the residence of the Archers of Saint Sebastian, to Helena, and to his domestic routine, which opens directly onto the realm of myth through the studio peopled with gods. The day begins with a Mass, which holds the same place in his life that church paintings occupy in his oeuvre, neither more nor less. It continues with works by Tacitus or Seneca, which one of his students reads aloud to him while he paints. In the evening he relaxes by taking horseback rides along the banks of the Scheldt, and this man who is so fond of skies doubtless revels in the hazy, ruddy tints of the sunset. Then comes the evening meal, which he likes copious but not excessive, and conversation with the few sensible, earnest, somewhat dull minds that Antwerp is proud to call its own. The day comes to an end with the almost mythological ardors of the conjugal bed.

In this routine, where all is order, luxury, calm, and sensual delight, how can we not see the prudent choice of a man who asks domestic life to facilitate his pleasures by legitimating them, leaving his eye and mind free to devote themselves to what is essential? The flame is no less present here than in certain other lives that are more turbulent or more secret; whoever says "hearth" also sometimes says "coals." But the end is drawing near: Rubens' last years remind us of those of Renoir, another painter of happiness. The rheumatic hand gradually refused to paint. In 1640 Helena became a widow at the age of twenty-six. She took a second husband—a gentleman who, like her first, held a respected position at the Spanish court. She is interesting to us only in her connection with Rubens.

In one of the last of the master's works, *The Judgment of Paris*, she is both Venus and Juno, two delectable nudes each trying to outdo the other. Elsewhere, she lends her sensual young face to Madonnas and saints. On the grounds of the little château of Steen, recently acquired by the artist, she does the honors in splendid attire; in front of the Italianate pavilion of her garden in town, she watches a servant woman throw grain to the peacocks. Seated beneath a portico, ravishing in her ball gown, she brushes one of the family's beautiful carpets with her ample skirt. Among all these canvases, the nude *Helena Fourment* in the Vienna collections is the only one that haunts us, but it does so for reasons that are more pictorial than erotic. Many a painter had depicted his wife or mistress without veils, but the subjects and the mythological settings (as was often the case with Rubens) placed these goddesses in a conventional Olympus. Above all, with the masters of drawing and contour, the ideal line that enclosed a nude body also clothed it, so to speak. In this case, it is a question less of a body than of flesh. This warm, dewy woman seems to be just emerging from her bath, or from making love. Her gesture is that of any woman who, hearing a knock at the door, hastily covers herself with whatever is at hand, but the noble style of the painter saves her from all lewd or insipid prudishness. You have to look at her twenty times, and play the old game which consists in finding eternal motifs in every work of art, before you realize that her arms are posed, with only slight modifications, like those of the Medici Venus; but this lush form is neither marmoreal nor classical. The fur cloak with which she covers herself and which her luxuriant figure escapes on all sides makes her seem more like a mythological bear cub. Those soft-looking breasts shaped like gourds, the folds of her torso, that belly perhaps rounded by the first stages of pregnancy, and those dimpled knees make one think of the puffiness of rising dough. Baudelaire no doubt had her in mind when, speaking of Rubens' women, he referred to the "pillow of cool flesh" and to female tissue "in which life flows"; it seems, in fact, that a mere touch of your finger would be enough to leave a pink mark on her skin. Rubens never parted with this canvas, which made its way into the Hapsburgs' collections only after his death; perhaps he felt a twinge of guilt for having played King Candaules. That monarch had exposed his wife's charms to no one but a close

Peter Paul Rubens, *State Portrait of Helena Fourment*, ca. 1631

Peter Paul Rubens, *Helena Fourment with Fur Cloak*, ca. 1638

friend; Helena, on display in Vienna, would henceforth belong to any passing tourist.

I would have preferred to have, as a great-great-aunt, Hendrickje Stoffels—the aging Rembrandt's servant, model, and concubine, who did her best to brighten the last years of that great unhappy painter and who, as ill luck would have it, died before he did: Hendrickje, with the slightly swollen eyes of a servant who has gotten up too early and with her tired, gentle body, tinged with gray shadows, which she lent to the *Bathsheba* in the Louvre. One would like to establish even the slenderest of ties with this man, to whom none of our troubles or fears were alien. I remember seeing, during a brief visit to the Hermitage in 1962, a peasant belonging to some delegation from the far reaches of the Soviet Union: he paused for a moment before a Christ by Rembrandt, which the mechanical voice of a guide had just perfunctorily identified, and quickly crossed himself. I do not think that a Jesus by Rubens would ever have elicited the same gesture. The sacred is not his domain. All Baroque art glorifies the will to power; his own echoes in particular the need to reign, to possess, and to enjoy membership in a privileged clique perched at the top of Europe during the Thirty Years War. Episodes from myth and from Roman history turn princely walls and ceilings into rows of double mirrors in which men and women decked out in plumes and pearls, weighed down by their heavy clothes and heavy flesh, are reflected to infinity in the form of heroes and gods. Like the gaudy machines of opera, allegories raise potentates to the heavens. Bloody martyrs and violent hunting scenes nobly satisfy their craving for spectacle and their taste for killing. The idiotic whims of crowds always demand gratification, but in this case the whims are those of a crowd of princes.

It is through his insatiable appetite for matter that Rubens escapes the hollow rhetoric of court painters. All takes place as if the layering and squirting of paint had little by little led the virtuoso far from the mythologico-Christian pageantry of his age, into a world where the only thing that counts is pure substance. Those ample bodies are no longer anything but solids that revolve (according to the still-condemned theories of Galileo) in the same way the earth revolves; the buttocks of the *Three Graces* are spheres; plump angels float like cumulus clouds in a summer sky; Phaeton and Icarus fall like stones. The horses and Amazons thrown down in *The Battle of the Amazons* are meteors arrested in their trajectories. Everything is volume that moves and matter that seethes: the same blood brings a rosy tinge to the bodies of women and infuses the eyes of the Magi's chestnut horses; the fur of Helena's cloak, the hairs of beards, the feathers of birds killed by Diana are no longer anything but modifications of basic substance; the rounded flesh of children bearing fruit is itself fruit; the waxy, flaccid flesh of Jesus descended from the Cross is but the final stage of fleshly life. In the presence of this powerful organic magma, the bombast and vulgarities, the tricks of the scene painter in the grand manner, become unimportant. The stout Marie de' Medici has the plenitude of a queen bee. The three Sirens welling up at the base of the vessel that bears this diademed fool cease to be the Capaio ladies of the rue Vertbois and little Louise, who served as models for them; their heavy charms do not evoke woman so much as they do the weight and the dull slapping of the waves against the prow. Like a lover in a bed, like a Triton in the water, he frolics in this sea of forms.

Claire Fourment left no traces; I don't know whether she looked more like her aunt Isabella or her aunt Helena. But we have a portrait of her son, Daniel-Albert Adriansen ("Daniel" by way of homage to the Fourment dynasty; "Albert" in honor of a well-loved archduke). A man of the sword like his father and an officer in the armies of West Flanders, this cavalryman in his crimson jacket has alacrity and fire. His eyes beneath their heavy brows laugh and speak. By the next generation, the blood has already lost some of its heat: Joseph-Daniel Adriansen, majestic in the red robes of a noble alderman, is engulfed by the blond curls of his Regency wig, which cascades down to his waist. This magistrate and ladies' man died young, leaving the three little daughters he had had by his cousin Marianne Cleenewerck, whose father was the purchaser of Crayencour. I've already described the eldest of these girls—the slender shade dressed as a canoness and holding a rose in her hand. Of the two who survived, one rejoined the network by marrying a Bieswal and died childless; the other, my great-great-great-grandmother Constance Adriansen, married her cousin Michel-Donatien de Crayencour, after obtaining dispensations for the second and fourth degrees of consanguinity. In addition to a substantial part of the Adriansen fortune, she brought him the lions of their armorial bearings (with which Michel-Donatien's descendants would quarter their bourgeois coats of arms) and a minor title of Spanish nobility handed down on the female side of the family. We'll meet Constance again further on, in her old age.

At the time of his marriage in 1753, Michel-Donatien, who later became a counselor to the king, could have been a handsome, well-built young man dancing exuberantly at the festivities to the music of violins. In 1789, at the age of fifty-seven, this paterfamilias looks like an ugly Louis XVI. The large, prominent eyes are pale and sleepy-looking; the lower lip curls disdainfully; the unbuttoned collar reveals one of those thick necks that seem to tempt the guillotine. My great-great-great-grandfather escaped that fate, but not without suffering his share of the unpleasantnesses that a revolution always brings with it. There exists a letter written to him from Cassel in 1778 which gives his estate name in its heading; and another, dated 1793, in which the lord of Crayencour, Dranoutre, Lombardy, and other places found himself designated as "Citizen Cleenewerck, self-styled Craïencour." Upon receipt of this letter, the curl of that scornful lower lip must have become even more pronounced.

In May 1793, at one of the estates of the de Gheus family, near Ypres, a group of people are conversing in low voices beneath an arbor. Michel-Daniel de Crayencour and his wife, Thérèse, are dressed in traveling clothes. Their five children, the oldest of whom is six, play at the edge of the canal under the eye of the nursemaid. Their host, Léonard de Gheus, who is Thérèse's brother, in one of those romantic "change partners and dance" movements which are highly characteristic of that day (and which, furthermore, tend to consolidate inheritances), has married Michel-Daniel's sister Cécile. From an array of family portraits whose subjects could not be identified, I chose the best, which was also the one that, in terms of age and clothing style, was most appropriate for my great-great-grandfather. Michel-Daniel could well have been that slightly insolent dandy, pale beneath his powder, who on this occasion has donned an old caped overcoat to conceal the fine coat of blue velvet in which he had himself painted. Charles, his younger brother, wears a wagoner's cloak that half disguises him. Their elderly father, Michel-Donatien, has taken off his club-tailed wig and looks like his own tenant farmers. I don't know whether he followed his sons into exile and, if he did, whether he was accompanied by Constance, then in her sixties. Whether she stayed or went, Constance was surely calm. I picture her quietly taking her enamel and silver étui out of her pocket and, at the last moment, mending a torn flounce on Thérèse's skirt.

The good-natured abbot accompanying the family is dressed as a bourgeois. This priest, whose amethyst ring was still in my father's possession, is said to have been Michel-Daniel's chaplain and the private tutor of his children. But the latter, at such a young age, had no need of a tutor, and I doubt whether the family would have given itself such airs as to have a chaplain. This priest, who refused to swear allegiance to the civil constitution in 1790, and whose portrait endows him with graces à la Bernis, was doubtless a distant relation or a friend of those people with whom he was setting out to take his chances on the roads of Germany.

Cousin Bieswal de Briarde, a small, lively man who has just covered on horseback, via side roads, the few miles that separate Bailleul from Ypres, is inquiring about routes to Holland, where he has decided to wait out the storm. It is agreed that he will go to Ghent and there take the coach to Rotterdam.

Léonard de Gheus and Cécile, as subjects of the Austrian States, are not emigrating; in principle, they have nothing to fear, even though the onrush of the *sans-culottes* terrifies them just as it does everyone else. At the château, all the objects of value have been hidden away. The arrival of a servant with refreshments interrupts the conversation, for no one trusts his servants anymore.

Those gentlemen and ladies have taken a while to become alarmed. In 1789 the petitions of grievance that communities presented to the king were quite moderate; since then, the mass conscriptions and the persecution of the clergy have greatly hardened the peasants' feelings toward the Republic. Certainly the news from Paris is frightful, and Santerre's drumroll has struck fear into well-placed hearts. But Paris is too far away for anyone to feel personally endangered. Ever since the guillotine began functioning at Douai, people have understood; the mayor of Bailleul was one of the first to decamp. Joseph Bieswal, figuring that in times of unrest women run less of a risk than men, has decided to leave behind his own wife, the ingenious and energetic Valentine de Coussemaker, who with the aid of a notary will perhaps be able to manage by selling some possessions or arranging fictitious mortgages, or by persuading the farmers, who will be reimbursed later, to buy the family's lands with already depreciated paper money, in order to return them someday to their masters.

Charles helps the driver load the carriage and climbs onto the seat, equipped with false papers in case there is a confrontation with any self-styled patriots. The family is supposedly going to Spa to take the waters. On her lap, Thérèse holds her little Charles-Augustin, who has not yet been weaned. The nursemaid sits in the rear with the baggage. As always, there are last-minute delays: a bag that has gone astray, a child who wants to get out to fetch a toy or take care of some other pressing need. Laughter and exclamations of impatience are mixed with sighs and tears of farewell. Cécile, weeping, waves her tulle scarf and blows kisses to the travelers.

Michel-Daniel and his family spent more than seven years living abroad, first in the château of Kalkar in Prussia, then in the château of Olfen in Westphalia. Alongside the émigrés burning to restore order in France or striving to make a career by serving a foreign country, there were those who, from lack of money, were forced to become fencing masters, private tutors, or pastry chefs. There were also less picturesque exiles who had enough cash to rent estates where they could live off the land as country dwellers. This, it seems, was the case with my great-great-grandfather and his wife. Thriftiness reigns. Michel-Daniel gives up wearing his handsome blue coat; they butter their bread sparingly, for blocks of butter wrapped in cabbage leaves sell briskly at the marketplace in town. From time to time visits by émigrés who are passing through the area do a bit to lighten the oppressive routine of exile. The family has little contact with local society, since language is something of a barrier, even though a knowledge of Flemish helps them speak a kind of broken German. The curé and the doctor, whenever they come (the latter comes only too often), communicate in Latin with these gentlemen.

As always in such cases, conversation centers on the differences—in dress, food, love, and manners—between the country that one comes from and the country where one is, the country where one is harshly judged. After meals, at which they have to swallow the bittersweet sauces of the German cook, they retire to the drawing room, where, to save money, the candles are not lit until very late, and moreover are made of tallow rather than wax. Shrewd cousin Bieswal, who found Holland rather unsafe, has come to spend a few days at Kalkar. Having visited France briefly under an assumed name, then made brief stops at the posting houses in Osnabrück and Bremen, he is brimming with political news, real or false. His heroic Valentine, taking advantage of a recent law that she finds abhorrent, has obtained a divorce, the better to safeguard the émigré's property—some of which, at least, she has successfully transferred to her own name. The Coussemaker woman, known prior to the Revolution as Bieswal de Briarde, has had to endure the compliments of officers of the Republic for this proof of her conformity to the ideas of the day. Even though the curé, whom she sees in secret and who has not taken the Revolutionary oath, has approved her actions, she suffers because necessity has forced her to act in violation of her duty as Christian and as wife. Fortunately, she has been able to send her children to safety in the Austrian States; little Reine in particular has grown close to an émigré canoness who is like a second mother to her. The visitor glances at young Charles-Augustin, who is playing with his top. Even during the Terror, it is never too early to begin thinking of fruitful unions between good families.

The faint sound of a cough coming through the open window causes Thérèse to raise her head. With slow steps, weighed down as she is by her pregnancy, which is now in its eighth month, she goes upstairs. The child, her eldest son, little Michel-Constantin, is lying in bed drenched in sweat, watched over by a German maidservant. The doctor has no more remedies for this consumption. Everyone except Thérèse has accepted the idea that the child will not live till autumn. The mother's grief bursts out as anger against the servant, who does not understand the orders she is being given.

Thérèse left two children in the cemetery of Kalkar, the consumptive and the newborn, who died while still in her cradle. The air of Olfen was no more wholesome: three other children died there. When the couple finally returned from their years abroad, they brought back with them only the young Charles-Augustin.

On the seventeenth of Nivôse, Year VIII, a letter from Fouché informed the prefect of Nord that the "Degheus woman," married name Cleenewerck, was authorized to return to her residence in "monitored freedom" and to reassume rights over her property, except for those lands that the state had previously sold, regarding which no attempts at reclamation would be allowed. The next day a document signed "Bonaparte" declared that among those removed from the list of émigrés were the Cleenewerck brothers, manufacturers, and stipulated the same prohibition regarding lost property. No similar documents have survived concerning Michel-Donatien and Constance.

The standing of "manufacturers" accorded the two brothers is explained by the fact that a small pottery works had recently been transferred to their name, perhaps to facilitate their return to France. This minor enterprise, employing only seven workers, supplied the local market with plates and cups in a rustic style. It is not known whether the family was counting on this business to reimburse itself for its losses, or whether, turning their backs on their pre-Revolutionary past, Michel-Daniel and Charles were seeking to insinuate themselves into the ranks of that commercial middle class which was proving to be, after all was said and done, the principal beneficiary of the upheavals. But the Do-littles had never had a talent for manufacturing and trade. The pottery works soon closed its doors.

Valentine de Coussemaker, the touching divorcée, endured those tragic years with difficulty; she died at the age of thirty-seven, in Year V, during her husband's second period of emigration. Thérèse de Gheus took leave of the world at forty-two, soon after her mournful return from Germany. Constance Adriansen, married name Cleenewerck, self-styled Craïencour, lasted somewhat longer: she died in her seventies in 1799. If she made the trip to Germany, she shared the sorrows and griefs of her daughter-in-law in exile. If, on the contrary, she stayed at home, perhaps too frail to bear the long journey, or, like Valentine, charged with doing her best to defend the family property, she spent her last years in the uncertain atmosphere of her little town—an atmosphere of secrecy, fear, official visits and interrogations in people's homes, increasingly harsh accusations by the republicans, and timid royalist jeremiads. It is not known whether she ever saw her émigré children again. Forty-six years spent in the company of the thickset Michel-Donatien do not make one envy her either. Finally, like so many others, she had had her share of children who died young, in those days when nature acted immediately to curtail excess fertility. But no life can be judged from the outside, especially not the life of a woman. The portrait that was painted of her in old age is not a sad one.

"Farewell pink skirts and gilded shoes . . ." Instead of the frills and furbelows she sported in her youth, Constance wears the somber-hued dress and wide scarf of the Revolutionary period; her only ornament is a gold cross, suspended from a velvet ribbon around her neck. Still, her bonnet remains a luxurious article. It is much like the one that all women wore in those days, from the widow Capet to Charlotte Corday and the wives who sat knitting during the deliberating assemblies; but hers, enormous and light, pleated and puffed, gives this reluctant *citoyenne* a kind of immense halo of tulle. The face covered with fine wrinkles is crumbling away at the bottom, like the faces of very old women. The clear eyes, which have remained youthful under their reddened lids, gaze at us with a cold benevolence in which there is both amusement and goodness. The sunken lips respond weakly to the smile in the eyes. This woman of the ancien régime appears to be no fool.

The trembling that seized an entire segment of French society after 1793 had not left those émigrés who returned to the fold. As we have seen, they had temporarily renounced their estate names, which they thought liable to draw the lightning down· on their heads. Reassured by the empire, and even more by the Restoration, they gradually began using these names again in daily life, on invitations and announcements, but did not do so on official documents until they had duly legalized them and had received authorization to insert them retroactively on all legal instruments registered since the Revolution.

Michel-Donatien did not die until 1806; Michel-Daniel and Charles, both octogenarians, passed away respectively in 1838 and 1845, during the reign of the usurper Louis-Philippe. Those old men who could still remember the coronation of Louis XVI doubtless continued to the end to play whist with the abbot, who, one hopes, was likewise able to witness the revival of throne and altar. One imagines them, around 1824, occasionally taking a cabriolet to Mont-Noir, whose fine sands furnished one of the raw materials for the ill-fated pottery works, and where Charles-Augustin, the "tall cavalryman," oversees the construction of a villa in a marked Louis XIII–Charles X style, perhaps a replacement for a lost country house.

It seems, indeed, that some of the family lands had been sold as the property of émigrés; Michel-Donatien could have transferred the titles of others in order to make it through hard times. But the history of the losses sustained during the Revolution is largely apocryphal: the legal records and what we know of the way of life of those plundered families show that they were quite well off. In times of unrest, to have suffered losses like other people is something to be emulated and boasted of: everyone complained about his lot. As for the venerable tradition claiming that the peasants spontaneously returned certain properties they had bought at auction, without aspiring to profits of any kind—this is perhaps more than a fanciful tale. In that corner of Flanders where owners and their tenant farmers still lived virtually side by side (since absentee landlords were mainly characteristic of the court nobility, which itself was fairly rare), envy, hatred, and bitterness were often rife; but sometimes affection and loyalty were, too. It seems that the Cleenewercks, with or without the French name they added to their own, were rather well liked.

PART II

THE YOUNG

MICHEL-

CHARLES

In a student room on the Left Bank, a young man is dressing for the Opéra ball. This low-ceilinged chamber—furnished with the flotsam of public auctions and as clean as possible for lodgings rented by the month, given that the landlady is an old woman aided only by an indifferent maidservant—is itself a commonplace and calls for description in the tritest possible terms. Above the fireplace, in which a few embers are dying, a slightly scorched engraving of Charles X's coronation proves that the landlady is a legitimist. Over the table strewn with young Michel-Charles's law texts is a shelf that displays a few volumes dearer to his heart: some Latin poetry, Lamartine's *Meditations*, Hugo's works from *The Orientals* to *The Twilight Songs*, but also books by Auguste Barbier and Casimir Delavigne, next to a dog-eared copy of Béranger's *chansons*. Nonetheless, all these details, especially the titles on the books' spines, are lost in the encroaching darkness of a February evening, which is alleviated only by two wax candles. One can scarcely see into the corner where, on the threadbare rug protected by a bit of absorbent cloth, sit two pitchers of warm water that my future grandfather, who at this time is twenty years old, has carried upstairs himself; there, too, is the sheet-iron tub in which he bathed, after his landlady sternly admonished him not to let any water drip through to the ceiling below.

On the bedspread he has laid out a pair of close-fitting pants from the best tailor, an evening jacket with tails, a domino (draped in such a way as to give an impression of mystery even before he has put it on), and, on the pillow, a black satin mask. Highly polished pumps seem to pirouette on the bedside rug. The student, although he prides himself on never spending all of the quite modest allowance his father gives him, is not stingy when it comes to his clothes—a trait that results to some extent, certainly, from the vanity of a handsome young man who wishes to please, but perhaps even more from his sense of what he owes to himself. Michel-Charles, who modestly regards himself as a simple fellow, is actually rather complicated.

In his undershorts and ruffle-front shirt, he gravely and curiously ponders his image in the little mirror on the dresser. This young man has one of those faces that seem to belong less to the individual, who has not yet proved himself, than to the clan, as if beneath his own features other faces that one might notice in passing on the walls of the family house in Bailleul rise to the surface and then disappear. In the well-defined bone structure, between the prominent cheekbones and the line of the thick eyebrows, his eyes gleam with a cold, intense blue, sometimes attracting the attention of beautiful women at the theater or on public promenades. The nose, with its slightly thick nostrils, satisfies him least. They're the sort of nostrils that a well-read mistress would describe as "leonine"; he wishes they were thinner. His mouth is wide and full-lipped, but the lower part of the face displays a childish softness, which of course this student who is winding two ells of fine batiste around his neck does not notice. In any case, he feels that his features are not Parisian and perhaps not even purely French. In sum, couldn't one take him for a Hungarian, a Russian, a handsome Scandinavian? Yes—a Ladislas, an Ivan, perhaps an Oskar . . . There's something about this face (he says to himself) that's bound to be intriguing to women.

But when all is said and done, for whom is he donning this costume? Since he first arrived in Paris, he has attended the Opéra ball every year with his friends, the upshot always being that he has left after a quarter of an hour, tired and disappointed. Like Frédéric Moreau, his contemporary, he finds that such hectic festivities leave him cold. Michel-Charles's goal is to graduate as quickly as possible, so that he can return to Bailleul and help his ailing father manage the family property. This ball is merely a whim to which he is in no way committed. Naturally he has read some of Balzac's novels—without, of course, knowing that he was dealing with masterpieces, since they have not yet been consecrated as such. But in none of the houses that he has been frequenting in Paris, not even at the home of his elegant cousins the d'Halluyns, has he met Diane de Cadignan, dangerous in her soft gray attire. No Esther has offered him the millions she has earned in her courtesan's bed; no Vautrin has given him the almost fatherly advice that would help him make his way in the world. A bit hastily, he concludes from this that novels are merely nonsense. What adventure could await him at the Opéra, amid a swarming crowd of people in hoods and black masks that flows and clusters as incomprehensibly as a column of ants or a hive of bees? A loose woman who plays the great lady disguised as a tart and who watches her pimp from a distance? A woman of the world who is disguised as a prostitute and is shadowed unwittingly by her jealous husband? A chambermaid adorned for the evening with her mistress's jewels and playing a woman of the world? It would have been better to devote the evening to the kind and compliant

Blanchette (I've chosen this name for her), a lacemaker (I've chosen this profession for her), whom it is so easy to entertain on Sundays, after an hour's intimacy in bed, by taking her to visit the Louvre if it's raining or for a stroll in the Luxembourg Gardens if it's fine. Those other women aren't the sort you should let yourself get involved with.

He thinks without pleasure of the bursts of foolish laughter inspired by repartee that isn't worth laughing at, the shrillness of the usual teasing, the stale odor of the women's perfumes and pomades. In the event he takes some nameless beauty to the Cadran Bleu or the Frères Provençaux for a late dinner, he knows what to make of the lewd fawning of the waiter who opens the door to the private dining room, the lingering odor of the preceding meal, and the little puff of dust that rises from the scarlet rep-covered sofa when the girl lets herself sink back on it. Will she even be healthy? Memories of the Dupuytren Museum soil the young man's mind for a moment; his father, Charles-Augustin, took him there during one of his regular visits to Paris to consult his doctors. Is it absolutely necessary that he make love with a nameless masquerader simply because today is Mardi Gras?

A bottle of champagne is chilling in an ice bucket that he himself has brought from the refreshment shop next door. As he finishes dressing he opens it—carefully, to prevent the cork from popping, which he has been taught to consider a vulgar sound. He fills his tooth glass with the sparkling liquid, coldly and deliberately drinks it down, refills the glass, and repeats until the whole bottle is gone. Not that Michel-Charles is a heavy drinker: his knowledge of fine vintages has made him a connoisseur and anything but an alcoholic. But he has acquired from his father a formula that he will pass on to his son: If you want to raise yourself to the level of a party that you really don't want to attend, the best thing is to consume, in small swallows, an entire bottle of fine champagne; without this, people and things will be merely what they are.

Almost immediately the beverage has the desired effect. His pulse beats more rapidly; his veins seem suddenly to be filled with golden flames. A young man owes it to himself to partake of the pleasures of his country and his time—to court adventure, run its risks, prove to himself that he can conquer something other than an amiable grisette, that he is capable of recognizing the elegance and charm beneath an ordinary hood and black lace mask. To choose, to amuse, to dare, to play, to satisfy . . . A marvelous agenda. When Charles-Augustin came to Paris recently to hobble about on his crutches in the waiting room of Dr. Récamier, who can do nothing more to help him, this intelligent father counseled his son not to let his youth slip by without tasting, in moderation, the pleasures of such a life. That day the two Charleses had one of those conversations that unite father and son in a masculine Freemasonry, far from the ears of mothers, wives, daughters, and sisters. Charles-Augustin would doubtless not have spoken so frankly at Bailleul. Since then, whenever Michel-Charles thinks of the "tall cavalryman" whose paralysis is little by little stiffening his limbs, he wonders whether his father might not miss other things from his past than the long horseback rides through the Flemish countryside. The sound of a carriage stopping before the door brings him back to the here and now: it's one of those coupés that the young man allows himself when he "steps out" on wet, muddy, or snowy evenings and that augment the landlady's good opinion of him.

Michel-Charles is just about to go downstairs when an idea occurs to him. He reopens a drawer that he closed and locked a moment ago, stows away his onyx signet ring (a gift from Charles-Augustin), and takes from his pocket several gold coins, which he hides under his shirts. The six louis that remain will be quite enough should he decide to offer supper to a pretty girl, whether duchess or bacchante. And if by ill luck the unknown woman turns out to be a swindler, that will be so much the less out of his pocket.

> Tomorrow, Sunday, May 8, when the or-
> namental fountains will be running at Versailles,
> trains will depart every half-hour . . . from first
> light until 11:00 p.m. All trains will be nonstop,
> with the exception of those departing earliest in
> the morning . . .
>   Tickets purchased in advance will be deliv-
> ered to the station on the rue du Plessis.
> —*Versailles Railway, rue du Plessis*

Three months later, the mildness of a certain May eighth fills Michel-Charles's room, making everything seem more beautiful. It is too early for the sun's rays to enter that narrow street, but obviously it will be fine weather—one of those spring days that counterfeit the summer to come. The year is 1842. It is Sunday; moreover (but Charles-Augustin would shrug his shoulders at this), it is the name-day of the Citizen King. The table, now covered with a white cloth, has been cleared of the student's law books. A coffeepot sits in state there on a burner, along with a stack of cups and saucers, all of which have been borrowed from the landlady. A large basket contains brioches.

By a happy coincidence, a friend from Cassel, Charles de Keytspotter, has chosen this moment to visit Paris, where his elder brother, another childhood friend, is also studying for a degree in law. The little group, which has been joined by two of Michel-Charles's former classmates from Stanislas School, is looking forward to spending this Sunday viewing Versailles and its fountains. Once they have made a tour of the grounds, they will take young Keytspotter to see the palace and the Tri-anons. They'll while away the afternoon in the woods, after lunching at some roadside tavern. The visitor from the prov-

inces, who arrived in Paris only a few days ago, has been
equipped for the occasion with an obliging companion, a girl
chosen by Blanchette. His brother is with the grisette who is
his recognized companion. One of the Parisian fellows is the
son of an architect named Lemarié; the other is a certain young
Monsieur de Drionville. Each brings (or perhaps doesn't bring)
his own girl with him. No one took the trouble to note down
the names of those two or three pretty girls; let's say they are
called Ida, Coralie, and Palmyre. Michel-Charles wants to begin
this fine day by inviting everyone to his lodgings for breakfast.

The young people arrive together, or perhaps one after the
other. Blanchette, who discreetly enters last, does the honors,
not without exchanging tender glances with Michel-Charles
from time to time. She wears a beautiful brand-new cashmere
shawl—a farewell gift, since it is understood that she will soon
marry a serious suitor, a bank clerk who lives in Moulins. These
young women are dressed in nainsook or organdy, with blue or
pink strings on their flowered bonnets; the gentlemen are sport-
ing light-colored trousers. The room is filled with rustling
sounds and little bursts of laughter.

Soon they head out into the streets, which are still nearly
empty, wending their way past the shuttered shop windows.
To add a newer pleasure to those they have planned for the
day, they have decided to make the trip to and from Versailles
by train. The Nord Line being only at the planning stage, this
is the first time that Charles de Keytspotter, who has come to
Paris by stagecoach, will have an opportunity to see a locomotive.
The Meudon-Versailles Line began operating only eighteen
months ago; even for the Parisians in this little group, travel
by rail is still a species of novelty. They have some trouble
finding seats in the cars, which are already quite full. Ida, or
perhaps Coralie, is frightened, or is pretending to be so out of
coquetry. The gentlemen reassure her, vowing that the railways

are eminently safe. During the journey, the Keytspotter brothers make the mistake of drawing Michel-Charles into a conversation concerning the momentous little events of Cassel; the two Parisians talk politics. The young women, who are a bit bored, discuss clothes and last year's boyfriends, laugh a good deal, and find that the train doesn't go as fast as people said it would. Michel-Charles gallantly helps Blanchette remove a cinder from her eye; though it is all but invisible, it is, she says, quite painful.

The spectacle of the great fountains is a triumph; likewise the Trianons. The palace itself is somewhat less so. Those enormous rooms overflowing with history and thronged with visitors weary them all, though no one will admit it. In the Hall of Mirrors, Blanchette remarks with a shiver that at night the whole place must be full of ghosts. The pathways through the gardens, bright with spring greenery and comparatively empty of people, are enchanting to the little band of visitors. They lunch gaily on omelettes and fried fish, which they find delicious because the hour is late and they are quite hungry. They drink to Blanchette's projected marriage, since she is definitely about to settle down. She has noiselessly taken off her shoes, which were pinching a bit, and, under the table, is stroking her fond boyfriend's ankle with her charming foot. They drink to the success of Michel-Charles and Louis de Keytspotter on their upcoming law examinations, and to that of Lemarié at the Ecole des Beaux-Arts.

They walk back at a more leisurely pace. The gentlemen offer their arms to the young ladies, who say that they are tired. They sing a sentimental ballad together, and with friendly tact they persuade Lemarié, who has had a little too much to drink, to stop humming bawdy songs. Coralie, who is thirsty, wants them to pause for a moment at a refreshment shop to buy an almond drink, but Michel-Charles points out that they have just enough time to get back to the station if they want to arrive in Paris in time to dine at La Chaumière, where he has reserved a table, and then to see the fireworks over the Seine.

The hubbub at the Versailles station is like a cross between a street fair and a good-natured riot. Michel-Charles himself suggests that they wait for the next train, which, after all, will delay them only slightly: to accommodate the crowd of travelers, departures are taking place every ten minutes. A train drawn by two locomotives enters the station. Middle-class couples in their Sunday best who have become dusty and disheveled by the unseasonable heat, high-school students, workers in caps, women with children in tow and their arms full of rapidly wilting jonquils dash toward the train's high steps. Lemarié has just enough time to draw his companions' attention to a much-decorated naval officer who is entering the compartment next to theirs: it's Admiral Dumont d'Urville, recently returned, after countless dangers, from an Antarctic expedition. He is accompanied by a well-dressed woman and a young boy who is doubtless his son. Aided by their gentlemen friends, the grisettes climb into the compartment, doing their best to protect their flounces and bonnets. Somewhat out of breath, they take a seat, or remain standing if there are no places left, just as the crewmen slam the doors and lock them, supposedly in order to prevent rascals who are traveling without tickets from slipping off the train before it enters the station. Paul de Drionville, seated opposite Michel-Charles, is a bit uneasy. His mother made him promise never to ride at the front of the train. Michel-Charles calms him: they're in the second car, not the first. He adds that they're definitely going rather fast. The train begins to lurch like a skiff in a storm. Suddenly a series of violent jolts tosses the passengers on top of one another, half laughing, half terrified. A gigantic upheaval, like that of an ocean swell, hurls the occupants to the floor or against the walls. A din composed of grinding metal, splintering wood, whistling steam, and boiling water drowns out the moans and shrieks. Michel-Charles loses consciousness.

When he partially regains his senses, he finds himself choking and coughing. He feels as if he's inside a smoke-filled oven. A current of fresher air seems to be coming from somewhere—whether a caved-in wall or a shattered window, he will never know. Crawling through the stifling darkness, shoving aside and thrusting away vague shapes that are bodies, here and there snagging on a piece of cloth that rips as he pulls free, he reaches the break, thrusts his head and shoulders through the narrow opening, struggles, falls outside at last, and tumbles down an embankment.

The feel and smell of the earth revive him; groping about, he discovers he is in a vineyard. Despite the long May twilight, it is almost as dark outside as it was in the hole from which he escaped. With the aid of his bleeding hands, he gets to his feet on the embankment and at last comprehends what he has thus far only experienced. The second locomotive has crashed into the first. The cars, constructed entirely of wood—heaved up, overturned, crushed, flung atop one another—have been reduced to a monstrous woodpile emitting smoke and screams. A few shadows move about and run along the tracks, having miraculously escaped, as Michel-Charles did, from the compartment-prisons. By the light of a fresh burst of flames, he recognizes a former classmate named Lalou, from Douai. He hails him, grips his arm, points to the place he has just torn himself from, and cries, "We have to go back in! There are people in there! People who are dying!"

The flames shooting out on all sides give the only reply to his futile appeal. A young woman, screaming, reaches out through a broken window; at the risk of his life, a man comes close enough to grasp her hand and pulls; the arm comes away and falls like a burning stick. An unknown passenger who has been hurled onto the tracks tugs off his burning shoe, and with it a crushed foot that remains attached to his leg by a mere scrap of flesh. A young man, not as lucky as Michel-Charles, has likewise fallen into the vineyard at the bottom of the embankment, but a vine stake has pierced his breast like a bayonet; he can do nothing more than take a few steps, and dies with a loud cry. The fire has been as capricious as lightning: along the rails, where rescuers with hooks and poles are busy retrieving charred remains, a young passenger, completely nude, eviscerated from throat to lower belly, has an erection in his death throes and looks like a monstrous Priapus. Toward the back of the train, where the fire has not engulfed everything, roadworkers have managed to break windows and locks and have freed a number of passengers. Some of these run away screaming, leaving the nightmare behind them; others, in contrast, plunge back into the smoke to search for their companions. But the cars toward the front are completely destroyed.

By the light of the fire, which now makes the smallest objects visible, Michel-Charles notices that the legs of his trousers are hanging in blackish tatters. Brushing his sleeve across his forehead to wipe away what he thinks is sweat, he discovers that his face is covered with blood. When he regains consciousness, he is lying in a room at the château of Meudon, where the wounded are being given first aid. Dawn is brightening the large windows; already it was yesterday that the catastrophe took place. Gently the attendants tell him that of the forty-eight people who occupied the four compartments in his car, he is the sole survivor.

Someone, perhaps Lalou, brought him back to his rooms in a hired carriage. Doubtless on the advice of Dr. Récamier, whose guidance the family had relied on for many years, it was decided that he should postpone until October the exams he had originally planned to take in July. On the basis of a broken watch case and a shredded passport, the authorities drew up death certificates for the Keytspotter brothers, which Michel-Charles signed. He may also have performed this service for Lemarié and Drionville. A bit of ribbon and a parasol handle recovered from that charnel house bring to mind the young ladies. I have pored over the list of victims, which is surely incomplete, searching in vain for names that might plausibly be theirs; Michel-Charles himself had perhaps known them only by their graceful *noms de guerre*. Little by little, the scars from his burns became less noticeable, but for a long time afterward a lock of hair over his forehead stood out stark white against the rest, which was thick and brown.

Nearly forty years later, Michel-Charles set down for his children, in a brief memoir written shortly before his death, the story of that disaster. He had no talent as a writer, but the precision and intensity of his account give one the feeling that beneath his bemedaled and well-tailored breast and in the depths of his almost inscrutable eyes, perhaps without his knowledge, that mass of wooden partitions, incandescent metal, and human flesh continued to burn and smoke. A man of the nineteenth century, respectful of propriety in all its forms, Michel-Charles did not state in writing that a few pleasant young women had joined the gay little group. He mentioned their presence to his son. He also spared his children a few hideous details, which I gleaned from the official reports.

Other people, close relatives of the victims, preserved for a time, deep within them, the memory of that catastrophe. The architect Lemarié, father of the dead student, had a chapel built on the fatal site and dedicated it to Our Lady of the Flames; he went mad soon after the ceremony at which it was consecrated. Apparently the building was quite ugly, but its beautiful name is richly evocative. Our Lady of the Flames: a father so pious could just as easily have erected a chapel to Our Lady of the Afflicted, or to Our Lady of Consolation, or to any number of others. More courageous than that, this man looked the holocaust full in the face, at the risk of being consumed by it himself. When I remember his Our Lady of the Flames, I can't help thinking of Durga or Kali, of the powerful Hindu Mother who is the source of all things and in whom all things are engulfed, and who dances upon the world, abolishing earthly forms. But Christian thought is of a different essence: "O tender Mary, protect us from the flames of this world! Preserve us above all from the flames of eternity!" Thus read the inscription on the chapel's pediment. For the souls who had passed from that earthly fire to the fires of Purgatory, four Masses a year were to be said. And so they were, for two decades. Then the memory of those ashes dissolved in forgetfulness: The chapel, constructed in troubadour style, was still standing thirty years ago. Today a modern building occupies the site.

The filaments of the spider's web in which all of us are caught are indeed fragile. On that Sunday in May, Michel-Charles nearly lost, or was spared, the forty-four years of life that remained to him. At the same time, his three children and their descendants, of which I am one, came very close to not existing at all. When I think that a defective connecting rod (according to the records, a replacement part had been ordered from England but was still waiting to be picked up at Customs) nearly annihilated these virtualities, and when I note, moreover, that so little remains of most of the lives that are actualized and lived, I find it hard to attach much importance to the caramboles of chance. Nevertheless, the image I retain of that disaster from Louis-Philippe's time is the image of a young man of twenty thrusting himself headfirst through a gaping hole, blind and bloody as on the day he was born, bearing his posterity in his loins.

Even for my father, who disliked anything that connected him with the family—and of course much more for my grandfather, whose ties to his kin were strong and close—the old house in Bailleul always meant beauty, order, and calm. Since it disappeared in the smoke of 1914 and since I had a chance to see it only as a very young child, it will remain forever in the ILLO TEMPORE of Golden Age myth. Balzac described a similar dwelling in his book *The Quest for the Absolute*, depicting it with his visionary genius but also with that megalomania which led him to overdo everything. Scarcely any families in French Flanders ornamented their drawing rooms with an ancestral portrait actually painted by Titian; very few boasted gardens containing valuable tulips of which a single bulb was worth fifty écus; none, fortunately, owned a series of contemporary panels representing in full detail the life of the brewer and patriot Van Artevelde, which was at most merely the naïve invention of a woodworker of Louis-Philippe's time. But reduced to its essentials, the Claes house, portrayed by a man who hardly set foot in the province of Nord, lives and breathes so vividly that I needn't bother to describe that house in Bailleul.

How Many Years

The shrill sound of the doorbell and the barking of his beloved dog Misca fill Michel-Charles with a sweet contentment that he thought he would never experience again. Then come the three virgins, Gabrielle, Louise, and Valérie, pink and white in their summer frocks, who have hurried ahead of everyone else to open the door for their brother. Then—superbly sure of herself, mastering her emotions, a comforting smile on her lips—comes the aptly named Reine ("Queen"), who presses her son to her ample bosom, which is clothed in taffeta gleaming like a cuirass. The embrace of the cook, Mélanie, who was present at the young gentleman's birth and who will eventually be laid to rest in the family tomb after fifty years of devoted service, is joined by the timid handshakes and bows of the two maids. Finally, a sharp thumping makes itself heard over this commotion: Charles-Augustin Cleenewerck de Crayencour, to honor his son, has risen from his armchair—the one he has scarcely quitted since a disease of the spinal cord, whose first symptoms appeared fifteen years ago, left him paralyzed in both legs. His long crutches go tok-tok on the tiles of the corridor.

Charles-Augustin's closely shaved cheek brushes lightly against his son's. His face furrowed with wrinkles and his keen gaze express a vivacity that his body no longer possesses. Impeccable in his well-tailored frock coat, supremely controlled despite his nerveless legs hanging limply beneath him, this invalid gives the impression of one of Ingres' bourgeois gentlemen. The worthy Henri, Michel-Charles's elder brother, has also come down from his room. He's not exactly retarded, not even slow-witted (or scarcely). The neighbors solve the problem by calling him an eccentric. From the time he was attending the parish school, it was recognized that Henri was not destined for Stanislas School or the benches of the Sorbonne. People already know that he will live out his days in the bosom of his family, without asking great things of life, without inconveniencing anyone, content to stroll around the main square wearing his handsome suits, which are sent to him by a tailor in Lille, and handing out bonbons and small coins to urchins who make jokes about him in Flemish as soon as his back is turned. He has excellent manners: at the dinner table he passes the salt or the mustard with a little bow to whoever has requested it. He likes to listen to his sisters sing romantic ballads as they accompany themselves on the piano; but he spends the better part of his time in his room, reading Paul de Kock, whom the young ladies must not be allowed to see. He directs his wide, slightly dazed smile at his brother.

At the end of the long corridor, the garden door opens onto shady greenery and the twittering of birds. The girls have left their games and their embroidery on a metal table. It was all just like this on a certain evening less than a month ago, when the inferno was raging and burning at Meudon. Let's not make any mistake here: it is not in the heart but in the mind that Michel-Charles has been wounded. We must not overestimate the pain he feels at the death of his four excellent companions: they weren't such extremely close friends of his. Blanchette's death is surely terrible to recall, but Blanchette herself was merely a likable girl whom he was preparing to bid farewell. What has for weeks left him stupefied and unnerved is his sudden recognition of the horror that lurks at the core of everything. The veil of appearances, so gay at that Versailles sparkling with fountains, has parted for a moment. Though he is ill-equipped to analyze his impressions, he has seen life's true face, which is a mass of flames. Reine notices that her son is growing weary; she takes him to a quiet room so that he can lie down, closes the curtains, and leaves him with Misca curled up at his feet.

Charles-Augustin Cleenewerck, Yourcenar's great-grandfather,
ca. 1840

"Reine Bieswal de Briarde, my mother," writes Michel-
Charles at the beginning of his memoirs, "was the daughter of
Joseph Bieswal de Briarde and Valentine de Coussemaker; she
was the granddaughter of Benoît Bieswal de Briarde, a counselor
to Parliament, and of the demoiselle Lefebvre de la Basse-Boulogne (a portrait showing the latter dressed as Diana the huntress
is still in my possession). My mother was of medium height,
had a rosy Flemish complexion, was very intelligent and very
good . . . She had been raised by a canoness of noble birth
whom the vicissitudes of the Revolution had drawn into the

106

Reine Bieswal de Briarde, Yourcenar's great-grandmother,
ca. 1840

family during its years abroad, and who afterward never left it. Everything in my mother bespoke the refined education of the old days." What he does not say (and this is neither the first nor the last time we will find him holding back hard-to-utter truths) is that this engaging woman was also formidable. There exists a painting of her by Bafcop, a fine portraitist who in those days was held in high regard throughout the Nord region. This fortyish woman in outdoor clothes of satin and fur, her hands tucked into an enormous muff, gives the impression of a frigate advancing under full sail. The former pupil of a high-born canoness has the face of an abbess from the ancien régime. One senses that her slightly jovial cordiality conceals a will that is as supple and sharp as a knife: this smile always has the last word. Reine is the masterpiece of a society in which women have no need to vote or to demonstrate in the streets in order to reign. She plays to perfection her role as regent by the side of an ailing king. It is assumed that she defers to Charles-Augustin in all things; in reality, she rules.

These inseparable spouses are divided by shades of opinion that their good upbringing almost always prevents them from expressing. In Charles-Augustin's eyes, there is only one King of France, and he is at Frohsdorf. For him, the imperial epic (or escapade) took place at a great distance. This man who was married the year of Waterloo did not exactly deck the house with flags when Wellington's victory was announced, but the only pang of grief he felt was at the death of Reine's brother, a member of the emperor's honor guard during the French campaign. Without ever saying so, Charles-Augustin perhaps deplores the fact that this glorious end, which augmented his wife's share of the inheritance, had not taken place instead under the folds of the white flag. Later he acquiesced when Reine—a legitimist, certainly, but imbued with the realism of the mother of a family—proposed that they marry their daughter Marie-Caroline to young P., scion of an honorable bourgeois clan in which the title Deputy from Nord would prove to be virtually hereditary throughout the nineteenth century under the various regimes. He even lets Michel-Charles visit, in Paris, that brother-in-law who is highly regarded in the ministries, but he will not hear of letting his son "feed at the trough" of the Citizen King. Reine, in contrast, dreams of a fine administrative or political career for her gifted boy. But enough talk: it's better to wait until Michel-Charles has passed his law examinations. Who knows? This man and this woman, both fifty years old, have already seen eight governments hold power in France. Before Michel-Charles has defended his thesis, the senior branch might possibly be on the throne again or, what is more difficult to believe, Charles-Augustin might change his mind. It is also possible—and even the most devoted families make such calculations at the bedside of an ailing loved one— that Charles-Augustin may no longer be there to impose his opinion.

Friends and family have not arranged any informal reception for the student's return, as on the already distant day when he came home with his bachelor's degree—a title so rare in Bailleul in those days that he was nearly regaled with a public celebration. People know that the accident on the Versailles railway has caused him great suffering. But the oppressive, even unctuous routine of family life continues. Every Sunday Reine presides at a meal to which she has invited all the relatives, meaning just about everyone who is of any consequence in the town. The tablecloth that is laid for this ceremony, which is hardly less sacred than High Mass, is resplendent with silver and gleams softly with fine old porcelain. The chicken quenelles are served at noon, the dessert and sweetmeats at around five. It is understood that between the sorbet and the saddle of lamb, the guests are entitled to take a turn about the garden, and perhaps, with a few apologies for indulging in such a rustic entertainment, even play a game of *boules*. Discreetly, a few of them take advantage of this diversion to slip away to a pavilion tucked among the trees. Charles-Augustin, deferring to the orders of the Faculty of Medicine, rises with the aid of his crutches and goes to lie down in the next room. The young ladies adjust their ribbons and gaily bring their girl friends up to their rooms or into a charming little nook on the mezzanine, which has a well-scoured wooden bench along one wall. Three people can sit side by side there, and it's the custom among the women to repair to that spot for their intimate chats. The soft sound of trickling water, which flows as if in the basin of a fountain, does not (so I've been told) offend these good-natured women. The little corner receptacle in which a broom is stored is made of old Delftware, like the vases in the drawing room.

Everyone celebrates the betrothal of young Louise to her cousin Maximilien-Napoléon de Coussemaker, who comes from a family that has enjoyed a spotless reputation for four hundred years. Charles-Augustin approves of his daughter's intended, even though one of his given names is a somewhat too vivid reminder that Reine's relatives fell into the imperialist trap. Those given names so characteristic of their milieu and their time are worthy of comment. Charles-Augustin doubtless owes one of his own to the Jansenism of his ancestor de Gheus. The name Reine, for a girl born in 1792, has only one meaning: loyalty to the threatened daughter of Maria Theresa. The Josephs and the Charleses, the Maximiliens, Isabelles, Thérèses, and Eugénies are traditional in the family, and some of these names, certainly, are common in France. It happens, though, that all of them belonged to emperors and empresses or to Spanish and Austrian regents of the Low Countries, or retain traces of Jansenist Augustinism. It is not completely an accident that two brothers who came from Arras to Paris in 1789, destined to leave their marks—one deep, the other quickly effaced—on the history of France, were named Maximilien and Augustin de Robespierre.

Still suffering from nightmares and insomnia, the young man nevertheless returns to Paris, where he passes his October examinations with great distinction. We will never know if the subsequent two winters bring him anything other, or more exciting, than study. In any case, he resumes living in his room on the rue de Vaugirard and dining for thirty-six sous in a restaurant on the rue Saint-Dominique, which, for a student, is a form of modest luxury. Did he meet his Diane de Cadignan or his Esther, or did he content himself with a new Blanchette? The men of the nineteenth century keep an entire side of their lives cloaked in mystery.

It is out of the question that a young doctor of law who graduated with highest honors should open a private practice. The liberal professions, so highly prized by a certain segment of the bourgeoisie, are considered inferior by this family, which approves of only a few occupations—namely, managing its own assets and serving the state. Despite Guizot's dictum "Enrich thyself," which is the present government's motto, business and industry are placed several rungs farther down: Charles-Augustin cannot see his son managing a spinning mill. The knowledge and the diplomas brought back from Paris will be useful to Michel-Charles as he carefully draws up contracts with his tenant farmers or resolves without too many difficulties some dispute over a boundary wall. The father who years ago had to give up inspecting his own farms is eager to train his successor.

But Reine finds the boy nervous. He flinches at the slightest noise, takes Misca on long solitary walks, and closets himself in his room like Henri—not, however, to read Paul de Kock. As is the rule, these parents don't know their son very well, but Michel-Charles has his sisters for confidantes. Reine learns from them that the young man who suddenly has time on his hands speaks often of blue skies, Roman ruins, and Swiss chalets and envies his cousin Edmond de Coussemaker, who is a student at Jena. He has shown his poetry to his favorite sister, Gabrielle; it closely resembles Lamartine's, and describes the joy he would feel if he could someday view the sea of Sorrento.

Reine's only experience of the world took place in the Paris of Louis XVIII, where she strolled on the arm of her young husband, visiting shops, fine restaurants, a pantomime or melo-

111

drama on the boulevard du Crime, the Bois de Boulogne at the hour when fashionable people congregated there in their carriages, and those very fountains at Versailles which, with nearly tragic results, she had recommended to her son. The young ladies have spent three years in the capital confined in their convent on the avenue de l'Observatoire, where their brother would come fetch them every Sunday for High Mass at Saint-Sulpice, a classical play at the Comédie Française, or an occasional informal dance at Deputy P.'s house. But these women who will be content to live out their entire lives in their little town have a vague intuition: the student, now returned home and tormented by the desire to travel, feels a legitimate need. A well-born man owes it to himself to see the world before settling down in the country where chance or Providence has placed him. A Grand Tour, of the sort that young gentlemen of the eighteenth century indulged in, would not only restore to Reine a son cured of his craving for travel but give her the time to set up her maternal batteries for arranging an advantageous marriage and (who knows?) a government career for her beloved child.

Charles-Augustin imposes only one condition: his son may not leave until the following year and must spend the intervening time perfecting his knowledge of the geography, history, and literature of the countries he will visit and learning something of their languages. During that winter, nighttime passersby—rare in that town where people retire at an early hour and the rain and cold discourage late evening walks—could have seen a lamp burning into the wee hours in Michel-Charles's window. But the young man forbids himself to read or reread poetic descriptions—travel accounts perhaps infused with an artificial enthusiasm that might prevent him from seeing and judging with his own eyes. He's probably making a mistake. Stimulating the mind with lyrical evocations of the countries one will visit is no more foolish than drinking champagne before a ball.

The day before his departure Charles-Augustin gives his son, already furnished with the funds necessary for the initial stages of his trip, a draft on the Albani Bank in Rome for ten thousand francs. He stipulates, moreover, that Michel-Charles should use some of this money to buy a few tastefully chosen gifts "for the ladies." As to the rest, he hopes that the young man will spend only three thousand francs for his personal needs and will show proof of his levelheadedness by bringing back the remainder. Let it be said here and now that his hope was fulfilled.

A carriage finally bears away the two travelers, Michel-Charles and his first cousin Henri Bieswal, a decent fellow who upon his return will settle down comfortably into the life of a wealthy country landowner, and who by the time of his death will be president of the agricultural society. Michel-Charles, intoxicated with joy, admits that he is leaving without any of the regrets that in those days were obligatory when bidding goodbye to one's family. The parents on the doorstep do their best to look cheerful. At fifty-two, Charles-Augustin knows that his days are numbered. Will he ever see his son again? The robust Reine thinks of the accident at Versailles. The new means of locomotion are not the only ones that are dangerous: stagecoaches can tip over; horses can seize the bit in their teeth; boats can capsize; brigands are said to infest the Roman Campania and Sicily; almost everywhere, Circes and Calypsos are on the lookout for young men, deceive them, conjure away their money, infect their blood with a life-destroying poison. Reine tells herself it is a miracle that, all those years ago, Charles-Augustin returned from Germany, leaving his brothers and sisters in the cemetery. It is likewise a miracle that he was able to found a family before some incomprehensible illness took possession of him. Though she is not naturally inclined toward anxiety or bitterness, it occurs to her, as she glances at her good Henri, that Charles-Augustin in his turn has only one son. Gentle Henri, standing on the threshold behind her, blows kisses to the travelers. Gabrielle keeps a tight hold on Misca, who is straining at her leash and wants to follow her master.

Paradoxically, this happy journey begins on a gloomy note. At Péronne the coach is forced to stop for several hours and undergo repairs. The weather is cold. The coachman suggests that the two cousins take shelter in the warmth of a rundown tavern frequented by wagon drivers. After being served with a pitcher of beer, which he is careful not to drink from, the young man listens and looks about him. The room reeks of stale tobacco smoke; his neighbors are laughing, drinking, quarreling, spitting on the floor, swearing hoarsely and obscenely. "They weren't men—they were animals," the young doctor of law noted with disgust. I'm almost grateful to him for not letting himself be carried away, as one of my maternal great-uncles was not long afterward, by saccharine images of greathearted workers: such clichés are likewise insulting to the people. There is a certain honesty in Michel-Charles that makes him describe what he sees exactly as he sees it. Coarseness and obscenity will continue to haunt him, accustomed as he is to a well-ordered household. Arles and Nîmes are "dirty towns," despite the beauty of their classical ruins; the port of Toulon is "sickening," and here he is doubtless not mistaken. His description of the prison resembles his description of that squalid tavern. Fresh from his readings in Dante, he is quite aware that he is looking at Hell. But once again, he feels mainly horror and disgust instead of compassion. When the lament of a convict claiming to be innocent evokes a pang in his heart, the mocking smile of a guard quickly brings him back to reality. "Fool!" this representative of authority seems to say to him. "The only pity here is to be pitiless." The young man does not gainsay this, and leaves with an uneasy feeling rather than utterly demoralized. In the fallacious battle between order and justice, Michel-Charles has already allied himself with the forces of order. All his life he will believe that a man who is wellborn, well brought up, well washed, well fed, well watered (within reason), and educated as befits a respectable man of his day is not merely better than those wretches but of another species, almost of another blood. Even if he encountered, amid many errors, a small bit of truth in this view—which, overt or tacit, has been that of all civilizations up to the present—the falseness it contains will always end up splitting apart any society that relies on it. In the course of his life as a privileged man (but not necessarily a happy one), Michel-Charles has never experienced a crisis so acute as to make him realize that he is, in the last analysis, the double of these human bits of refuse, and perhaps even their brother. Neither will he admit that every man, sooner or later, will find himself condemned to forced labor in perpetuity.

Forty years after his return from Italy, in the last months of his life and in the relative peace of an autumn at Mont-Noir, Michel-Charles carefully recopied into a handsomely bound volume the few hundred letters he had written to his family during his travels. The task no doubt gave him the somewhat sad pleasure of an aged invalid who leans for support, so to speak, on the young man he once was. As a pretext for his efforts, Michel-Charles modestly cites the fact that his son, and the one daughter remaining to him, may someday enjoy looking through those unpretentious pages to learn how people traveled in Italy long ago. Marie, so far as I know, never had occasion to read them. Michel, my father, did no more than glance at those pages covered with fine, pale writing and found the content to be fairly insipid. In a prefatory note, Michel-Charles asks that the book be thrown into the fire if it ever leaves the family. I disobeyed him, as you can see. But aside from the fact that those inoffensive letters are not worth such precautions, it so happens that at a distance of 130 years, and in a world more greatly altered than Michel-Charles could ever have imagined, they have in many respects become a historical document, and not only concerning the way in which people used to contract for the services of coaches and drivers.

Reine had made her son promise that he would write to her every day, even if he mailed her the pages only once a week or whenever the opportunity to send a letter to France arose. The result was what one might expect: an extra task that a well-intentioned youth performed willingly but without enthusiasm. All of us at around the age of twenty-two have sent letters to our families or to whoever stands in their stead, in which we wrote that that morning we'd visited a museum and seen some famous statue, that we'd then eaten an excellent meal, not too expensive, in a nearby restaurant, that we were planning to go to the opera that evening if tickets were available, and that we'd like our best regards conveyed to various people. In those reassuring accounts, there was no word about what excited us, unsettled us, perhaps thoroughly bowled us over. One can scarcely believe that such flat, somewhat childish summaries could have come from that handsome youth with the lovely eyes who was traveling rapidly through a country he would never forget as long as he lived.

Of course, the principal litotes is the one concerning the sensual adventures of the French *cavaliere*. Good parents in every age believe that their children "tell them everything." If by chance Michel-Charles ever really confided to his family a small part of what he experienced, it was surely not by means of a letter that would be read in the evening under the linden tree by lamplight. Sometimes we get a glimpse of passion in a remark on the beauty of the women of Avignon, or in the obviously quite vivid impression that was made on him, at a ball at the French embassy, by the young Muscovite princesses and ladies-in-waiting who were serving as travel companions to the Empress of Russia, the wife of Nicholas I, the very German Charlotte of Prussia. In Sicily, afterward, he will again mention the charming Princess Olga, later Queen of Württemberg; but the lovely Italian girls, more accessible, remain invisible. Very soon the two cousins join a group of three or four young Frenchmen—to save money, Michel-Charles tells us, but one hopes they do so also for the pleasure of the companionship. These youths—who, like him, are seeking education amid their amusements—quickly teach him how to stretch his money well beyond his father's expectations by staying at inns far from the hotels frequented by English misses and their imperious or aloof parents. In the big cities they rent an apartment and hire a local servant. For the fun of it, they make part of each excursion on foot, up to the point where the exhausted young travelers are only to happy to be offered a ride in some village *carrozza*.

But we will never know anything about the amorous adventures of those young men wandering the roads in the land of the *Satyricon* and Boccaccio's tales, where love readily granted (but not as romantic as expected) has always been an attraction or a mirage for foreigners. We see not a single procurer roaming the streets, having stepped straight out of a classical comedy and now proposing to lead these Illustrious Lords to reputable addresses; not a single pretty laundress bending over her tub, showing off her bottom or her breasts; none of those passionate glances exchanged along a Corso during evening promenades; not a single beautiful woman smiling behind a window blind. There are no local wines (or very few), no heated discussions of politics or the arts, no occasional quarrels among friends, no jokes offered in a straightforward way, as people liked them in those days, no student ditties or guardhouse refrains sung while bumping along in a cart and bawled out all the more lustily as the driver understands not a word. Only once are we present at one of those choral exercises that students everywhere indulge in, but what we hear is not Béranger or Désaugiers or some popular tune; it's a ballad by Alexandre Dumas entitled "The Angel," which exudes a bland idealism and which the young men toss to the echoing Tuscan hills. The ethereal emotions that it conveys are highly artificial, but perhaps no more so than those expressed in a song by Prévert or in one of Edith Piaf's heart-tugging and timeworn refrains.

The banal letters of this brilliant student reveal a great deal about a culture in which the subjects taught in schools had changed little since the eighteenth century and perhaps even the seventeenth. We have so long deplored the decline of the humanities that it is not disheartening to see how they themselves signed their own death warrant. Despite a memory that approaches the phenomenal and that will enable him throughout his life to recite impressive passages from Homer whose meaning he has all but forgotten, Michel-Charles, like the vast majority of literate French people of his time, knows scarcely any Greek. He is, however, an excellent Latinist, which means he has read four or five great historians, from Titus Livy to Tacitus; a comparable number of poets, beginning with Virgil in his entirety and ending with selected works of Juvenal; and two or three treatises by Cicero and Seneca. Nearly all cultures founded on the study of the classics limit themselves to a very small number of authors, and the intrinsic merits of these seem less important than the fact that people are familiar with them. Once an average man has read them, he is stamped as the member of a group and almost of a club. They furnish him with a modicum of quotations, justifications, and examples that help him communicate with those of his contemporaries who are equipped with the same baggage—and this is no inconsiderable thing. On another level, one that few people attain, the classics are of course a good deal more: the buttress, module, plumb line, and T-square of the soul, an art of thinking and sometimes of living. In the best of cases, they liberate us and incite us to revolt, seemingly despite themselves. But let us not expect them to have such an effect on Michel-Charles. He is not a humanist, a species that was in fact rare around 1845. He is merely a very good pupil who has studied the humanities.

The country he visited is an Italy we can no longer see today. Its ruins were still magnificent vine-covered relics that inspired meditations on the fall of empires; they were not those specimens of classical architecture that have been restored, labeled, glamorized after dark with floodlights, and dwarfed by nearby buildings which the next bombardment will flatten along with them. The Meta Sudans, point of departure for all the roads of the Roman Empire, with its spring in which gladiators bathed their blood-covered arms, had not yet disappeared in the aedilic upheavals under Mussolini; visitors still approached Saint Peter's through a labyrinth of little streets that made Bernini's colonnade an immense and harmonious surprise. The Victor-Emmanuel monument, that enormous block of lard, was not yet competing with the Capitoline. And not until much later would the sputtering of motor scooters drown out the splashing of the fountains. Michel-Charles roamed on horseback through a city that was dirty and often fever-infested, but not polluted as it is today; it was still fit for humans, and for ghosts. The vast gardens, which real-estate speculation would destroy at the turn of the century, were still green and flourishing. The working-class neighborhoods were overflowing with a noisy, squalid mass of humanity, which Belli evoked almost tenderly in the poems he composed in dialect. The contrast between the wretchedness of the poor and the luxury of the papal and banking families was brutal; the contrast today between the gilded underworld of *la dolce vita* and the inhabitants of the city's grottoes and shantytowns is no less so.

Michel-Charles's eye was less jaded than ours, but also less sensitive. On the one hand, he had not already seen those sites reproduced a hundred times and clothed in the allure of Technicolor. He owned no photographs of Great Art, in which tricks of lighting and perspective may change the proportions and exaggerate or soften the features of a sculpted marble face, so that the visitor often has difficulty recognizing, in some corner of a museum, that same bust reduced to what it actually is. On the other hand, his knowledge and his taste often reached their limits. Accustomed as he was to the green woods of Nord, he was disappointed when he first encountered the Italian countryside. Its dry hills had fewer flowers than he expected; the olive tree seemed to him a poor, stingy plant. What would he say today if he could see that pylons have too often replaced the trees, and that the waters of the Clitunno, dear to the great white bulls of Virgil, now flow beneath a roaring highway? The dark Florentine streets, their palaces adorned with outlandish carvings, saddened this traveler, who as yet had only a veneer of Romanticism. If he had dared, he would have confessed that the musculatures of Michelangelo struck him as exaggerated. In any case, in Florence he devoted more time to describing the tomb of the Grand Dukes, with its beautiful facing of gray marble, than to *Dawn* or *Night*. At Paestum the powerful, stocky-looking columns, which seem to have grown straight out of the depths of the soil, made him feel almost afraid. He was quite typical of his people, who, when they revived the architecture of the Greeks, preferred to endow it with the graces of the Louis XVI period or the cold elegance of the Empire style. The robust Greece of preclassical times, with its gods, monsters, and dreams, was known in the first half of the nineteenth century only to a prescient old man and a few young visionaries: the Goethe of *Faust*, Part II; Hölderlin and Gérard de Nerval, both insane; and the fever-racked Maurice de Guérin, who heard within himself the hoofbeats of the Centaur. We cannot ask as much of a young doctor of law.

You can imagine with what curiosity I deciphered, in one of the letters to Mother, the passage concerning Hadrian's villa—a lovely site today defiled by obtrusive restorations, shapeless statuary dotting the gardens and arbitrarily grouped beneath renovated porticoes, not to mention a refreshment stand and a parking lot just a few feet from the great wall that Piranesi sketched. Gone is the old villa of Count Fede as it still looked when I saw it as a teenager, its long allée bordered by a praetorian guard of cypresses leading step by step to a silent realm of shadows, haunted in April by the cry of the cuckoo, in August by the hum of cicadas; but where, on my last visit, I heard mostly the din of transistor radios. Between the abandoned ruin—accessible only to a few intrepid amateurs such as Piranesi, cutting his way through those enchanted solitudes with a hatchet—and the tourist trap swarming with busloads of visitors, how little time has passed! The young visitor of 1845 stumbled about in what seemed to him merely a vast confused landscape strewn with irregular blocks of stone. Hadrian belongs to the period following the great classical historians that Michel-Charles had read. My grandfather surely did not plunge into the dust of chronicles such as the *Augustan History* in order to form—as one reassembles a mosaic from scattered tesserae—an idea of the most modern and complex of those men who were cut out to rule. At most, his guidebooks told him that Hadrian had traveled widely, patronized the arts, and waged war in Palestine; and Bossuet's *Universal History* informed him that Hadrian "dishonored his reign with his monstrous passions." This was not enough to induce a young man to linger among the broken arches and olive trees that had so little appeal for him. He hastened to leave that uninteresting place for the Villa d'Este—for its fountains ornamented with fleurs-de-lys and its gardens that conjured up visions of lovely maidens harkening to a *cavaliere* strumming airs on a lute.

This young man who was acquainting himself with the arts confessed that he preferred sculpture to painting—perhaps, although he did not realize it, because the mind can make sense of sculpture more easily. In fact, he wandered almost exclusively among what people in those days called "antiques": Greco-Roman or, at best, Alexandrian copies of lost originals. The public no longer feels such attachment for these works, now considered cold and redundant, in any case secondhand. No one still goes to the Vatican seeking a revelation of the sublime from the *Apollo Belvedere* or learns about the role of the emotions in art by gazing at the *Laocoön*, that opera in stone. Even with regard to what is properly called "Greek" art, the fashion has gone backward, leaving in its wake the Venus de Milo (brought to France by the same Admiral Dumont d'Urville whom Michel-Charles nearly accompanied to the grave), passing from the canephoroi and ephebes of the Parthenon to the archaic *kouroi* and *korēs*, and from these to the geometric masks of the Cyclades, preclassical versions of African masks. So as not to make Michel-Charles seem like a philistine, which he was not, we must remember that Goethe and Stendhal did not view "antiques" any differently: those gods and nymphs with noses straighter than ours, nude, but contained in their formal perfection as in a garment, are the hostages of mankind's Golden Age. If they have been restored and repolished, if their missing feet and arms have been replaced, it is because the wounds in their marble contradicted the image of happiness and harmony that we expected of them.

These pagan gods were so inoffensive that a good Catholic like Michel-Charles could—indeed, if he had any culture, was obligated to—follow his visit to the pope with a visit to the

The Young Michel-Charles

Vatican Museum. The princes of the Church who amassed these artworks did not collect idols (only a few illiterates referred to them this way); they collected sublime and soothing objects of luxury, proof of their owners' culture and wealth, adorned with the nostalgic charm of all that is preserved, catalogued, and imitated but that will never again be spontaneously created. In turn, the prestige of the great collections reflects back on these beautiful pieces: the *Hercules* would make less of an impression were it not also *Farnese*. People did not ask them, as we ask works of art nowadays (that is, whenever we take such works seriously enough to ask something of them), to banish unsatisfactory images of the world, to convey the personal cry of the artist, to "change life." Although the respect accorded them prevented people from perceiving their subversiveness, these works continued to advocate, in the middle-class world of the nineteenth century, types of behavior that elsewhere no longer prevailed. The *Dying Gaul* commits suicide in the presence of a young man who would never have dared take the liberty of killing himself; philosophers who denied the immortality of the soul, and "good" emperors who nonetheless were supposed to have fed Christians to the lions, were enthroned in the majesty of marble—and "bad" emperors as well. In an age when a nude woman was a bordello treat, when even new brides wore nightdresses with buttoned collars and long sleeves, when the slightest allusion to "loose morals" caused mothers to turn pale, Michel-Charles could without embarrassment write to his own mother that the *Hermaphrodite* and the *Venus* were the most beautiful ornaments of the church service. He was allowed to ponder the graceful nude foot peeking out from disheveled drapery, and the guard who was hoping for a tip would take the trouble to have the charming Venus rotated on its pedestal for the benefit of the young traveler.

In Naples he was shocked by the Museo Segreto. The two

small rooms that in those days contained the *"raccolta porno-grafica"* had nothing to teach a boy who had read Catullus and Suetonius, but images are always more traumatizing than words. The few sententious phrases he wrote to his worthy mother on this subject ring true, if not accurate. To a youth of twenty-two who is chaste, or nearly so, the spectacle of debauchery is an affront, the more so if he is tempted. Even if, "in a moment of aberration," he has engaged in one of those actions he disapproves of, it is vexing to be brought face to face with them portrayed in marble. Amid those more or less realistic images of Priapus, did he think of the ithyphallic cadaver of the accident at Versailles, symbol of the life force expressing itself even in death? Probably not. But when Michel-Charles pointed out that sensual excesses were not surprising in those people, because they were not Christians, he had come a long way. Not only because the merest glance at Paris, or even at Bailleul, would have taught him that mores have changed little, whatever their cloak of hypocrisy, but because it is self-deceiving to make Antiquity into an Eldorado of the senses: austere middle-class people, or those who claim to be such, have always existed.

Any indecency that was displayed too openly offended him. In an out-of-the-way spot in Italy, he happened to meet his "noble and worthy cousin d'Halluyn" (as he scornfully referred to him), a dashing officer who had deserted his regiment in order to live abroad with the wife of one of his superiors. In Michel-Charles's letters, this romantic d'Halluyn is treated much the way Vronsky, living in Italy with Anna Karenina thirty years later, would have been treated by any of his Saint Petersburg cousins traveling on the peninsula. For a man to have a mistress is one thing; for him to abandon his career and renounce his stripes is another. Michel-Charles was unable to see things from two perspectives, or he would have spoken less harshly of a man who had thrown away his uniform for the sake of an ardent love.

This "Flemish patrician," as he called himself, was rarely taken in by social displays, however brilliant they may have been. He had enjoyed the formal elegance of the balls at the French embassy, but those of the Torlonias, owners of the Albani Bank, did not impress him greatly; he noted only that the parquet floors were not ideal for dancing (as someone quite skilled at waltzes, he found this annoying) and that there was an abundance of English guests, which in his opinion always discredited a gathering. He appears not to have seen other remarkable details: the immense mirrors that, according to Stendhal, the miserly and ostentatious banker bought cheaply at Saint-Gobain while posing as his own steward; the crystal chandeliers reflected to infinity; the gloomy *Albani Antinoüs* sequestered in a room too small and too ornate for it, like a young wild creature in a gilded cage; the shade of the murdered Winckelmann prowling about amid the slightly maleficent masterpieces that he had collected and deeply loved. The English visitors hid the phantoms from my grandfather. At Palermo, despite Princess Olga's lovely eyes, he listened as the duke of Serra di Falco, who all the while kept dipping into the golden snuffbox that the czarina had given him before his departure, spun tall tales about the filth and coarseness of Moscow. He found it pointless to have gone to Loreto, half tourist and half pilgrim, to make a votive offering as Montaigne had: in the sort of Tibet that was Italy in those days, he still saw the priests' shortcomings all too clearly—though it must be admitted that these were scarcely hidden. He was offended by the monsignor who treated himself to a "Protestant meal" on a meatless day, and he perhaps noted other, more serious lapses. As they were about to leave Rome, the young gentlemen, who were all good

Catholics, agreed that a person would quickly lose his faith there if he did not pay close attention to his soul. Theirs was the eternal reaction of men from the north when confronted by Italian Catholicism's blend of pageantry and abandon. Behind Michel-Charles and his scandalized friends, I discern the powerful form of an Augustinian friar who, disembarking in sixteenth-century Rome, nearly fell to his knees and kissed the ground sanctified by so many martyrs—and who left the city ready to become Luther. But those young, well-brought-up Frenchmen would have found it pretentious to try to reform the Church. They merely lit up a cigar and spoke of something else.

"That journey developed my mind in an almost tangible way," said my grandfather modestly. The pages that attest most clearly to this progress are addressed to Charles-Augustin and deal with the subject of politics. Earlier, in a letter to his mother, Michel-Charles had ventured an original prose poem (though he'd claimed it was translated from the Italian) in which he'd expressed pity for decayed Florence in terms quite similar to those that Musset had used for the Florentine exiles in his *Lorenzaccio*. That bit of Romantic eloquence had been nothing more than a schoolboy's plagiarizing. Now he was writing as an adult and was directing his words to a man. In the course of his travels, being a foreigner who spoke good Italian, he had met some young men who had confided in him, telling him of their resentments, their hatreds, their sacred hopes that were to some extent vain. It is always a serious moment when a young mind previously indifferent to politics suddenly discovers that injustice and mistaken self-interest are all around us in the city streets, strolling back and forth decked out in cloaks and uniforms or sitting at café tables in the guise of good bourgeois who always stay on the sidelines. For me, 1922 was one of those moments, and Venice and Verona were the site of the revelation. Michel-Charles, who was disgusted by the insolent customs officers and police of the odious Neapolitan Bourbons, understood what was seething in those youths so like himself. With the slight pang that always strikes the heart at such times, the young man saw that France had ceased to be a torchbearer for his enthusiastic young friends. The great hopes that it had raised in 1830 had been disappointed, he felt. Charles-Augustin, for whom 1830 marked the twilight of legitimate rule, must have shuddered as he read that letter. Every era has its generation gap, even when the flowers of worthy feelings bloom on the edges of the rift.

The liberal fervor that preceded the Risorgimento in Italy is one of the century's finest phenomena. Since the days when efforts to revive humanism and Platonism inflamed minds in Italy, that country had rarely been seized by so pure a passion. When we remember that in addition to these great outpourings and tragic individual sacrifices, a vast amount of collective blood was spilled on the battlefields of the nineteenth century, we are again resigned, if only out of habit, to the scarlet flood that soaks all history. But it is harder to accept what followed: the bourgeois monarchy of the Savoys, bringing in its wake speculators and profiteers; the war in Eritrea, which prefigured the one in Ethiopia; and the Triple Alliance, corrected by the embrace of the Latin Sisters and by the futile deaths at Caporetto. Neither is it easy to accept that after the turmoil which ought to have given rise to reforms came the bombast of Fascism, culminating with Hitler ranting in Naples (I hear him to this day) flanked by two rows of eagles in simulated stone, with the rats devouring the corpses in the Ardeantine mass graves, with Ciano shot to death in his armchair, and with the bodies of the Romagnolo dictator and his mistress swinging by their heels in a garage. Yet things wouldn't be so bad if the disorder, this time irreversible, were not continuing: Venice corroded by chemical pollution, Florence damaged by erosion that no one is effectively combating, eight million migratory birds killed each year by the brave Italian hunters (ten apiece—that's not so serious), the Milanese countryside reduced to a memory, the villas of actresses on the Appian Way, the "cities of art" that have become stage sets amid sterile zones of industrial forced labor, human anthills, and dust. Other countries, I know, offer a nearly identical balance sheet; but this is no reason not to weep.

Let's return to Michel-Charles. Thirty years later he would say to his son that, thanks to judicious management of his funds, he had succeeded in living more than three years in that enchanting Italy. In fact, he spent only about ten months there, and the rest of his Grand Tour, devoted to the mountains of Switzerland and the universities of Germany, was much briefer. But even if we assume that my father was not himself exaggerating, such an error shows to what extent that period of freedom, in a country Michel-Charles was destined never to see again, quickly became fixed in a mythical time having no relation to calendar dates. All of us make mistakes in such matters: it always seems to us that we have lived for a long time in those places where we have lived with great intensity. "Fifteen years with the army passed more quickly than a morning in Athens," I had Hadrian say as he recounted his life. To relive, alone with himself, the joy of those mornings in Italy: it was for this that an exasperated husband, an unfortunate or disappointed father, a Second Empire official thanked by the Republic, an invalid who knew that his days were numbered and perhaps did not care to add to the total, recopied in his small precise hand, today almost completely faded, those letters that in his eyes glowed with the fires of memory.

An episode from the trip to Sicily merits discussion on its own. When confronting an event that shook him to his very core, Michel-Charles, in the solid and rather flat realism of his prose, occasionally and at exceptional moments manages to attain the goal of every writer, which is to convey an impression that the reader will never forget. The episode in question is the one in which he climbs Mount Etna. At Versailles we saw him fall prey to the forces of fire and the risk of violent death; here he is contending with the snow-covered slopes of a volcano and with the more insidious danger of death by exhaustion.

Toward nine o'clock on a cold, windy evening, Michel-Charles and his friends departed on mules, accompanied by some goatherds and mule drivers who were familiar with the mountain and were serving as guides. The first few hours of the journey were merely arduous, taking them through woods of chestnut trees that more or less protected them from the wind but that intensified the blackness of the night. I myself, not more than two or three times in my life, in Greece, have taken part in such nocturnal expeditions that climbed single file along a trail bordered by trees, where the great plant-creatures, often sparse and crooked in those regions that are nowadays anything but lushly forested, recover in the darkness their tangled, terrible strength. Michel-Charles, who has little poetic talent or at least little gift for expressing poetry, nevertheless feels, as anyone would in a similar situation, that as soon as man is dislodged from his habitual routines and exposed to the night and the wilderness, he is a paltry thing, or rather nothing at all. Does the thought of Empedocles cross his mind? I expect not, for he has certainly never read those sublime fragments scattered throughout two or three dozen works of antiquity, *membra disjecta* of one of the very rare texts in which Greece and India come together in a fulgurant view of life. He has never heard the unforgettable lament of the soul mired in the earthly swamps, or the voice in the night that, according to tradition, called the philosopher toward another world. The only thing he must have known about Empedocles was the legend of his *mors ignea*, reduced of course to its crudest version and attributed to the vanity of a man who wishes to give himself the prestige of a miraculous end. Michel-Charles is nonetheless following in his footsteps, just as he is unwittingly following in those of Hadrian, who climbed this mountain at a time when —powerful, loved, brimming with plans and dreams, scarcely touched by old age—he was still on the upward slope of his destiny.

When they reach the end of the woods, the zone of ice and snow begins. They stop to rest for a while at the climbers' cabin, then continue beyond it. The patient mules find it extremely difficult to move over this terrain: they slip, fall, get up again, sink up to their bellies in the snow. The mule drivers urge the young foreigners to lash their animals without mercy, and they shout furiously to spur the creatures on. The night is filled with whistles, blows, snorts, and cries. The mules merely sink further and lie down in the snow. Finally the mule drivers themselves give up. The young men dismount; the unburdened mules are led by their harsh masters back to the cabin, which is only a short distance behind them. Michel-Charles is glad for the poor creatures, and we are grateful to him for this.

But the youths henceforth have only their own muscles to rely on, and we must remember that they embarked on this adventure without any of the equipment that the most casual hiker would have today. They walk single file in snow that comes up to their knees, then up to their waists, and with each step they must tear themselves from the soft, loose drifts. Michel-Charles is convinced that his hands and feet are frozen for good. He feels himself dying, and we know that he has never been one to dramatize. I, too, have had the experience of being overwhelmed by snow and fatigue—the feeling that the engine of bodily life is stopping, that your breath is coming in irregular gasps, that your panic is that of someone face to face with death, and that death, if it comes, will merely bring the struggle to an end. I thus understand all the better the mortal cold that has seized Michel-Charles. The goatherds hoist him under their arms and carry him—just as two helpful neighbors, one day during a snowstorm, will carry me from their house to mine through a mass of white drifts that I could no longer manage to negotiate. They are too far from the cabin to get back to it, but a few steps from the cone of lava and slag that separates them from the summit squats the tiny *casa dell'Inglese*, a stone hut that a farsighted British climber has had built as a shelter. The caretaker keeps a fire burning inside. In the stupor of extreme fatigue, Michel-Charles wonders why no one puts him close to the burning logs, but his rescuers have other ideas. Along a wall, in the lee of the wind, the men dig a rectangular pit the length of a human body. They fill it three-fourths full with warm ashes and cover them with a thin cloth. In this species of tomb they lay Michel-Charles, wrapped in a faded old cloak belonging to one of the goatherds, and they spread a few more handfuls of warm ashes over him. All of this takes place by torchlight, since it is still dark. They even cover his face with a flap of the cloak.

Little by little the humble warmth returns to his body, and with it thought and life. He even lifts the flap of fabric to see if dawn has come. But instead he glimpses the sagging forms of two young Englishmen who have climbed too rapidly in the wake of his group and who, seized with mountain sickness, are vomiting in the doorway. He covers his face again, with the gesture that dying men made in classical art and life, and sinks back for a moment into the warm ashes. On his very first visit to the museum in Arles, this student discovered he was avidly interested in the most minor objects and appurtenances of Roman life. But does he know that his hollow is precisely the shape of an *ustrinum*—that rectangular pit, scaled to the human body, in which citizens cremated their dead, or at least the dead who had no one to buy them a sumptuous funeral pyre? Does he think of initiations using embers and hot ashes—of the young Demophoön, whom Demeter laid on a bed of glowing coals and who died because the cries and gesticulations of his mother broke the magic spell? But here there is no woman to disturb the goatherds' rite.

After a little more than an hour, the young man feels sufficiently recovered to try to join his friends at the edge of the crater. He clambers up the cone on his hands and knees, slipping on pumice and ash; this quarter of a league takes another hour. It is already broad daylight when he arrives at the summit, but his friends assure him that the sunrise was a disappointment.

The adventure at Versailles had resembled a birth ritual: the young man had been thrust headfirst toward life. The adventure at Etna is a ritual of death and resurrection. These two nearly sacred incidents would do well as early chapters in the biography of a great man. But Michel-Charles is not a great man. I would describe him as an ordinary man, if experience did not teach us that there is no such thing as an ordinary man. It teaches us, too, that all people in the course of their lives undergo a series of initiatory trials. Those who undergo them with full knowledge of their situation are rare and in most cases quickly forget. And the exceptional ones who remember their ordeals often fail to derive any benefit from them.

The taste for the arts that Michel-Charles acquired or developed in Italy can be gauged by the objects he brought back from his travels. Fortunately, mass production for tourists did not yet exist; the manufacture of souvenirs was still a craft. Among these articles is a little coffer whose mahogany trays, nested one on top of the other, contain images stamped from intaglios. The impressions, each of which has a different classical subject, are arranged in the box like bonbons from a fine confectioner's. The collection is both a type of parlor game ("Look! It's Jupiter!"—"No, it's Neptune! There's his trident!") and an inventory of what people liked best in museums around 1840. It's a fine-art curio, even though it was sold in large numbers to Russian, German, and Scandinavian amateurs making their Grand Tours. I replaced two or three missing pieces with the aid of other sets that had doubtless been purchased by nineteenth-century Yankees. A more unusual item, the fruit of a visit to some antiquarian, is a Renaissance copy of the bust of a third-century emperor; the neck is draped in onyx, and the whole has the scaled-down proportions of an "article of virtu" such as the ones Rubens brought back from Italy to adorn his house in Antwerp. In contrast, an abandoned Ariadne, copied in bronze, has the coldness of the Empire style. No matter. Relegated to the billiard room at Mont-Noir, she taught me the beauties of drapery as it flows softly over a reclining body. Last, forming a dark patch against the light-colored panels of the drawing room: a painting, only one, suitably chosen by this young man who thought he knew nothing about painting. The work of some student of Luini, it shows "Modesty and Vanity," or perhaps "Sacred Love and Profane Love," both with that mysterious smile, slightly taut at the edges, which can be seen on the lips of the women and androgynes of Leonardo. I don't think I ever asked the names of those two figures, but I sensed in them an austere, indefinable sweetness that was lacking in people and in the other paintings displayed on the walls.

Still in my possession are two gilded bronze door handles in the form of classical busts: a Tiberius, ravaged and worn by the empire and by life, and one of Niobe's young daughters, her mouth open wide in a cry of innocent despair. Analogues of these can be seen in Venice in their original settings, on the doors of the Doges' palace. These two small bronzes cast in Italy nearly four centuries ago—this Tiberius and this Niobide, transformed into items of Baroque luxury (which itself has had its day), gilded with the nearly unalterable gold of ages past—were touched by the hands of hundreds of unknown people, who turned the handles and opened those doors, behind which something was waiting for them. An antiquarian sold them to a young man in pearl-gray trousers; old and ailing, my grandfather perhaps stroked them affectionately. I had them mounted on two pieces of timber that once formed part of the American house I had made my own. The wood of those bases had grown before Michel-Charles himself was born—had grown amid the great silence of what in those days was truly Mount Desert Island. Felled by the man who built this little house, the tree was floated on the sparkling ocean inlet whose waters, in the wintertime, boil and smoke when they come in contact with air that is colder than they are. The "locals" who lived here before me wore down its grain with their heavy shoes, scuffing the thick floor as they walked from the small, plain living room to the kitchen, or to the bedroom containing a cradle. Some people will tell me that any object could inspire similar musings. They will not be mistaken.

I shall do no more than mention the jewels that Michel-Charles purchased "for the ladies": a brooch with a mosaic depicting the Colosseum by the romantic light of a full moon, a cameo displaying a model profile for Canova or Thorvaldsen, another cameo showing frolicking nymphs—all of these pieces in massive gold settings. Reine pinned them to her ample shawl, Gabrielle and Valérie to their light scarves. But Michel-Charles kept for himself, and had mounted in a ring, a classical cameo of the purest style: it bore an image of the aged Augustus. He bequeathed it to his son, who in turn gave it to me for my fifteenth birthday. I myself wore it for seventeen years, and owe a great deal to my daily contact with that specimen of severe glyptic perfection. All disputes over classicism and realism seem pointless when one is gazing at their complete fusion in a Roman cameo. Around 1935, in one of those bursts of emotion that must never be regretted, I gave it to a man I loved, or thought I loved. I am a bit annoyed with myself for having placed that beautiful object in the hands of an individual (who doubtless soon passed it on to someone else), instead of finding it a permanent haven in a public or private collection, which is where it in fact may have ended up. Yet (must I confess it?) I might never have parted with that masterpiece had I not discovered, a few days before giving it away, that the outermost edge of the onyx had been marred by a slight crack, the result of some careless blow. To my eyes, the object thus seemed to have become less precious, imperceptibly damaged, perishable. In those days that was, for me, a reason to cherish it a bit less. Today it would be a reason to cherish it a bit more.

The album of dried flowers that Michel-Charles compiled during his travels is certainly not the work of a botanist. The specimens do not appear in it under their Latin names, and it does not give the impression that the miracle of plant forms meant anything to him. His teachers at Stanislas School taught him rhetoric and history such as they understood them, rather than the natural sciences, just as educators today often sacrifice botany to nuclear physics; and the fashion for such albums is as dead as the fashion for keepsakes. But Michel-Charles seems to have loved flowers instinctively, like any person who is struck by the beauty of a cornflower growing amid the grass. His aim, he says, was to use those floral "compositions" to fix the memory of each lovely place he had visited; he was not unaware that a world of supposedly dead emotions and impressions can live forever in a dried leaf or flower. All that he could not or would not say in his letters is there: the mood of the moment, gay or sad, thoughts that are profound but that give rise only to commonplaces when expressed, a few words exchanged with a charming peasant woman. Each carefully glued petal has remained in place, a little patch of pink or blue, the ghost of a fragile plant form sacrificed to the glories of history and literature. Flowers from the ancient stone quarries of Syracuse and from the Forum, plants from the Roman Campania and the Lido (Musset's "dreadful Lido" where the "pale Adriatic" dies, and which only a handful of people still frequented—a few Venetian fishermen, and Jews who buried their dead there), sprigs of boxwood and Tuscan cypress, leaves from beech groves in the Apennines, flowers from Clarens in memory of Julie d'Etanges and the most beautiful and unusual love story in all of French literature—a novel that is nowadays misread by graduate students or not read at all.

Accompanying the flowers are bits of verse, taken sometimes from Latin lyrics and elegies, sometimes from famous or virtually unknown Romantic poets. Horace and Tibullus are the most quoted in Italy, Schiller and Klopstock in Germany, Byron and Rousseau in Switzerland; but Hégésippe Moreau is quoted at least as often as Lamartine. These calligraphed lines frame the flowers of memory with garlands and rosettes, concentric corollas analogous to the genuine corollas, or else press like waves around each dried-flower island, reminding one of the so-called Celtic curves in Irish manuscripts, which Michel-Charles certainly never saw. Whatever artistic talent the young man may have had was expressed there.

After the flowers, the animals. Arriving in Florence, Michel-Charles called for his general-delivery mail and found a sad note from Gabrielle informing him that Misca, his beloved dog, had been stricken with a mysterious illness and was dying amid torments that no one knew how to ease. "Poor little thing!" mourns Michel-Charles. "What have you done to deserve such suffering?" Years later he will ask the same unanswerable question at the bedside of a girl of fourteen, his oldest child. He evokes all the humble happiness that Misca has given him, her silky coat, so soft to the touch, her big, clean paws that jumped from one patch of pavement to another to avoid the mud in the streets, his long nights of insomnia after the accident at Versailles, when the little creature lying curled up at his feet had been such a comfort to him. I have no illusions here: if he is yielding to a lyrical impulse, it is partly because in school he read Catullus' poem on the death of Lesbia's sparrow and the tale of Odysseus' dog. But his sincerity is undeniable. The fact that Misca will not be there to greet him will cast a cloud over his homecoming. The little dog has become the model of canine perfection. Michel-Charles knows that all the dogs he may have in the future will be mercilessly compared to her, and that however much he may love them, her leaping, barking shade will always come first in his affections. He is clearly my grandfather.

THE
RUE MARAIS

When Michel-Charles returns to France, the ship of state (as a contemporary joke has it) is sailing on a volcano. Louis-Philippe is at his last gasp. Ever modest, like all serenely self-confident people, the young man is surprised at the warm welcome accorded him by those who hold power in his native region of Nord. He sees quite clearly that such astute politicians cannot be counting on his competence, since no one knows whether or not he has any, or on his experience, which is nonexistent. Very simply, these somewhat beleaguered gentlemen wish to secure for the cadet branch of the Bourbon line the services of a young man who comes of good family, who is quite well-off, and whose name carries weight in the district. They offer him a post on the prefectural council, which he accepts, and when his nomination is announced in *L'Officiel* the liberals raise cries of favoritism. This doesn't bother him in the slightest. He takes up residence in Lille and finds it a pleasant place to live—all the more so, he says, since he has been going out in society there and has just met a young woman who embodies his feminine ideal. We'll soon see how things turned out.

145

At Bailleul, the legitimists who have come to spend an hour at Charles-Augustin's bedside do not reproach him, as they might have done not long ago, with letting Michel-Charles "eat the government's oats." The rumblings of the workers' revolt, the proliferation of secret clubs and societies, and the word "communism," which has just been coined, strike fear into all hearts: people agree that it's better to use whatever skills they have on behalf of the forces of law and order. Moreover (and such contradictions are, as always, the quintessence of politics), everyone fervently hopes that the disturbances will go just far enough to bring the savior Henri V back to France. In that case, Michel-Charles, already established in the administration, will be in an even better position to render service to the legitimate king. For Charles-Augustin, this repudiation justified by a future betrayal seems to have been a bitter pill to swallow.

Reine's plans for their son's marriage have upset him almost as much. Well before Michel-Charles's return, the farsighted Reine took pleasure in drawing up a list of possible matches, and "matches" is to be taken here in the matrimonial sense. Contrary to what one might think, she attaches no importance to the prestige and age of the families: those of Charles-Augustin's family and her own seem sufficient in her eyes and have no need of any borrowed luster. In the vivid language of a well-born woman of the ancien régime, Reine would say that the sow does not ennoble the hog. It's important, though, that Michel-Charles be very rich. Actually, he already is: he has just inherited, or will soon inherit, two or three legacies that will augment his sizable fortune. But his realistic mother knows that, given the times they live in, there is a significant difference between a sizable fortune and a great fortune. Mademoiselle Dufresne, daughter of a judge on the Lille Tribunal, comes to exactly the required weight on Reine's scales.

This young woman dresses well and has an attractive figure. Despite her slender wrists and ankles, one can see that someday she will be an imposing person. Her thick hair and her plump arms and shoulders attest to her flourishing good health: an essential point. Her father, a future public prosecutor, will be able to use his influence to help Michel-Charles. He owns two or three of the most beautiful houses in Lille and speaks of giving one of them to his daughter for her dowry. He has acquired several farms in the region, and part of his portfolio is said to consist of coal-mining stock.

At this point Charles-Augustin interrupts his wife to ask how she can explain that a mere member of the bench could be so wealthy. He himself has made a counter-investigation, which he initiated as soon as Reine checked off the name of Mademoiselle Noémi on her list. The late Dufresne and his wife, Philippine Bouilliez, both the children of farmers, were natives of Chamblain-Châtelain, near Béthune. The mother of the said Dufresne was named Poirier, or Pénin—it's not really clear; the parish register is barely legible and seems to show that the curé was as illiterate as his flock, most of whom signed their names with an X. If you go back in time this way, laboriously, from X to X and from Dufresne to Dufresne, to the late seventeenth century, you encounter a Françoise Lenoir and a Françoise Leroux, both wives of farmers, and an Ursule Thélu (a fine peasant name which, though Charles-Augustin doesn't know this, means "star" in dialect), whose mother's family name was Danvin.

Let's be clear about something here: if it were profitable to do so, Charles-Augustin would willingly marry his son (or so, at least, he thinks) to the daughter of one of those worthy farmers who, never expecting a sou for their generous action, gave back the lands belonging to their masters after the latter returned from their exile abroad. Old Man Dufresne, on the contrary, a rustic who became a notary, traded in black-market

goods, most often (cunning fellow that he was) through inter-
mediaries. The money that enabled his son to build a career
was made in this way. Who knows whether the old fox might
not even have trafficked in military supplies? Some people said
he had, and many people in those days did. So long as Charles-
Augustin has anything to say about it, the heiress of the Dufresnes will not marry Michel-Charles.

Reine is careful not to answer. She changes the subject
and speaks of the judge's wife, Alexandrine-Joséphine Dumesnil, whose estimable parents lived and died in Lille, on the rue
du Marché-au-Verjus. Reine asked to be shown the miniature
of François Dumesnil, a magistrate during the Directory and a
handsome man, with his powdered club-tailed wig and benign,
somewhat conceited air. His wife, Adrienne Plattel, outfitted
in her own miniature as an elegant woman of her time (Reine
remembers with an indulgent smile that, as a little girl, she
admired the filmy tunics and frivolous bonnets which a respectable woman wouldn't dare wear nowadays), has a roguish eye
and the mouth of a gourmande. One trembles a bit, in retro-
spect, for the conjugal happiness of the good judge. But there's
nothing to be said against Alexandrine-Joséphine, who has
brought up her daughter well and who runs a very proper household in the beautiful mansion between court and garden that
her husband owns on the rue Marais. They have few callers,
it is true, no doubt because they extend few invitations. In the
drawing room hangs the portrait of a great-uncle of the lady of
the house: a certain Abbé Duhamel, a canon who refused to
take the oath of loyalty to the Republic and who allegedly lan-
guished and died in prison during the Terror.

Nothing could have had a better effect. Charles-Augustin
points out that Old Man Dufresne and his wife doubtless never
set foot in that lovely dwelling, which prior to the Revolution
belonged to the comte de Rouvroy. They were never seen in

Lille, where their son, certainly, was not eager to introduce them. The old fellow ended his days in his chambers in Béthune, listening to the hammering of his neighbor to the right, a tinsmith, and the drinking songs of his neighbor to the left, a tavernkeeper, and of those who frequented the latter's establishment. His widow eked out an existence there for several more years. It was the tinsmith and the tavernkeeper who signed the couple's death certificates. One can picture them returning home from the registry on those occasions, walking arm in arm and not saying goodbye until they'd had a drink, to banish dark thoughts and to toast the old skinflint and his crone of a widow. It's doubtful that portraits of the deceased are hanging in the drawing room of the handsome residence on the rue Marais.

Reine goes downstairs to prepare the medicinal potion that her invalid takes every night. Nothing has been resolved. But before long, political events will relegate the list of marriageable young women to a secondary plane. Noémi's wedding presents will not be arriving anytime soon.

Let's pause a moment to consider this marriage, which will of course take place. It gave me Amable Dufresne for a grandfather (Amable, meaning "lovable," was a misnomer) and, for a great-grandfather, the notary from Béthune who was so adept at lining his pockets in times of unrest. His legend, of which I am the sole repository, may or may not be true—but this scarcely matters. For my father and grandfather, it was virtually an article of faith; still, my grandfather thought of it only on days of conjugal bitterness. On the side of the ancestors extending back from Alexandrine-Joséphine, lady of the Dufresne household, the visibility is quite limited: I can see no further than the judge who served during the heyday of the Directory and a somewhat acerbic-looking canon posed in a crimson armchair, his elbow near some large volumes that doubtless contain the Fathers of the Church. Beyond these individuals is, I assume, a set of people belonging to the Lille bourgeoisie and, even further in the past, perhaps to the merchants' or craftsmen's circles of old Lille or to Nord's French peasantry, which the Dufresnes moved out of only at the very end of the eighteenth century.

The line extending back from the notary of Béthune has left some names—a few more of them, as we have seen, but scattered like bits of straw on bare ground. The trail sinks yet again into the vast anonymity of the peasantry. Those generations that succeeded one another in Chamblain-Châtelain beginning in late classical times and perhaps even earlier, those people who for centuries tilled the soil and collaborated with the seasons, have disappeared as utterly as the flocks they once led to pasture and the dead leaves from which they made humus. Certainly we needn't go back any further than three or four centuries to see that the ancestors of all "good families" ultimately are engulfed in the same anonymous loam. Moreover, there is a certain grandeur about those peasants who have vanished thus without a trace, except perhaps for a line in a parish register that fire or rats will someday destroy, or a wooden cross, soon to be supplanted by others, that stands on a grassy mound. Charles-Augustin would nonetheless say, not without a touch of solid good sense, that it's something to have been able to read, write, and do sums (especially the last) ten or so generations before those people. But it's also something not to have left in one's wake an enormous litter of bourgeois bric-à-brac and noble collections of arms.

If I did not mention these rustic folk when I was trying to trace the network of "my families," it is first because they did not connect up with that network until well in the middle of the nineteenth century, through Michel-Charles's marriage; and second because, between Béthune and Lille on the one hand and Bailleul and Cassel on the other, we clearly see the considerable distance that separates French Flanders from Flemish Flanders. Despite the fact that these individuals experienced the same historical vicissitudes, the same wars, the same changes in reigns and regimes, they give the impression of being not merely from different social milieus but from different peoples. To begin with, for the Cleenewercks, Cousse-makers, and Bieswals (until the nineteenth century, at least), French was an acquired language and Flemish the language of childhood, whereas from time immemorial the families of Lille and Béthune spoke only French, even if this French was reduced to a patois. Their children did not "make their First Communion in Flemish," as Michel-Charles did. Approaching those strangers through their descendant Noémi, I seem to find in them a certain aridity, a certain greediness for work and profit, a certain keenness yet at the same time a narrowness, which are characteristics that one finds to some extent everywhere in the French province and that differ completely from the expansiveness and slow fire of the Flemish.

But my soundest reason is that I know so little about them as people. Certainly, with the aid of a background composed of various literary ingredients and without using a model, I could paint a portrait of poor laborers cheered now and then by a bit of insurrection and a lot of poaching, show my ancestors making merry at village dances and feasts, or depict avaricious peasants filling wool stockings with their hoard. Nothing in these images would come directly from the Dufresnes, Thélus, or Danvins. Still, by dint of imaginative sympathy, let's try to get a bit closer to one of these people, chosen at random—Françoise Lenoir, for example, or her mother, Françoise Leroux. Even their names don't really belong to them, since millions of women in France had, have, or will have the same ones. Concerning Françoise Lenoir, we know only that she married for the first time at the age of forty. Let's try Françoise Leroux instead. Hey, Françoise Leroux! Hey! She doesn't hear me. But with a good deal of effort I manage to catch sight of her, there in her house with its floor of beaten earth (I saw some like it in the vicinity of Mont-Noir when I was a child), watered with beer, nourished on brown bread and cream cheese, wearing an apron over her woolen skirt. On the one hand my need to simplify life and on the other the accidents of circumstance bring me closer to her than to my ancestors in frills and furbelows.

Living amid the commodities and even the luxuries of a different age, I still make the gestures that she made before me. I knead bread; I sweep the doorstep; after nights of gusty wind, I gather dead wood. I don't sit on the pig that's being bled, to prevent it from thrashing about, but once in a while I do eat ham (doubtless not as flavorful as the ones she smoke-cured) that comes from an animal just as brutally slaughtered, albeit not before my own eyes. In winter she and I both have swollen hands. But I'm well aware that what was for her a necessity is for me a choice, at least until the moment when every choice becomes irreversible. Hey! Goodwoman Leroux! I'd like to know if, in her youth, she worked as a tavern maid or a servant in a château, if she loves her husband or cuckolds him, if she lights candles at church or disparages the curé or does both at once, if she looks after her ailing neighbors or slams the door in beggars' faces. It is by the most ordinary deeds and gestures that we must initially try to circumscribe a person, as if making a rough sketch. But it would remain a crude portrait if we denied this unknown woman the subtler, almost purer emotions that seem to spring from a refining of the soul, in the sense in which we think of an alchemist refining gold. Françoise could have been as fond as I am of the music of fiddlers and hurdy-gurdy players, popular tunes that have today become treats for overrefined tastes; could have found beauty in a sunset casting its ruddy light on the snow; could have sadly picked up a baby bird fallen from the nest and remarked what a pity it was. Whatever she thought and felt regarding her joys and sorrows, her bodily ailments, old age, approaching death, her loved ones since departed—all this is neither more nor less important than what I myself have thought and felt. Her life was doubtless more difficult than mine; but I suspect it was average. She is, like all of us, caught in the inextricable and the ineluctable.

In February 1848 the revolution in Lille began with a ball at the prefecture. The telegram bearing the news of the uprising in Paris had arrived too late for the festivities to be called off, but according to my grandfather all the guests looked as if they were in mourning. To secure the great courtyard, the prefect summoned a battalion of troops, whose presence angered the populace: whistles and catcalls greeted the richly dressed men and women as they got out of their carriages. Next day, the funereal expressions became even more pronounced when people heard that Louis-Philippe had abdicated and fled. This elderly bourgeois gentleman, shabbily dressed but equipped with a satchel full of gold, was traveling incognito to Honfleur with all possible speed.

Two days after the ball, a crowd excited by the news from Paris surges into the courtyard of the prefecture. This rabble probably comes from the notorious "cellars of Lille"—damp, unhealthy basements where workers and their families have been rotting for several generations and that yield a large income for the owners of the buildings. As Michel-Charles is worming his way through the incoming crowd in the direction of the iron gates, he is surprised to notice a man wearing old clothes and an old hat: it's the prefect himself, Monsieur D. de G., who is unwittingly imitating the behavior of the King of France. Seeing that the young councillor has recognized him, Monsieur D. de G. begs Michel-Charles to accompany him discreetly to the military headquarters on the rue Négrier, where the army will ensure his safety. With his mind still full of images of Roman senators sitting in their curule chairs and waiting for the barbarians, the young man is privately astonished but hastens to oblige his chief. During their short walk, the prefect tells Michel-Charles he is relying on him to protect his wife and daughters, who are still at the prefecture.

Back at the scene of the disturbance, Michel-Charles sees that the tide of the crowd has spilled over the threshold; an unkempt mob fills the ground floor and the level above. An old servant stands before the door leading to the prefect's apartments: "There are women in there! You can't go in!" Michel-Charles, whose writing is sometimes stilted but whose speech is rather vigorous, will later declare that that valet "had guts."

In the courtyard a man is haranguing the crowd, speaking of the dead bodies lying on the sidewalks of Paris and inveighing against the people in office "who have danced to the sound of our brothers' blood." Michel-Charles, who is in the habit of polishing his metaphors, cannot help smiling. The yelling crowd, which is brandishing a red flag, demands the tricolor decorations from the ballroom so that it can make a bonfire with them. They were hastily taken down, to efface all memory of that ill-fated gala; no one now knows, or wishes to know, where they are. For lack of anything better, the crowd makes off with the ground-floor curtains, intending to burn them in the main square—a form of waste that brings the exasperation of the wealthy to its peak. The fact that the rioters abscond with a bust of Louis-Philippe and throw it on the fire along with the curtains attracts less attention.

A few days later a certain Antony Thouret of Douai, special commissioner of the Provisional Government, arrives in Lille to bring the Republic to the town. He is "dirty, fat, and vulgar," and so zealous about fulfilling his duties that he boasts of having slept in his clothes and boots for four nights running—a fact that is only too apparent. He calls a meeting of the prefectural council, to find out if its members will agree to cooperate with the new regime. An awkward silence fills the room. Michel-Charles has made his way to the front row, so that he can be seen and heard by the commissioner.

"I agree to continue to fulfill my duties, but I shall keep my political opinions."

This lone voice infuriates the representative of the new order. Already there are traitors! Already there are rebels! He launches into a panegyric on behalf of the Republic. These faded flowers of rhetoric, this poor-man's oratorical richness, annoy the young councillor, who is on the verge of responding. The official next to him, a middle-aged fellow named Monsieur de Genlis, gently puts his hand on Michel-Charles's shoulder.

"Take care, young man! Remember what they did to our people during the Great Revolution!"

These words, which are like a confirmation of his letters patent of nobility, calm Michel-Charles, and he lets the commissioner finish without interruption. The audience streams out of the room. People are anxious to avoid speaking to young Crayencour and give him the widest possible berth. It's no advantage to be the only one with the courage to speak up.

The following day he receives notice of his dismissal, signed by the commissioner and by the vice-president of the prefectural council—a certain Baron de T., highly respected within the conservative party. For the first time, the baron has omitted his title on an official document. The discovery of cowardice, too, is an initiation. Michel-Charles, who will be dismissed three times in the course of his life, is learning. All he can do now is return to Bailleul.

When he appears before his father, Charles-Augustin welcomes him with unexpected warmth. In the legitimist's eyes, Michel-Charles, by being fired from his position, has been cleansed of a stain.

"At last I've got you back!" he says to his son, clasping him in his arms.

But the bourgeoisie's Great Fear persists, not without good reason. Cavaignac doesn't have what it takes to be a savior; Changarnier is nothing but an old saber full of nicks. The accession of Louis-Napoleon to the presidency reassures everyone, even if a Bonaparte (albeit a false one) inspires little enthusiasm in serious people. In any case, the repression has begun. In Lille, after the uprising of May 1849, which was sparked by famine, the Correctional Court, presided over by Amable Dufresne, condemns forty-three individuals to punishments totaling forty-five years in prison and seventy-four years of probation. Most of those found guilty are children. One teenager who had stolen some bread was treated especially harshly: two years in prison. A widow, who on her income of one franc twenty per day was doing her best to support a family of four, burst into tears when she was given a similar sentence. Another beggar made as though to commit suicide right there in the courtroom. A certain Ladureau, a lawyer from Lille, defended this riffraff, regrettably sparing them even more severe penalties. People agree that Amable Dufresne, who will soon become head of the civil court of Lille, is an upholder of law and order.

Michel-Charles has said that this troubled year was, for him, a period of vacation. He spent his time sorting his notes and mounting the souvenirs he'd brought back from his travels. If my aim were to paint a favorable portrait of him, I'd prefer to say that he felt more outrage in the face of injustice, which in those days was on the right. Nevertheless, at a time when everyone was lying or talking nonsense, when the only choice was between the defenders of order, adamant in their pitiless, heartless morality calculated for display, and ideologues forcibly bringing an era of dictatorships onto the scene, between well-fed wolves on the one hand and enraged sheep on the other, the young man who amused himself making a paperweight from fragments of classical marble was perhaps a realist.

He was nonetheless quite happy to be reappointed to his post in December 1849. His father on this occasion said nothing: he was gravely ill. Around the same time, Michel-Charles was offered the subprefecture of Hazebrouck, which he declined because Lille seemed to him a better stage and because he was seriously courting Mademoiselle Noémi. He married her in September 1851. Charles-Augustin had been dead for a little more than a year.

It wasn't a grand marriage; it wasn't even a stylish marriage. It was a very good marriage. I'm speaking, of course, from the public's point of view. Like Charles-Augustin, a few old people made reference to fortunes that bring bad luck; but this was nonsense. Reine, who had devoted a great deal of time to the customary negotiations with the future parents-in-law and the notaries, returned to Bailleul with her two young ladies, pleased to have done well by her son. Whether he had gone up or down one rung on the social ladder is a question we shall not debate here, Europe's caste system being as complex as India's. In any case, the decisions had been made. This man of twenty-nine had already reached the point where an individual's choices, which at the outset seem limitless, are reduced to just a few. Everything that came afterward had its origins in that day.

For the time being, he was fully satisfied to have his young wife, the respect of society, and his creature comforts. Lacking much ambition (in which he differed from his mother), he contented himself with diligently fulfilling his duties, which entailed taking care of the legal matters of the *département*. Lille seemed a large city compared to sleepy Bailleul, and he prided himself on cutting a good figure there. As we have seen, he had once again begun to use what he somewhat naïvely called his "noble name"—better referred to as his French-sounding estate name—which an official decree had restored to his family. He had not resurrected the old-fashioned title of "chevalier" (*"I don't use it, because it's no longer the custom"*), which seemed frivolous and a bit dissolute, and certainly wouldn't have been appropriate for the serious-mannered husband of Noémi, but which the traveler who had made his Grand Tour could, strictly speaking, have used. The Chevalier de Lorraine, the Chevalier d'Eon, the Chevalier de La Barre, the Chevalier de Saingalt, the Chevalier de Valois, the Chevalier Des Touches . . . "The Chevalier Cleenewerck" wouldn't have fared badly in such company.

Amable Dufresne transferred the handsome residence at 26 rue Marais to Noémi's name; subsequently it passed to that of his son-in-law. Amable was also the owner of the houses at 24 and 24A, the latter of which he seems to have partly occupied himself, renting the other rooms to one of his colleagues. I lived in that 26 rue Marais during the first two winters of my life; deep in my bones, I must still retain traces of the warmth that emanated from its large heating stove. As a little girl, I went back there two or three times to visit my grandmother—in the spring, before she had left for Mont-Noir, or during the first cold weeks of the fall, after she had returned to the city. I vaguely sensed the deconsecrated atmosphere of the place: the home of an elderly lady whom scarcely anyone still comes to visit. In the depths of my memory I spy the marble steps of a staircase, a curving banister, the tall trees of a spacious garden, and an arcaded gallery that must have reminded Michel-Charles of eighteenth-century Roman porticoes. Those gloomy, slightly cold mansions which were built in impeccable rows in the days of the French Intendants and which took the place of Lille's old houses, with their gables carved and gilded by the master craftsmen of the dukes of Burgundy—those old mansions have their mystery as well. Legend has it that this house, before it belonged to Monsieur de Rouvroy, was the sumptuous home of a tax farmer who took in young girls from the opera. Around 1913, after Noémi's death, the uncle who had inherited 26 rue Marais discovered, on the mezzanine, several hidden rooms lit only by a few almost invisible apertures and filled with the slightly dubious, musty smell of the past. Dresses from the days of the notorious Madame du Barry were hanging in wardrobes: satin and taffeta, flowered chintz and striped Chinese silk. The women who had worn them must have spent delicious hours strolling beneath the trees in the garden. Erotic books and engravings were discovered in a drawer. My uncle, an austere man, had all those things burned.

Passing through Lille in 1956, I saw that the garden had been replaced by some featureless buildings, but the old concierge said he still remembered the lovely trees. The mansion itself was occupied by an insurance agency; the arcaded gallery was still there. About twenty years have passed since then. A friend from Lille wrote me recently to say that the neighborhood has changed greatly, has become a sort of North African ghetto. "I thought I had taken a trip to Mecca," added that kindly man, who mourned the passing of his old city. The insurance agency has moved; the house has been put up for sale. I tell myself that for Amable Dufresne, who was an Orleanist until the day he rallied behind the empire, the conquest of Algeria had doubtless been one of the glories of the century. Today, the distant aftermath of that military exploit is flowing back upon his handsome residence.

It was in this courtyard that Michel-Charles, a few days after his wedding, saw a fissure appear in his comfortable existence. A great lover of horses, he had just bought a thoroughbred that he intended to ride every morning on the paths near the Citadel, which in those days were beautifully cared for. A groom who had recently been hired (since the Dufresnes' coachman couldn't do everything) was waiting for instructions when the judge, who was just leaving the house after visiting his daughter, approached Michel-Charles and said sarcastically:

"You're losing no time in turning my daughter's money into horse manure."

Several replies are appropriate to this sort of witticism. Michel-Charles, with one blow, could have sent the judge sprawling on the front steps; he could then have had the gate opened, ridden away on his horse, and never come back. This is what his son would have done. Or he could have protested, with reason, that he had the wherewithal to maintain a saddle horse without relying on Noémi's dowry, or could have continued to give orders to his groom as if nothing had happened. But he was the type of man who, when confronted by ill-will or malice, simply backs off, not out of cowardice (we have seen that he was no coward) but out of distaste for arguing with an insolent or boorish person; out of pride; or perhaps out of a fund of indifference that made him relinquish whatever he possessed or desired, with the feeling that after all he wouldn't have owned it very long or didn't really want it that much. I've sometimes observed that same reaction in my father and in myself. Michel-Charles decided to send the horse to Mont-Noir and never again went riding in Lille.

And now let's peer into that abyss of pettiness, Noémi. Women who treat their husbands like consorts, when they're not treating them like valets, can be found in every age—most of all, perhaps, in the nineteenth century. Such an attitude doesn't even exclude feelings of genuine warmth: Victoria, who was very fond of her Albert, nevertheless kept him in a subordinate position. Michel-Charles, who always tended to present things from the most reassuring angle possible, asserts in the memoirs he wrote for his children that Noémi was intelligent (in her own way, she was), beautiful (we'll see about this shortly), matchless at running a household (he was not exaggerating), and "genteel"; and I'm afraid that this unfortunate word primarily evokes affected expressions of courtesy, measured out with great precision according to rank, wealth, and the current value of a person's social stock—qualities in which the ladies of good society vied with one another, or rather against one another. Michel-Charles was not unaware of his wife's essentially crass and limited nature, and spoke of it frankly to his son. If we wish to find Noémi beneath the litotes on the one hand and the exasperation and bitterness on the other, we must first clear away the myth that surrounds her, even if the myth takes shape again afterward.

I myself knew her only when she was in her eighties, hunched and thickened by age, coming and going in the corridors of Mont-Noir like Seaton's aunt—the unforgettable woman in Walter de la Mare's story who prowls about her empty house and who, in the eyes of the young boys observing her, has become the stout incarnation of Death or, even worse, of Evil. But Noémi's prosaic nature did not inspire mortal terror. She had ceased to be on speaking terms with her son, got along poorly with her son-in-law (whom she feared), and was both affectionate and sardonic in her relations with her grandson. Toward me she was a tireless nag, without being able to penetrate the cocoon of indifference that sometimes envelops childhood and shields it from the provocations of adults. After her three meals, the old lady would repair to the drawing room and sit in an alcove, where, without being seen, she could watch a whole row of rooms and hear what was being said against her down in the basement, thanks to a heating duct that served as an acoustic pipe. Alert to all this, as one might expect, the servants spoke about her only when they were far from the place in question, or chose their words carefully, knowing they were being overheard. If a malicious remark came wafting up from the vent, Madame would find some agreeable excuse for a scene. Her chambermaid, Fortunée, who served her badly but whom she was used to, would engineer at will the firing of the delinquent and his or her return to grace. The nuns who nursed my grandmother in her last days were subject to the same disciplinary regime. This old woman who had feared death all her life was alone at Mont-Noir when she met her end, which came as the result of a heart attack. "A *heart* attack?" exclaimed a facetious country neighbor. "But she never made much use of hers!"

The earliest picture we have of Noémi shows her at about the age of fourteen, in a short skirt and pinafore. Around 1842 Amable Dufresne had the idea of commissioning a local artist to do two complementary works—half portraits, half genre paintings. One shows the judge sitting in his handsome library on the rue Marais. Tall, spare, aloof, clean-shaven, he has the pseudo-British air that men who held government posts used to affect in the days of Guizot. The walls around him are lined from floor to ceiling with handsomely bound books; a bust of Bossuet attests to his respect for sacred eloquence; through an open window we can see the tower of Saint Catherine's Church, with the tricolor of the Citizen King at its peak. Little Noémi, who has apparently entered to bring her father a message rather than ask permission to borrow a book, gives the painting that touch of familial affection which people had come to consider tasteful. In the second of the two canvases, Alexandrine-Joséphine, sitting stiffly under her fluted bonnet, is enthroned in an armchair next to a fireplace; on the mantelpiece is a set of ornaments that still exists. A young boy in a lace collar is standing near her. Some fancywork is within reach on a table, and the sheet music for a ballad is on the harpsichord. The fire screen is decorated with a classical scene in monochrome; the statue of a nymph embellishes the garden that we glimpse through a bay window. An immense Savonnerie carpet eclipses everything else with its gaudy colors.

The boy in the lace collar is named Anatole, or perhaps Gustave, or perhaps both. (The couple had at least one son who died young, and may have had two—the facts are unclear.) Gustave departed this life, a bachelor and a doctor of law, at the age of twenty-nine. His name figures in a document concerning a charitable foundation to which the Dufresnes contributed ten years later. Anatole, if indeed he existed separately, is not mentioned anywhere. My grandfather's memoirs are silent

Judge Amable Dufresne and his daughter, Noémi, ca. 1842

when it comes to this vanished fellow, or fellows, of whom Noémi must have been the sole heir. The worthy Alexandrine-Joséphine, in contrast, is referred to in those pages as "the best of women." My father, for his part, never spoke either of that uncle—who may have been one person or two, and who may have died too soon for my father to get to know him—or of "the best of women," even though she apparently lived almost to the turn of the twentieth century. We have no need to stroll through the necropolises of the Orient to take lessons in how to forget.

It is not out of a love for the picturesque that I have immobilized my reader before these two canvases in which objects matter at least as much as people. In fact all societies, whatever their nature, are founded on the possession of things. A great many people who have had their portraits painted have always insisted that their favorite knickknacks be represented next to them, just as in ancient times they would have asked for those objects to be put in their tombs. In one sense Alexandrine-Joséphine's clock and carpet are equivalent to the wooden clogs, the mirror, and the marriage bed of the Arnolfinis. But Van Eyck's models were still living in an age in which objects had meaning in themselves. Those clogs and that bed symbolize the intimacy of the spouses; that almost magical mirror is tinged with everything it has seen or will someday see. These interiors, in contrast, testify to a culture in which TO HAVE has taken precedence over TO BE. Noémi has grown up in a milieu where servants are kept "in their place"; where no one has a dog, because dogs dirty the carpets; where no one puts crumbs for the birds on the windowsills, because birds soil the cornices; where, if people give alms at Christmastime to the poor of the parish, they do so on the doorstep, for fear of lice and ringworm. No child "of the people" has ever played in that lovely garden; no book that is considered hostile to "good doctrines" has ever been admitted into that handsome library. For those Pharisees who consider themselves Christians, "Love others as you love yourself" is one of those precepts that sound fine when the curé delivers them from the pulpit; those who hunger and thirst for justice are rioters who are sentenced to hard labor. No one has ever dared tell Noémi that all unshared wealth is a form of abuse and every useless possession an encumbrance. She scarcely comprehends the fact that she will die; she knows only that her parents will die and that she will inherit from them. She does not know that every encounter with someone, even a vagabond who stops at the gate of 26 rue Marais, ought to be a celebration of kindness, if not of fellow feeling. No one has ever told her that things deserve to be loved for themselves, independently of us, their uncertain owners. No one has taught her to love God, whom at best she considers a sort of celestial Judge Dufresne. No one has even taught her to love. It's true that millions of people are in her situation, but many of them have a quality, a gift, that itself is able to move them beyond the realm of ingratitude. Noémi is not so fortunate.

She is virtuous, in the ignobly narrow sense that is given to the word in her day when it is used in the feminine form, as if virtue, for a woman, concerned nothing but an aperture in the body. Monsieur de C. will never be a deceived husband. Is she chaste? Only her sheets can provide the answer to that question. It's possible that this robust wife has a passionate nature which Michel-Charles is able to satisfy or, on the contrary (and I lean toward this alternative, since a woman whose every desire is satisfied is invariably ill-tempered), that a certain poverty of temperament, a lack of curiosity or imagination, or the advice that Alexandrine-Joséphine must have given her cause her to turn away from "illicit" pleasures and even from permitted ones. The carnal act might seem to her, as to many women of her day, merely a bothersome aspect of that married state outside of which a "person of the female sex" could not call herself "established" and would think of herself as "unsold merchandise." Though there is nothing unseemly taking place, she is nonetheless proud to be considered "a fine figure of a woman." Her body is precious to her not as an irreplaceable object that enables her to live, and even less, I imagine, as an instrument of sensual pleasure, but as a piece of furniture or a porcelain vase in her possession. It is less out of coquetry than out of a sense of what she owes to her "social position" that she clothes that body in taffeta or cashmere or, as the occasion arises, reveals it as fashion prescribes. She likes to show her "well-turned" shoulders and arms—no more, certainly, than the stylish women at the Tuileries or Compiègne, but a bit more than provincial modesty sometimes allows.

It seems that one night as they were leaving a ball, Michel-Charles, escorting his wife down the staircase of one of Lille's fine mansions, heard the vexing sound of silk fabric being torn. In the crush of people, Monsieur de N. (I've invented this initial), an elderly bachelor from a better social set and an arbiter of elegance in Lille, as ill-natured as the hunchback he slightly resembled, had carelessly stepped on the train of the handsome woman who was just ahead of him on the stairs. Noémi turned and said, with the mythological hiss of Medusa in her voice:

"*Fichu* [wretched] imbecile!"

"That *fichu* [shawl], Madame," replied Monsieur de N., "would do better on your shoulders than in your mouth."

Michel-Charles, after returning home, had to put up with his wife's reproaches, which he perhaps deserved. A husband with any self-respect would have challenged the impertinent cad. But one doesn't duel with an invalid. The husband was discreetly pleased to play the man who isn't listening, and refrained from exchanging a complicit smile with the guilty fellow.

One always hesitates to present a little story like this to the reader. It may be that Monsieur de N. took his repartee from some anthology of anecdotes, or even that Michel-Charles took the entire tale from such a collection so that he could entertain his son with it. True or false, it's characteristic of the period, like lace fichus.

I've spoken elsewhere of my grandmother's fondness for the possessive pronoun. The townhouse in Lille is "my townhouse," Mont-Noir is "my château," and the couple's landau is "my landau." Michel-Charles, who is "Monsieur" to the servants, is "my husband" the rest of the time; his first name appears only abruptly, coupled with an admonition ("Michel-Charles, you're going to make this carriage overturn!"). In public, he is often contradicted ("That story didn't happen precisely as my husband said it did") or scolded ("Michel-Charles, your cravat is badly tied"). An armchair that he thinks frightful and that she considers superb is reserved by the judge's daughter exclusively for paternal use ("Don't sit there, Michel-Charles; it's your father-in-law's favorite chair"). He never again uses that piece of furniture, which is upholstered in garnet (or perhaps buttercup) and which, incidentally, the judge isn't as fond of as all that; it remains empty, like Banquo's chair in *Macbeth*. The dates of their spring departure for the country and of their return to the city in the fall are set months in advance; if Michel-Charles or the children have a cold, then let them bundle up ("Myself, I never catch cold"). The Dufresnes have persuaded their son-in-law to entrust his financial affairs to their lawyer; they have a say in the composition of his portfolio. The judge has bought some land in the vicinity of Mont-Noir to round out the young couple's estate: Michel-Charles is no longer completely at home on those 130 or so hectares of woods, meadows, and farms. It seems that Amable took it upon himself to enlarge the country estate that was already a quarter of a century old; in any case, a secret report criticizes the magistrate for giving himself such airs as to have a small château built. Writing desks in the style of Louis XV and Eugénie clash with old Flemish cabinets and honest Restoration pieces. As in the days before his marriage, Michel-Charles likes to travel from Mont-Noir to his mother's house in Bailleul for midday dinner on Sundays. He goes alone; his departure and his return are the cause of angry scenes.

Their means permitting, he would like to spend several weeks at Nice or Baden-Baden, or even see his beloved Italy once again. This modest desire is the object of irony from Noémi ("I'm fine where I am"). He gives up the idea, and breaks his longstanding habit of murmuring lines of verse that seem to him beautiful and appropriate to certain occasions—greeting the moonlight with Virgil's *Tremulat sub lumine*, or, on the subject of children, evoking Victor Hugo's *Le Cercle de famille*. At table she cuts short, if she can, these inopportune quotations with a sharp rebuke to the valet de chambre ("This wine isn't sufficiently chilled"; "You haven't refilled the salt shaker"). Michel-Charles tries to soften the acerbity of the reproach with a pleasantry, but only aggravates his wrongs ("One must never become too familiar with such people"). If he leaves his *Journal des Débats* open on a hassock in the drawing room, intending to finish reading it later, he comes back to find it crumpled under the firewood ("Nothing looks more untidy than a newspaper that's been left lying about"). If he wants to use an empty boudoir in the Lille house to enlarge his library, it becomes absolutely necessary to transform that room into a linen closet. When he receives news from Bailleul concerning the death of his cousin Bieswal, a rich bibliophile nicknamed the Golden Calf who has made a bequest to Michel-Charles, a decision must be made as to whether he will sell or keep the celebrated collection of incunabula and books of hours, of contemporary engravings and romantic watercolors. Noémi favors selling it ("We already have enough books as it is"), and the impressive sum obtained from the appraiser makes her opinion seem the right one, even in Michel-Charles's eyes, though he regrets having to part with the La Fontaine of the Farmers General.

On all these occasions, my grandfather resembles a strategist who falls back on positions prepared in advance; Noémi triumphs like a conqueror over scorched earth. Michel-Charles tells himself that it would be grotesque to attach so much importance to cutting remarks, wheedling, and smiles. One can't have everything: at bottom, Noémi has solid qualities. As for him, he still has his official duties, his conversations with his colleagues, his books (he rereads more than he reads), and the lessons he gives to the children. In the morning, during the intimate moments over coffee and toast, Michel-Charles is silent when he is unable to hit on a topic they will be sure to agree on, or makes observations on the weather, though even these are often badly received. ("It's raining." "You're wrong; it stopped raining ten minutes ago.") Ultimately, this man and woman—who form a respected couple, who have two lovely children, who sometimes still pant in the same bed, who basically wish each other well, and of whom one is destined to see the other die—will share in this way, amid polite silence or with conversation that is scarcely worthy of the name, a total of almost twelve thousand breakfasts.

One topic of conversation, though, is never exhausted: the large formal dinner they give every Tuesday. *"She was in her element on those occasions,"* remarks Michel-Charles with his almost imperceptible raillery. Indeed, it's not only a question of holding conferences with the cook; writing to the florist, the fishmonger, the provisioner, and the dressmaker, who usually has to touch up one of her Parisian gowns; and overseeing the pressing of the damask napkins, in which every wrinkle would be as jarring as a sour note. The most serious business is the drawing up of the guest list. It's crucial that no one below a certain social level be offered those turbots and pineapples. Some personages are invited *ex officio:* the prefect; the commander of the Citadel; the directors of the Nord Line when they are in Lille; Parisian bankers who have come to town to take the pulse of local industry; a few representatives of good families who are supporters of the government, or at least whose legitimist sympathies are merely a harmless idiosyncrasy; the bishop, who always makes a good effect at table; and the nuncio, when there is one. From time to time the judge, in lordly fashion, will invite colleagues who are passing through town—

for example, little Ernest Pinard, the imperial public prose-cutor, who had Monsieur Baudelaire's *Flowers of Evil* censored as being offensive to wholesome morals, and nearly had the same success with *Madame Bovary*. This defender of public decency collects lascivious epigrams from antiquity. Judge Dufresne, who indulges in the same hobby, vies with him in coming up with spicy and erudite quotations; fittingly, Michel-Charles lends him assistance.

The rest of the time, the coarse jests that the men exchange come from Paris or the army. The women who are invited are not the worldly sort, but they are all used to hearing such jokes at the end of the meal, when the five long-stemmed glasses at each place have put them in a rainbow mood. ("The family gatherings had real bacchic spirit," an octogenarian cousin as-sured me a few years ago. He could scarcely have been present at those Second Empire feasts and was instead recalling the family's Sunday dinners in Bailleul, where an elderly guest who was suffering from cancer of the cheek would let champagne trickle from his lesion.) In the sparkling atmosphere of those Tuesdays in Lille, everyone thought himself a wit, and all gave themselves over to the optimism of the day. Paris, which Michel-Charles and Noémi visit at least once a year, has never been so gay or so rich. Unearned income is rising; dividends are increasing before one's very eyes. The workers' housing that has just been built at Roubaix is yielding a return of 25 percent. It's true, though, that the dwellings have no windows, or even doors. Michel-Charles, who would have had to intervene in the matter, privately realizes that they ought to have been con-demned as unhealthy and dangerous, but tells himself that, after all, the laborers in the spinning mills must be housed one way or the other and that investors will not lend money unless they are assured of substantial profits.

The count of Palikao, a regular at these Tuesday dinners,

recounts a few incidents from his Chinese campaign. The French cannons triumphed gloriously over bands of yellow horsemen, armed, like the savages they were, with spears and arrows. In their dealings with the civilized nations, those barbarians refuse to make any concessions, even though these would facilitate matters. The Arabs, too, are staunchly opposed to progress. In Algeria, Bugeaud's soldiers no doubt went a bit too far: rebellious hamlets captured in the evening were often nothing but a pile of ashes next morning. Those brutes even let themselves be burned along with their huts. In the smoking room, where there was no fear of shocking the sensibilities of the women, the hero goes so far as to recall that there were a few incidents involving babies spitted on bayonets. What do you expect? War is war.

A government informer, who evidently attended these family feasts to gather material for his secret reports, has nothing but complimentary things to say about Noémi's kind and gentle nature—enabling us once and for all to appreciate the value of secret reports. *"Despite her extreme modesty, she does not go unnoticed in society. Moreover she does not wield great influence there, and will never seek to exercise any."* It may be that Noémi was limited in ambition, just as she was limited in her capacity for love. It may also be that her indifference was the result of an admirable and robust provincial pride, the pride of someone who is content to be what she is and nothing more. I'm grateful to her for not putting herself forward in the salons of the prefecture.

The writer of those reports, who seems to have formed an unfavorable idea of the people and things of Nord, notes almost reluctantly that Michel-Charles, *"who is related to the best families of the region,"* displays *"impeccable attire"* and that *"his manners do not lack a certain distinction."* But *"he shows the effects of his Flemish origins."* *"His wit is not of the liveliest, yet beneath his genial air he is not without subtlety. His facility in speaking is remarkable."* He has no *"political acumen,"* adds the anatomist of human marionettes, who is correct on this point, whatever the meaning, favorable or sinister, that may be given to these two words. But *"he has a good grasp of business, and his diligence leaves nothing to be desired. His position and his connections make him useful."* What is more, he is *"sufficiently educated,"* doubtless for the vice-presidency of the prefectural council—a position that this report, despite its ambivalence, will secure for him. The government spy is not mistaken. Michel-Charles is only sufficiently—which is to say insufficiently—educated. Certainly in this domain as in any other, it is not essential that one be "up to the minute," and it is even an advantage not to be lured into the trap of fashionable opinions. Nevertheless, in the age of Darwin on the one hand and Renan and Taine on the other, this well-lettered man who rereads Condillac's works because his teachers at Stanislas School made him read them, who occasionally reopens his Tacitus so as to prevent his Latin from getting rusty, and who teaches his daughter the history of the world in six periods from the Fall of Adam to the reign of Louis XIV is not, in the strict sense of the word, an "educated" man. I fear, though, that the Parisian informer is judging him by the fact that he's never read *La Fille Elisa* or heard the latest couplet by Offenbach.

Concerning his morals, the powers above give him their official blessing: Michel-Charles, staunch family man, devotes himself exclusively to his wife and children. Of which formal evidence is given, along with the handful of qualifications that always exist. But alas—and the scribbler returns to this point with an insistence that would justify every form of separatism —*"he's a Fleming."* *"His expression is frank and open, despite the very Flemish cast to his features . . . His character is very Flemish. He is doubtless quite loyal, and I in no way wish to claim that he would be capable of distorting the truth; but he does not always speak the whole truth."* Here, the informer has hit the nail on the head. But in the France of the Second Empire, duplicity is scarcely the appanage of a single despised ethnic group. Michel-Charles's duplicity is, rather, the result of a tendency acquired in certain religious schools where litotes and mental constraints have flourished since the seventeenth century and where individual expression is still afflicted by a too prevalent vice: an obliquely manifested sincerity.

But what matters most to the official spy is how deep this fellow's pockets are. After the death of his mother- and father-in-law, the income of the above-mentioned will rise to one hundred thousand francs annually. This fortune which is so solidly based (or seems to be so) is the leash that will keep the dog from straying: *"He is too attached to what he possesses not to be a loyal servant in the emperor's government."* The word "loyal" evokes a smile in this context. We should interpret it to mean that Michel-Charles will never make the mistake of aligning himself with the liberals, whose *"disguised socialism"* is a threat to property owners. The empire is guarding itself on the left.

People have not forgotten his family's legitimist sympathies, or his Orleanism, or that of his father-in-law, who in another official report is severely taken to task. *"Satisfied with his Legion of Honor rosette and with the important post of presiding judge of the Lille Tribunal, and reassured (he's not the only one) by the fact that he has been appointed for life,"* Amable Dufresne supported the candidacy of an Orleanist, Deputy P., the brother-in-law of his daughter's husband, and gave vent to sarcastic remarks on the subject of the government. In sum, the son-in-law, firmly established in *"his position and his connections,"* is no more reliable; fortunately, at least, he covets the Legion of Honor. Despite the recent decree of the Hazebrouck Tribunal, the informer persists in calling Monsieur C. de C. only "Cleenewerck," which no doubt strikes him as better suited to those Flemish features. Because the fellow insists on adorning himself with that Old Regime name, the spy reproaches him for wanting *"to rub elbows with the self-styled nobility of the region."* The phrase "self-styled nobility," which he seems to spit out like a feather lodged in his throat, reveals that this servant of the self-styled emperor Bonaparte harbors the deep-seated Jacobinism that always lies in the hearts of so many Frenchmen. Try as my grandfather might to perform his administrative duties with zeal, to fulfill his temporary posts such as subprefect of Douai and prefect of Lille, and to take *"the necessary measures"* (whatever these might be) *"on the occasion of Gérenchies' attack against His Majesty the Emperor,"* the government has its eye on him. The empire is guarding itself on the right.

Noémi, dressed in a low-cut black velvet gown and wearing a red velvet rose in her hair like a Doña Sol at the Comédie-Française, plays with her delicate scarf of Indian muslin without suspecting that a guest who has had two helpings of asparagus in hollandaise sauce is coolly writing that *"this household is passably well run."* (One hasn't dined at Mornay's in Paris in order to admire the provincial splendor of Nord.) Michel-Charles, who at this moment is serving curaçaos and brandies to his guests, does not know that he is a figure—held in somewhat low esteem and respected only because he is rich—in the secret reports of a police system. If he found out, his sagacity would lead him to say that all governments are like that. In a miniature corresponding to the portrait of Noémi as Doña Sol, he looks a bit constrained, gazing into the distance beyond the viewer. He appears neither frank nor open, and especially not genial. The informer took the warm exterior of Flemish hospitality as the essence of his temperament. Despite the favorable indications that are seen in him (*"Perfect health; no infirmities"*), Michel-Charles has suffered from stomach ulcers since his marriage. One of his son's earliest memories will be of watching his father, not at the Tuesday dinners, which the little boy was not allowed to attend and at which the master of the house surely made a pretense of eating, but at the family table, during the long and copious meals that were the custom in those days. To keep himself in countenance, Michel-Charles would repeatedly stir his food: oatmeal smothered in cream, the only form of nourishment that, sometimes for months at a stretch, his doctors would permit him. In spite of everything, he eventually got well. A specialist would no doubt hesitate to establish a cause-and-effect relationship between those lesions so slow to heal and the stomach cancer from which he would die at the age of sixty-four.

The photography of the nineteenth century, that age of bombastic portraitists, makes no claims to deserve the label "art." It has every right to be called art, however. Those bourgeois people who hold interminable poses, and who thus imprint their likenesses on plates treated with silver nitrate, unwittingly have the severe frontality of primitive statues and the vigor of Holbein's portraits. To this nobility—the nobility of every great art that has just been born—is added a disquieting touch of magic. For the first time since the world began, light directed by human ingenuity is able to capture the specters of the living. These people, who in our own day are truly phantoms, stand before us as their unquiet spirits might have, clothed in spectral frock coats and ghostly crinolines. It has perhaps never been noted that the first great photographic portraits date from the time of the first séances. The success of the spell requires, in the latter case, a rotating table; in the former case, a sensitized glass plate; in both cases, the intervention of a medium (for every photographer is a medium). Precisely because everything is present in these images—for there has been none of that winnowing and sorting which a painter or sculptor would

Noémi Dufresne, Yourcenar's grandmother, ca. 1868

Michel-Charles Cleenewerck de Crayencour, Yourcenar's
grandfather, ca. 1868

have begun with—they are as difficult to interpret as the faces themselves seen in life. In most of them we confront worlds that are opaque and closed. Certain shots reveal, without our knowing if that revelation pertains to actions or tendencies, aspects of what these people could have been and done, or of what they were and did. It might even happen that various characteristics, slowly developing as if through some chemical reaction, do not become visible until our own day, and to our own eyes. After the splendors of Compiègne, for example, the defeated-looking face of Napoleon III enables us to foresee Sedan, as if he already bore his disaster on his body. And despite the dithyrambs of her admirers, the beautiful Castiglione, costumed as the Queen of Hearts, reveals her thick ankles and her feet squeezed into satin mules, as if this idol of the salons had exhausted herself walking the streets. Contemporary viewers did not see such features, doubtless because they were blinded by habit or fixed opinions based on respect or infatuation; had the parties concerned perceived the slightest trace of them, they would have torn up those costly visiting cards. But to us the lacunae, flaws, and vices are revealed as if the photographs were X-rays.

Noémi is no longer the Doña Sol of the families: she looks proper and ordinary in her high-cut taffeta gown. Only her lips, which are stiffly pressed together like the clasp of a lady's purse, betray her lack of kindness. Her well-kept hands are those of a woman who has never performed the slightest domestic labor; thus, in the parlance of her day, they are the hands of a "respectable" woman. Michel-Charles in the 1860s appears to us only as a gentleman with a thin, almost emaciated face, in frock coat and goatee. His tall, very erect body and his slightly raised head give the impression of painful self-control. His gaze, intense and dark (for nothing is darker than the gaze of certain light-colored eyes), gleams with a cold brilliance between the

DATE   TIME
03/09/97   15:02

HALF PRICE BOOKS
ST. PAUL, MN 55116

87990023101   0000000000

ACCOUNT NUMBER   EXP
4190087719235029   0399

SALE $ 17.59

136   APPROVED 18788

SIGNATURE X _Dorothea M Robert_

THANK YOU!

TOP COPY-MERCHANT BOTTOM COPY-CUSTOMER

line of his brows and his high cheekbones. One might think this the image of Ibsen's Solness or Rosmer on the eve of a crisis, or Tolstoy's Ivan Ilych already worn by illness yet continuing to resist it. We would know nothing about this man who suffers and perhaps thinks, if we did not have a few anecdotes told by his son. Michel-Charles himself has obliterated Michel-Charles.

The children, too, were taken to the photographer, as was fashionable in those days. There are two of them. We can't help being grateful to the Lille couple for having stopped at this number. The desire to avoid carving up the estate into too many pieces was doubtless more of a factor than the desire to avoid overburdening the earth; nonetheless, something tells me that Michel-Charles did not approve of the way humans were swarming over the planet. He was certainly a good father. As for Noémi, her attitude toward her children is one of the mysteries of that woman who seems incapable of having any. She grieved violently for her little Gabrielle, who died young, but such emotion does not necessarily prove that she would have showered the girl with affection had she lived. Toward her son, Michel, she seems to have displayed, as far back as one can go, only an ill-temper that closely resembles hatred.

We are so attached to the cliché of a loving mother, so moved by the sight of the warmth and devotion (albeit brief) of mothers in the animal kingdom, that Noémi's attitude surprises us—all the more because it was rare, in those days and in that social milieu, that an only son should not be treated like a crown prince. Noémi's hostility toward her second child makes one suspect that there was some sensual conflict which had become irreconcilable, or else that Michel-Charles had committed some peccadillo at the time, despite the official testimonials to his excellent morals. Later, Noémi will not lack reasons for vilifying her rebellious son, but she will be largely responsible for inciting that rebellion. For the moment, the two little nestlings upstairs at 26 rue Marais are objects, virtually her personal belongings; they are "my daughter" and "my son," until the day that Michel, when Noémi is speaking about him to his father, becomes "your son." But she has surely gone up to the third floor to oversee the maid who is washing, dressing, and brushing the two little ones for their sitting.

Here they are, then, as the photographer captured them —and "captured" is the word: captured in their fine clothes, amid the handsome furniture and graceful accessories of the professional's studio, captured in the manners and customs of their century. But compared to the adults—stiff, wooden, already marked to be felled someday—these young shoots have the inexhaustible force of all that is still fresh, lithe, and adaptable, of the slender stem that can, if necessary, pierce a thick layer of dead leaves or pulverize rock. Like other children of their time, they already have, at least in front of the camera lens, the dignity of little grownups; they live in an age when childhood is still felt to be a state that one should leave as soon as possible, so as to accede quickly to the rank of Gentleman and Lady. There would be much to say in favor of such a view if the gentlemen and ladies offered as models to the children were not, far too often, merely tailor's dummies themselves. At six or seven at the most, Gabrielle is already a lady in miniature. Standing in her short crinoline and plaid blouse, she rests her hand with a gesture at once firm and light on the shoulder of her younger brother, who is seated next to her. Her perfect self-possession, her already worldly air, the indefinable self-assurance in her small, proud head make us slightly uneasy about what Gabrielle will be at twenty. But such worries are pointless: she will not live to be that old. Scarcely five, the well-behaved boy sitting in the chair and holding a book is dressed like a little man. Nothing is lacking—not the vest, not the

Michel de Crayencour and his older sister, Gabrielle, ca. 1858

carefully tied cravat, not the well-polished shoes. His head is quite round, like those of Donatello's putti; his robust little body makes one think of the bodies of young dogs, which seem to contain in their plump fullness all the elements that will enable them to grow. His face is stamped with an honesty and seriousness that are almost grave, but his clear eyes are laughing like water in sunlight.

Let's turn quickly through the leaves of the album. Soon we see Michel at the age of seven, fragile and slight. We need only throw a dalmatic over his shoulders to turn him into an angel by Fouquet or Roger van der Weyden, but his eyes already contain sadness in their depths: at seven, one knows what life is. Later we will see the slightly stout high-school boy, nourished on good thick soup, with a mischievous glint in his eye; the handsome hero of twenty, enveloped in Byronic gloom, driven by a rather restless sensuality, harassed by worldly and fleshly phantasms; the soldier who is trying out his new uniform and his new mustache; the fin-de-siècle man of the world, a cigarette between his fingers, pondering some private unfinished business; the horseman with his head shaved in Hungarian style; the fifty-year-old gentleman in a morning coat, not the slightest bit incommoded by the height of his detachable collar, which one feels is appropriate attire for giving orders and distributing tips—the image of a milieu at least as much as of a man; the same gentleman on a beach, in white flannels, walking in step with the lovely woman of the moment.

But the snapshots taken at the end of his life interest me even more. A pensive old man, properly dressed in English fabric, seated at a table in the garden of a hotel in Cap-Ferrat, his tall figure leaning toward a little dog with which he has struck up a friendship, curiously isolated from the woman seated in the chair opposite, whom he has just taken as his wife, partly to repay her for her loyalty and partly because it's convenient

Michel de Crayencour, Yourcenar's father, 1870s

Michel de Crayencour, ca. 1909

Michel de Crayencour, 1920s

Michel de Crayencour on the bridge
at Aricia, 1920s

to have her as nurse and companion. The same old man alone, seated this time on the steps of an Italian palace or cloister, his hands hanging between his knees, with his air of gentleness and depleted strength. The same man, finally, leaning on the parapet of the bridge at Aricia, his back to the immemorial landscape of Latium. He is very weary, which I didn't notice when I took the photo. This souvenir of an excursion through the countryside around Rome is, above all, the image of the end of a journey: in his clothes of grayish wool, Michel has the air of an old beggar in the sunshine.

The older I get, the more I realize that childhood and old age not only are connected but, in addition, are the two most profound states that it is given us to experience. The essence of a being is revealed in them, prior to or after the efforts, the aspirations, the ambitions of life. The smooth face of Michel as a boy and the strongly marked face of the elderly Michel resemble each other, which was not always the case for the intermediate faces of his youth and maturity. The eyes of the child and those of the old man gaze at us with the serene candor of someone who has not yet joined the masked ball or who has already left it. And the entire interval between them seems a vain confusion, an agitation with no point, a useless chaos that makes one wonder why it was necessary to pass through it at all.

Late one afternoon in April, the children are awaiting the arrival of their first English governess. They're approximately as old as they are in their photograph. The mail train from Boulogne has been delayed: the young stranger does not arrive at the house on the rue Marais until the little ones are just about to begin their supper upstairs. She removes her bonnet, freeing her blond hair, slips off the short traveling cloak that covers her simple dress, then takes the siblings in charge and makes them say their *Benedicite*. She is of course Catholic, perhaps Irish, and her new employers have been assured that she comes of good family. She has been recommended to them by the Mother Superior of an English convent, who vouches for her irreproachable conduct and her impeccable accent and manners.

This is the first time she has ever left England. Crossing the Channel was a new experience for her; the train ride in second class from Boulogne to Lille was another; this opulent, gloomy French house is a third. She has been shy in Madame's presence, and shy as well in front of the servants who bring the trays and hot water upstairs; they've been told to call her

"Miss" but refer to her among themselves as "the English girl." While undressing the children at bedtime (and the maid who until now has had this job does not give it up without grumbling), she amuses them by talking about her trip: she saw seagulls on the water, cows in the fields, French dogs along the roads. After the little ones are tucked in, she puts their favorite toys beside them—the boy gets his stuffed monkey made of plush and the girl her doll—with droll and tender remarks that they have never heard anywhere else. When she speaks French they laugh, and she laughs with them. When she speaks English ("You will begin teaching English to my children immediately"), they feel as if she is making them a present of something entirely new—a wonderful secret entrusted to them alone. ("Here's something you don't know: where I come from *une poupée* is called *a doll*.") Michel will later become partial to this playful whimsy so typical of Englishwomen. She wishes them sweet dreams; no one has ever wished them sweet dreams before.

Early next morning they are awakened, as usual, by the bugles of the regiment which marches through their street every day. Dressed only in her petticoat and camisole but throwing a shawl over her shoulders, the English girl runs to the window, her curiosity piqued by the unfamiliar music and the soldiers in red pants. The men down below catch sight of her little blond form leaning over the sill. A few high-spirited fellows blow her kisses. She withdraws in confusion and closes the window. But the sound of the window being closed is accompanied by that of the door being flung violently open, to admit an enraged Noémi. She has seen and guessed everything from the dining room downstairs, where she was buttering her toast.

"Worthless girl! Slut! Soldier's whore!"

Michel-Charles has come upstairs more slowly and now intervenes on behalf of the pretty girl, who is sobbing. It's quite

natural that the newcomer should go to the window to watch
the French soldiers march by; and also quite natural (he adds
with a cautious smile) that those boys should have blown her
kisses. This ill-considered remark merely causes the mistress
of the house to become even angrier at the girl.

"Get out! Pack your trunk! You're corrupting my children,
you wretch!"

Michel-Charles goes back dowstairs with a sigh. Through
her tears, "Miss" gathers up the few things she has unpacked
from her trunk, buttons her dress, puts on her traveling cloak
and her bonnet. No one bothers to remember that she hasn't
had breakfast. Taking advantage of a moment when Madame's
back is turned, she gives the petrified children a quick kiss,
and goes down the stairs followed by the sneering valet, who is
carrying her trunk. Below, Michel-Charles comes noiselessly
out of his study and slips two napoleons into her hand; she takes
them, forgetting to say thank you. She climbs into the hired
carriage that has been called. ("You certainly don't think I'm
going to hitch up our horses for such a tramp, do you?") The
carriage drives off, with the trunk swaying on its roof.

Noémi insists on writing an indignant letter to the convent
in Brighton whose Mother Superior had recommended the governess. Michel-Charles succeeds only in persuading her to
soften her wording a bit. ("Naturally that shameless girl caught
your fancy.") The children wept over the pretty "Miss" for a
quarter of an hour and then forgot her. But at a deeper level,
Michel remembered. The image of the little Englishwoman
probably played no part in drawing him, when he was much
older, into one of the most tempestuous love affairs of his life
(though I couldn't swear to this). Twenty years later, on a foggy
evening in London, did he consciously think of her? It's doubtful. And if the poor girl had ended up adopting the profession

toward which that shameful dismissal could have pushed her, after two decades she would have been nothing but a very faded night-flower.

At Mont-Noir, where Michel-Charles is a man of leisure, father and son are together almost constantly. He takes Michel to visit Reine, who continues to reign at Bailleul with her daughters as ladies-in-waiting. Neither Valérie nor Gabrielle has married, doubtless because it was impossible to find suitable husbands for them in the few châteaux in the district. If they suffer from their celibacy, which is by no means certain (they don't yet live in an age in which women have been persuaded that making love can cure all ills), they perhaps console themselves with the thought that their share of the inheritance will devolve intact upon Michel-Charles. Their life flows by in a convent-like tranquillity. They adhere so closely to religious principles, such as they understand them, that if they happen to play checkers on a Sunday and if one of them wins a stake of ten sous from the other, she won't pay it back until the next day, because all monetary transactions are improper on the Sabbath. The two demoiselles perform many good works and find ample outlet for their charitable impulses; an official report tells us that many poor people live in Bailleul and that their lot would be pitiable if worthy women from the town's best circles did not come to their aid.

These two pious spinsters are growing old with dignity in their fine dresses of pearl gray or autumn-leaf brown, with their tuckers, their ruching, their point lace, their wide sleeves of white silk peeking through slashed satin, their little purses suspended from their waists and filled with cone-shaped packets of sugared almonds. Valérie, the more severe of the two, has Reine's authoritarian side without her coaxing ways or her velvet gloves. Gabrielle has a melancholy gentleness; one might easily imagine there was some unrealized romantic tale in her life. As for the worthy Henri, he continues to stroll about the town's main square, with his mother or one of his sisters on his arm and the key to his room in his waistcoat pocket, so that no one, not even a servant, will enter that sanctuary in his absence.

The inspection tours of the farms are the boy's greatest pleasure. It was agreed in the marriage contract that Michel-Charles would manage Noémi's properties as well as his own. In this land of fragmented estates, such visits take hours on horseback, and sometimes it's even necessary to spend the night on one of the farms. When the boy is small, he sits astride in front of his father on the placid, gentle mare that they take on these excursions; later, Michel will ride behind or will have his very own pony. We already know that Michel-Charles is not much of a naturalist. No matter: the boy at least learns to distinguish couch grass from wild oats, and Jerseys from the heavy cows of Flanders. He becomes familiar with the damp undergrowth, the newly hatched birds in the hedgerows, the fox cubs in the grass. Michel-Charles is not a hunter, so the boy does not see these living creatures from the outset as objects for killing. Sometimes, when they return home late, at one of those foggy or windy sunsets that enable peasants to predict the weather, a star that they at first take to be the light of a distant house rises in the sky and the little boy asks its name. Michel-Charles is no more an astronomer than he is a botanist, but he can recognize Venus, Mars, and a few clearly visible constellations. He can explain the difference between a planet and a star, and why the moon appears larger on the horizon than it does at its zenith and assumes an orange or reddish hue. What he knows best of all are the myths associated with the constellations, and he often spins fine classical tales that delight his son.

The little boy likes to eat his share of the basketful of provisions using only his fingers and knife; to urinate against a tree, as his father does, and watch the hot steam rise from the moss. The peasants' food is good, or seems so to him. In honor of the visitors, the farmer's wife has augmented the family's ordinary fare, a thick soup, with the grilled bacon or the omelette they usually have only on Sundays, or perhaps a tart made with fruit or cream cheese, if the necessary ingredients are at hand. The boy falls asleep with his head on the well-scoured wooden table. His father, even as he's swallowing his medicinal powders, thinks that this food is every bit as good as the grand Tuesday dinners, forgetting that this frugal repast is a luxury for his hosts. The importance of the farms is calculated by the number of horses each one has: a farm with one horse yields just enough for the peasant couple and their children to live on and to pay the landlord; the farms with two horses are already better off; those that have a greater number of horses also have better-equipped stables and employ workers who are treated and fed as well as (or as badly as) the family. The thousand hectares of land that Michel-Charles and Noémi pride themselves on owning comprise about thirty farms.

My grandfather is well aware that this exploitation of the field hand by the farmer, of the farmer by the landlord, of the patient animals and the even more patient land by everyone, does not exactly constitute Paradise. But where is Paradise to be found? His archaic fondness (which I find touching) for landed property at least prevents him from participating to a great extent in the beginnings of industrial development; he has gotten too close a view of the manufacturing regions not to know that it is better to labor in the open air behind a single horse than to suffocate in the dust of the spinning mills. He sometimes thinks that it would take very little to make the peasants' lot acceptable and even happy; but if he agreed to reduce the rent for this small tenant farmer burdened with debt because of a poor harvest, or to compensate a farmer for a cow he has lost, Noémi would say, perhaps rightly, that he is taking bread out of his children's mouths. One could slightly lessen the distance between owners and farmers by renouncing certain luxuries. But which ones? For him, the height of superfluity is represented by Noémi's footmen; for Noémi, it's a winter at Sorrento. Besides, he is only too familiar with the perpetual complainer who invents illnesses and frustrations that he doesn't have; with the sly or cunning fellow who regards his master's kindness as a weakness to be taken advantage of; with the brutal or improvident man who beats or starves his animals; with the skinflint who puts his few sous of profit into a woolen sock and refuses to buy even one more measure of seed. You can't remake the world. Tonight he sleeps in the best bed, which the farmer and his wife vacate for him; the dampness that rises from the floor of beaten earth creeps into his joints, always susceptible to rheumatism. The little boy, happy to be spending the night with his father, falls into a sound and untroubled sleep.

The next day the complaints continue around the bowl of chicory juice flavored with coffee. Here Monsieur de C. is Monsieur Cleenewerck, not because anyone wishes to challenge his Old Regime fiefs (as the government informer thought he could do), but because farmers and owners have known each other, from generation to generation, since long before the family began using an estate name. Moreover, the tenants appreciate Michel-Charles's good manners: he removes his hat in the presence of the farmer's wife, even when he is outdoors; he pats the animals and knows the children's names. But above all, he is one of them: he speaks Flemish.

Charmed as always by the pleasant faces, he lingers to exchange a few words with a fresh-looking young dairymaid. The old farmer sitting on the doorstep takes the little boy, who has been exploring the poultry yard, on his knee. He lifts him with outstretched arms, just as good peasants raise their lord's son in sentimental eighteenth-century engravings, and murmurs with admiration:

"Mynheer Michiels, you will be rich!"

At an early date, Michel-Charles begins to take advantage of his son's school vacations to travel abroad with him for brief periods. The boy must learn to see the world. Noémi makes no formal objections to these escapades, but the family calculates the smallest expenditures in advance, to the last penny. Monsieur de C. and his son owe it to themselves to stay at good hotels, but Michel-Charles keeps track of their most trifling expenses in a notebook and haggles with the coachman when they treat themselves to an excursion. The boy recalls having heard his father complain about the sacristans in Antwerp, who made visitors pay them ten sous to draw back the serge curtain in front of the altar paintings by Rubens. In Holland everything is so expensive that Michel-Charles at the last minute decides against taking a boat ride along the coast of Zeeland. But he doesn't have the heart to refuse to buy his son a native costume, which is pronounced ridiculous when they return home.

There are also unexpected incidents. One summer they make an excursion on the Rhine. The boy sees his first castle; and from the tourist boat he gazes with vague wonder at the Lorelei, where a fairy seated on a high rock is combing her golden hair. Having passed this famous site and having left behind them the last echoes of the ballads sung by hearty German voices, they go below to the dining room to eat a copious meat-and-potatoes meal while watching the river's banks glide gently by. At dessert, Michel-Charles hands his son a postcard and says to him, "You really should write a few words to your mother." The boy sets about it diligently, mentions the castle and the Lorelei, and finishes with a description of their dinner. Returning to Lille at the appointed day and hour, they pull up to the house at nightfall in a hired carriage. Noémi, waiting in the vestibule, is wearing her storm-cloud face. She shows the postcard to Michel-Charles.

"You were deliberately trying to offend me by sending me this postcard from your son. You can't even be trusted to look after a child."

Michel-Charles doesn't understand. She draws him over to a gaslight and raises the incriminating card toward the livid flame. The boy wrote of having eaten a cold chicken wing and a slice of excellent roast beef. She points an accusatory finger at the date: a Friday.

An incident such as this might give the impression that Noémi is extremely devout. Actually she's one of those good Catholics who attend eleven o'clock Mass on Sunday, perform their religious duties at Eastertime, and avoid eating meat (and make others around them do likewise) on fast days. When a gale is raging and lightning bolts are playing about the summit of Mont-Noir, she also reveals the depth of her piety by taking refuge in a closet with her rosary.

Early one summer Michel-Charles decides to take the child to Ostend for some sea bathing, to help him shake off the last traces of a lingering cold. As usual, Noémi stays home, convinced that the edifice of domestic life would collapse if she failed to supervise her servants for eight days. One evening father and son sit down to eat in the dining room of the still-half-empty hotel, near an open window that looks out onto the seawall. The breeze coming off the ocean makes the curtains billow. Dusk is just beginning to fall. The maître d'hôtel waits until dessert to light the little lamps, which glow under their rose-colored shades; the boy has been looking forward to this great moment. A charming young lady is sitting all alone at the next table. Her skirts are pale pink, and her tiny bonnet seems made of genuine roses. On this fine evening everything is rose-colored, even the sky above the sea in the distance. Monsieur de C. rises with a small bow to hand the menu to the lovely lady. A conversation ensues which the boy pays no attention to, immersed as he is in the enjoyment of his food and his view of the seawall promenade, with its well-dressed people strolling by, laughing among themselves and often speaking languages he doesn't understand. The women who sell shrimp are returning home at the end of the day, their baskets on their heads. The boys selling the evening papers are crying out the latest headlines. When the coffee is served, Michel-Charles changes seats so that he is facing his charming neighbor, who is still eating her ice cream and fruit. Michel thinks he has heard his father propose that the pretty lady accompany him to the theater this evening.

"Go upstairs to our room," Michel-Charles tells him gently. "Leave the key in the door and don't turn the lock, or else I'll have to wake you up to let me in. You're old enough now to be by yourself without feeling afraid. If something happens, ring for help or knock on the wall to call the neighbors."

The boy thinks he hears the young woman murmur that he is charming, which offends the little man's dignity. But this is made up to him a hundredfold by the fact that his father has entrusted him with the key to their room. He obediently goes upstairs to bed.

The footsteps of people returning to their rooms nearby wake him from his first slumber. He's a bit afraid. Nothing but that door stands between him and the almost unknown world of the corridor, with its red carpet and its potted palms. His father's bed has been turned down by the chambermaid; to his eyes, it looks empty and sad and somewhat frightening, with its starkly pale pillows and its brasswork that glints in the light coming through the breaks in the curtains from the gas lamps out on the seawall. Cries and conversations drift up from the pavement, less gay than they were earlier in the evening; some of those people have apparently had too much to drink. The boy thinks he hears the clock on the landing strike twelve times, then once several times, then twice. How long that play is! Eventually sleep overcomes him again.

When he wakes, it's broad daylight. Papa, who returned without his being aware of it, is still sleeping. The boy gets out of bed and washes noiselessly, or almost noiselessly. Deep down, he wouldn't be annoyed if the clink of the water jug against the basin were to wake his father. The breakfast period is almost over.

At last, Michel-Charles opens his eyes. He immediately orders coffee and croissants: they'll breakfast together on the balcony, which looks out over the ocean. He is (if this is possible) even more gentle than usual. The day passes quickly, like all pleasant days. Only once, in the lobby, does the boy again encounter the lady in pink from yesterday: his father kisses her hand. That evening he again goes up to bed by himself. He's no longer afraid and falls asleep right away.

The next day is the day of their departure, as well as the occasion of their last sea bath. The tide is low. As always, they have themselves taken to the edge of the water in a wheeled cabin drawn by a fine big white horse, for whom the boy has saved some sugar cubes from breakfast. ("You must hold your palm very flat.") Father and son disrobe together; the boy, who is ready first, jumps out by himself to brave the ocean's powerful surges. Neither of them knows how to swim, and Michel will never in his life learn how. Both of them suffer from a circulatory deficiency that makes them subject to cramps if they remain immersed too long; and on this fine morning in late June the water is still ice-cold.

They put their clothes back on in the little cabin, carefully wiping their bodies, which are slightly sticky from the salt water, and brushing off the patches of sand.

Suddenly his father says: "When I folded my clothes a little while ago, a dozen louis that I took along for the trip must have fallen out of my pocket. Look—the latticework of the floor has enormous gaps in it. No, it won't do any good to search under the cabin. The tide is coming in; the horse is already up to his hocks in water. You'll explain all this to your mother when I mention it to her."

The boy nonetheless insists: he jumps out bare-legged and wades around for a moment, without feeling anything against his toes but the surging water and the sand being sucked back and forth by the currents. It's time to roll the cabin back to the dry part of the beach. Does he daydream when he looks through the little window and sees glimmers of gold on the water? Michel-Charles is silent. I don't think the boy suspects the lie immediately, but he senses that his father feels ill at ease, as he himself so often is when he has to tell grownups stories that they perhaps won't believe. He feels a bit sorry for his father. As for the pretty lady in pink, Michel-Charles has no need to tell his son not to say anything about her at home. The boy knows instinctively that the topic mustn't be raised.

On September 22, 1866, Monsieur de Crayencour and his children are preparing to leave Mont-Noir for Bailleul, where they will spend the day in the old house. Michel-Charles is on horseback; Gabrielle and Michel are riding together on a fine donkey that has been outfitted with the pretty saddle adorned with tassels. Gabrielle is holding the reins, aided, or perhaps hindered, by the efforts of her little brother, who is sitting behind her and whose interference provokes "words" between the two children from time to time. She turned fourteen last May; since then, she has doubtless not been permitted to sit astride. I assume she rides sidesaddle, her knee raised, her skirt carefully tucked in so that the wind will not lift and swell the fabric. The little cavalcade sets out gaily, making its way down the lane bordered with rhododendrons that leads to the iron gate. They pass by the mill, located on a knoll and set back from the château, in a spot where there is always a bit of a breeze, even on the calmest days. The great arms, as they turn in the wind, sound like the sails of a ship on the open sea. A light one-horse cart has stopped in front of the wooden steps, which are shaking and vibrating. The miller is standing on the

narrow platform, exchanging banter with a woman who is waiting down below for the flour that has been made from her sacks
of grain. Beyond, there is only the little tavern shaded by two
young linden trees and likewise located on the hill; it's a favorite
destination of villagers out for a stroll. The sunken road de-
scends steeply toward the village of Saint-Jans-Cappel. The two
animals walk single file. The road is so narrow that Michel and
his sister can reach out now and then and pluck a tempting
spray of hazelnuts.

They are already three-fourths of the way down the hill
when they hear the sound of galloping hooves and rumbling
wheels approaching rapidly behind them. The woman with the
cart has lost control of her horse, which has been goaded by a
horsefly or perhaps one too many whiplashes and has seized the
bit in its teeth.

Michel-Charles pulls over to the extreme edge of the road;
the frightened donkey jumps onto the embankment and throws
its two riders. Gabrielle falls under the wheels of the cart, which
rolls over her shoulder. Michel comes through with one foot
dislocated and a long shallow wound in the calf of his leg, where
it was torn by a stone. The cart horse comes to a stop, its sides
heaving; the woman gets down from her seat crying, or rather
screaming, with grief and fear. Michel-Charles, always self-
controlled in emergencies, has dismounted. He gently places
Gabrielle on the sacks of flour in the cart and decides to drive
to a nearby farm. There he borrows the farmer's two-horse
wagon and continues on to Bailleul, where he summons a surgeon and a physician. One can imagine the anguish of that last
remaining mile, covered at a crawl so as not to jostle the already
dying girl. Not only is her shoulder broken but a horrible wound
gapes at the base of her neck, as if someone had clumsily tried
to decapitate her. The girl moans and suffers; she seems lost
in the confusion and delirium of a bad dream, no longer aware

of who she is or where she is going. Her father, seated next to her on the straw, experiences one of the cruelest quarter-hours of his life.

Immediately after the accident he told the little boy to run back to the château and alert everyone there, without even noticing that Michel, too, is hurt. The boy doesn't suspect it either. He will never cease to marvel that despite his dislocated foot, he was able to sprint back up that long hill without stopping. Gasping for breath, he hurries back along the lane bordered with rhododendrons and comes out onto the terrace, where his mother is occupied with some embroidery.

"Mama, Gabrielle . . ."

At the sound of the boy's call, she leaps to her feet. From his very first words she understands everything.

"Wretched child! Why did it have to be her?"

The little boy, tottering, clings to the back of a garden chair. He loses consciousness.

Reine and her two daughters were admirably calm and attentive. They set up an improvised bed for Gabrielle in the drawing room. The physician and the surgeon hurried to the house, but were unable to be of any help. One could do nothing more for the girl except wish her the speediest possible death. Unfortunately, the child lingered for several hours.

Noémi had hastened to have the horses and carriage readied for her, after quickly gathering up all that Mont-Noir contained in the way of bandages, lint, and tonics, on the off chance that they might be needed. Arriving at Bailleul, she found the girl already in the throes of death. The mother expressed her despair in indignant recriminations.

"What did I ever do to the Good Lord to deserve this?"

In that milieu, with its narrow notions of Christianity, Noémi's question was understood; but it clearly reveals her egotism, which saw everything in terms of the self. The doctor finally found a way to be useful: he prescribed a sedative for her.

The father and mother remained at Bailleul until the funeral. Michel learned of his sister's death from the surgeon who came to treat his dislocation. He was confined to his room on the third floor of the château, which seemed strangely empty and where the servants now spoke only in lowered voices. An old nursery maid sat by his bed, sewing mourning clothes. Early on the day of the burial he was left alone, everyone else having gone to the cemetery. His mother, upon her return, did not come upstairs to see him. The sight of this living son aggravated her grief. In contrast, his father soon came to sit by him; he helped him with his vacation schoolwork, sought to keep him occupied by giving him his first lessons in Greek, and in this way recovered a bit of his own inner peace. This affectionate father was not, however, an indulgent father. The boy would remember all his life the time he refused to eat one of the meals that had been sent upstairs to him on a tray (I think it was sweetbreads). He was not given any more food for two whole days, until hunger drove him to eat every last morsel of the dish he detested.

It seems that, for a time at least, the disaster brought the husband and wife closer together. Perhaps on the advice of the doctor, who was worried by Noémi's depression, they resumed their physical intimacy. Fifteen months after the accident, Madame de Crayencour, at the age of thirty-nine and after an interval of twelve years, gave birth to her third child, which fortunately was a girl. "This little one will be the comfort of your twilight years," exclaimed the worthy and somewhat solemn Dr. Cazenave as he showed the newborn to her father. For once, the prophecy was fulfilled. From the outset Michel-

Charles believed that, in Marie, he had found Gabrielle once again; for a brief time he thought, like the grieving mother in Hugo's poem, that the dead girl had been reincarnated in the living one. But he would have made himself a laughingstock if he had ever suggested such a thing. As for Noémi, these whims of the imagination never occurred to her.

Marie died a violent death, like her sister, at the age of thirty-three. At the time of her fatal accident, Michel-Charles had been long in his grave and Noémi had arrived at the age when most people scarcely mourn their dead. But this tragic end would make an impression, just as Gabrielle's had. In Lille and elsewhere, there were plenty of old people who whispered to whoever would listen that the fortune of the Dufresnes, founded on black-market goods, had brought unhappiness to their descendants. Even if one were inclined to believe in mysterious forces of retribution, one would find it difficult to put any credence in this. But Michel, throughout his life, was never far from believing it.

There were consolations, however. Gabrielle's death did not exactly win the Legion of Honor for Michel-Charles, but apparently it at last persuaded the authorities to grant him that ribbon, which he had believed himself entitled to for many years. *"Such a misfortune, however great it may be, cannot in itself be a reason for bestowing honors on a civil servant. But when the services rendered have already been noted, a justly earned reward is an appropriate way to lighten the sorrow of a father so grievously stricken in his deepest affections."* The empire could occasionally be good-hearted. Besides, the husband and wife, seconded by the grandparents Dufresne, decided to take some acreage from their properties around Mont-Noir and construct a school on that site for the girls of the district. A black marble tablet bearing Gabrielle's name was displayed on it until 1914. The school was burned down and was rebuilt, but I don't know whether anyone paid to have the memorial tablet replaced. Establishing the school seems to have earned Michel-Charles the decoration he wears in his portraits, between his Cross of Valor and his Belgian Order of Leopold (clearly, there was a point to his owning property across the border). Of the unfortunate Gabrielle herself, nothing remains but the photograph of a little girl seemingly destined for a happy future, and a thick notebook bound in black fabric. On its vellum pages the teenager had carefully calligraphed, sometimes printing and sometimes in cursive, the history of the world from the time of Adam, as her father had told it to her. The story began with the Creation, in the year 4963 B.C., and ended in 1515 with the battle of Marignano. If Gabrielle had lived, she would doubtless have continued her enumeration of monarchs and battles up to Napoleon III, indeed up to the Third Republic. Almost a century later, attracted by that yellowed vellum, I copied onto the remaining blank pages a few of my favorite poems.

The episode of the unfortunate little governess marks the point at which I can begin drawing on a rich oral source: the stories that my father told and retold in the course of our long walks through the countryside of Provence or Liguria, and in later years as we sat on garden benches at various hotels and Swiss clinics. Not that he set great store by his memories; for the most part, they mattered very little to him. But a random incident, a passage in some book, a face glimpsed in the street or on his travels would bring them to the surface in fragments, somewhat like the classical tesserae that he would handle for a moment and then push back into the soil with his foot. Listening to him, I received some invaluable lessons in detachment. Those bits and pieces of the past interested him only as residues of an experience that would never be repeated. "All of that," he would say, with one of those barracks expressions that a former soldier often employs till the day he dies, "all of that was useful on furlough."

As I jotted down his recollections every evening in the notebooks I kept during those years, and especially later, as I repeated to myself those anecdotes I had come to know by heart, a bit the way one keeps playing an old record, it seemed to me that Michel had managed to tell the story of his entire life in this fashion. But now I realize there are a great many gaps. Some of these (the plural is misleading: there is perhaps only one) can be explained by his sacred dread, his fear of letting the ghosts out of the closet. The rest entailed nothing so gloomy: uneventful periods of time had merely slipped into oblivion. I know that in saying this I'm contradicting all our licensed psychologists, who claim that every act of forgetting serves as camouflage for some secret. These analysts are like the rest of us: they refuse to confront the dismal emptiness that every life comprises to a greater or lesser degree. How many of our days might just as well never have been lived! How many events, people, and things were scarcely worth bothering about, and even less worth remembering! Many old men, when telling about their past, inflate it like a balloon, embrace it like an elderly mistress, or, on the contrary, spit on it; they highlight a mass of confusion or an absence, for lack of anything better. Michel did not indulge in any of this; he never even tried to draw up a balance sheet. "I've lived several lives," he said to me on his deathbed. "I can't even see what connects them all." Neither was his memory (in contrast to that of most old men) prone to exaggeration. His accounts of the past say only what he wanted to say. This is what allows me to study them.

The first gap concerns school—his years in grammar school and high school. None of that was of any interest to him. Many great writers, especially nowadays, have used those years as a mold in which they have shaped virtually all of their work. In high school they discovered love, sensual pleasure, ambition, lofty thoughts, and base actions—life in miniature. Sometimes it seems as if they never learned anything after this, and as if the essence of their being died when they were twenty. Michel's life is neither *Fermina Marquez* nor *The Land Whose King Is a*

Child. He retained very sketchy memories of rivalries, teachers' injustices, classroom ruses, stupid jokes, vulgar tricks, and brutal or violent games, at which he excelled without feeling the urge to boast about his skill later; on the contrary. He even remembered without pleasure his successes as the leader of a gang. He could name no instructor whom he liked, respected, or hated enough to remember; no teacher to whom he was grateful for introducing him to some great work or helping him understand it; no classmate or friend (with one exception, who, as we shall see, scarcely counts). In this barren landscape two memories survive as specimens.

First of all, a memory of violence. The young Jesuit who is responsible for teaching Latin likes to read the students' translations out loud in a mocking voice, to make everyone laugh. Michel, as a newcomer recently expelled from a secular institution, is singled out as a target.

"Here, gentlemen, is an example of public-high-school Latin," sneers the teacher.

"That will convert you from your church Latin!" Michel retorts.

The student grabs his translation and angrily tears it to pieces. Little butterflies—bits of Montalembert rendered into the language of Cicero—flutter at the whim of the air currents and alight on the desks. The young teacher thinks he can bring an end to the uproar by sending for the Superior, who will take disciplinary measures. Michel draws his knife from his pocket. The Latinist takes to his heels, lifting the hem of his cassock, which flaps against his skinny shanks. Doors divide the quadrangle at regular intervals. He can be heard opening them as he runs, then banging them closed behind him; then they're opened and banged shut again by the pursuer and his pack. At the far end of a corridor, the door to the grounds stands open. The victim dashes through and turns the lock, to the accompaniment of laughter and shouts. The student with the knife is expelled the next day.

Second, a memory of desire. In another school Michel, hopeless at algebra, is having a lesson in the office of a young teacher in a cassock. They're sitting side by side. Under the table the young priest gently places his hand on the boy's bare leg, then slides it a bit higher. The boy's shocked expression puts an end to his maneuver. But Michel will never forget that look of supplication and shame, that air of absorption and near-sorrow which is the look of half-fulfilled desire and pleasure.

Neither of these two episodes is responsible for his first escapade; boredom and an aversion to routine are sufficient. Fifteen-year-old Michel, equipped with one or two louis he has obtained somehow or other, has plans for the future: he will cross over into Belgium (which is attractive only because it is on the other side of the border), head for Antwerp, hire himself out as a deckhand, dishwasher, or cabin boy aboard one of the steamships or freighters moored in the harbor, and thus make his way to China, South Africa, or Australia. The train he catches at Arras (which is where his school is) takes him only as far as Brussels—and even then he has to change trains several times. Arriving at the Gare du Midi, he learns that the trains for Antwerp leave from the Gare du Nord: he has to go to the opposite end of the city. Night is falling, and with it a cold rain that seems to make things wetter than the rain in Lille. He remembers a Belgian classmate named Joseph de D., who has come back to Brussels to complete his schooling. Michel once told him briefly about his idea, and Joseph obtained from his parents an invitation for Michel to stay with the family for one night—provided, of course, that he tell Joseph's parents nothing of his Great Plan. A porter assures Michel that the street he's looking for is not far away. It's not close by, either. He arrives just as the family is finishing dinner. He invents a story about an elderly cousin whom he was going to visit in Brussels; unfortunately, he doesn't dare ring her bell at such a late hour. The family offers him leftovers from their dinner on a corner of the table and a bed in a room on the mezzanine, half storeroom and half servants' quarters. Joseph (who, now that he is home in Belgium and surrounded by his family, has become more of a little boy than Michel thought he was) bids him good night with an air of embarrassment. The unusual guest is locked in his room, as if the family suspected him of having come to steal the porcelain vases belonging to the master of the house, who is an avid collector. Michel is certain that tomorrow they will put him on the train back to Lille, whether he likes it or not. It isn't difficult to climb out the window: he lands in a muddy flower bed. The garden wall is likewise only a slight obstacle.

Outside, it is blackest night. He avoids the streetlights and the occasional tavern that is still lit up, so as not to let himself be seen by the police, whose sole task in life, it seems to him, is to arrest a French boy of fifteen. To this student who knows his classics by heart, the labyrinth of streets in which he loses his way evokes the Minotaur. He arrives at the Gare du Nord chilled to the bone, and just misses the first train of the morning. In the third-class compartment in which he at last finds a place, he forces himself to speak a halting Flemish, with the vain hope of attracting less attention.

In Antwerp he allows himself to be carried along by the flow of people in the streets, and this is sufficient to bring him to the harbor. Soon he spies the smokestacks of the steamships and the tops of the masts. But no one wants a deckhand or a cabin boy. In the stern of a German freighter, coarse heavyset men are amusing themselves, roughhousing and dealing each other great blows. An officer who is just climbing back on board sends the vagabond away: *"Nein, nein."* The broad red faces look down at him, full of laughter. The boy weaves his way around the shrill prostitutes, dodges with one bound the thunderous wheels of a dray cart. These gigantic vehicles and the slender, swaying masts are the only beautiful things in this dirty gray landscape. A mass of horseflesh slips on the paving stones and falls. The driver brings it to its feet with a hail of whiplashes. Michel relieves his feelings by shouting invective in French: "You swine! I'll punch you in the nose!" But in a squalid tavern on the harbor where he eats a ham sandwich, he doesn't dare protest when the serving girl cheats him of some of his change.

The gas lamps are already being lit in the yellow fog. In front of a tobacconist's window a well-dressed man puts his arm around Michel's neck while whispering propositions that seem to the teenager less obscene than demented. He frees himself from this satyr of Antwerp, runs across the roadway that separates him from the docks, and comes to a halt, panting, behind a stack of barrels. Fear and brutality are everywhere. Should he take refuge for the night beneath one of these tarpaulins? He knows that clever fellows sometimes succeed in boarding outbound ships and aren't discovered until they're on the open sea. But these dark, cramped vessels, tethered to the dock by a single rope that alternately tightens and slackens, seem inaccessible. And what will become of him in mid-ocean when hunger forces him to emerge from his hiding place? He resumes his wandering, doing his best to avoid the policemen on the one hand and the prowlers on the other, and comes to a smaller basin where tugboats and barges are moored. A woman on the deck of a little coasting vessel is taking in some towels forgotten on a clothesline. Michel hails her: Could he sleep on board, for a fee? Her husband comes on deck with a lantern.

The request makes them guffaw: their boat isn't a hotel. And they're leaving tomorrow at dawn for Ostend. No matter —Michel reels off a story that he invents on the spot. He is from Ypres (he doesn't dare admit that he comes from the other side of the border); his father and he spent the day in the city and got separated in the crowds; he searched for him all day without success. Now he has to make his way home on foot, since he has almost no money, but it's not far from Ostend to Ypres. He trusts these good people. He shares their supper; and when the husband and wife retire to their little cabin gleaming with copper fittings, he falls asleep on a heap of sacking amid the bales.

The following day is one of the loveliest of those closing days of childhood. Lying up in the bow, on that gray morning in March, he delights in the powerful flow of the river; the barges they meet, with children who run the length of the vessel; the flags at the stern, waving over the foam; the smoke frayed by the breeze, and the cinders fallen on the deck; the gulls greedy for household refuse; the large ships that they miraculously avoid just in time; all the gaiety of life on the water. At the mouth of the river they pass through a flotilla of fishing boats. The sea is rough; Michel, a novice as a sailor, struggles heroically against his seasickness. At Ostend, where they arrive only after nightfall, he jumps to shore without lingering too long to thank his hosts. Who knows if, out of kindheartedness, they haven't decided in the meantime to turn him over to the police? He feels in his trouser pocket for his last five-franc coin: it's still enough for several days' worth of adventures.

But Ostend off-season is unfamiliar to him. The big hotels are empty, shuttered hulks. Passersby redolent of beer, brandy, and fish elbow one another in the narrow streets. He notices a shabby restaurant-bar where there are rooms for rent. A mechanical organ is playing in a small room where sailors, walking about with their rolling gait, have a girl on their arm, or perhaps one on each arm; the landlady shows the "little one" (as she calls him) into the scullery. She's a kindly woman, with abundant blond hair and rosy cheeks that can turn bright red. Michel would be greatly surprised if someone told him that she's the same age as his mother. She speaks scarcely any French; he has trouble understanding the Flemish of Ostend. She gives him something to eat and refills his empty plate. She points upstairs, to the door of a room. He climbs into bed half-dead with fatigue, without even noticing that there are women's shoes under the chair and a skirt hanging on a nail.

The creak of a floorboard awakens him. The fair hostess is unhooking her corset. By the light of the candle, he sees her coming toward him in her chemise, her long blond hair cascading over her ample bosom. She laughs and says a few halting words that are comprehensible in all languages. She's at just the age when extreme youth inspires the greatest desire and the greatest tenderness; she knows what she's about. For the first time Michel discovers the warmth and depth of the female body, and the sleep of shared pleasure. They even end up revealing their secrets to each other, mingling their patois just as they mingled their bodies. Next morning she gives him good advice over his cup of café au lait.

"Your father must be terribly worried about you. You ought to send him a telegram. Would you like some money?"

He has no need of money. Writing his telegram at the post office on the rue des Soeurs Blanches, he's well aware that he's locking the door to further adventures: he won't be seeing Africa or Australia anytime soon. But he'll have other opportunities. While waiting, he has lived some very full days during which he felt keenly alive. He now knows what women's clothing conceals; he will no longer be ignorant of what the girls he meets in the street expect from him and what he is able to give them. He can return their bold gaze as an equal. And the rest of today, at least, is still entirely his own.

At this time of year, the wheeled cabins are nowhere to

be seen on the beach. He stretches out in a hollow in the sand, where he is sheltered from the wind. He lets the grains run through his fingers and builds sand castles that he afterward destroys. He fills his pockets with seashells, which he empties a little later into a tide pool that he wades through barefoot. At noon he goes to a food stall and eats mussels seasoned with vinegar. For him Ostend will be one of those singular places that one generally has no reason to visit, that one does not like very much, but that one ends up falling back into as a token falls into the box in a game of goose. He will spend a gloomy October there, then an Easter week that will be a bit pleasurable, a bit romantic, and ever so slightly cynical. He will also spend a certain painful and tragic day there one August. But things that have not yet come to pass are even more unreal than things that have taken place. Until sundown the teenager meanders over the dunes, where one loses all sense of distance. He watches some fishermen mending their nets on the sand, sheltered from the wind by the hull of their sloop. When he returns to his current lodgings, he thinks how nice it would be to spend a second night there, so that he could show himself more skillful than he was on the previous occasion. And if his father doesn't answer his telegram? He could find work on a fishing boat. But that wouldn't last. He realizes for the first time that moments of freedom are rare and brief.

Michel-Charles has come with all possible speed. The boy is almost relieved to see him there in the room, sitting in his fine traveling cloak, pretending to drink a glass of beer, and chatting politely with the hostess. This intelligent father has understood everything immediately. But the woman in question seems like a good sort; things could have turned out worse. In other circumstances—who knows?—he himself might have tried his luck with this attractive proprietress. But this is not the time for lovemaking. He pays the bill for Michel, whom the pretty hostess now calls "the little gentleman," and takes his son to spend the night in town in one of the hotels that are open off-season. The next day, in the train that is bringing them back to Lille, he makes the expected speech on the dangers of chance encounters. He keeps it short, for which his son is grateful to him. It is tacitly understood that Noémi will never learn anything of this lesson in love in Ostend. But Michel does not tell his father everything: he does not say that he wanted to run away from home forever.

The Second Empire was, to the very end, a golden dream for Michel-Charles. *"The emperor was the arbiter of Europe; agriculture, industry, and trade were flourishing; money circulated in abundance, easily earned and easily spent. From the lowest to the highest, everyone seemed happy. The winter was nothing but balls and dinners; in summer the spas and seaside resorts overflowed with visitors. One winter in Lille, I remember, there was a ball or a formal dinner every evening for fifty-eight straight days, either at our house or at a friend's or at the home of some high-ranking military or civil official. Every week there was a ball at the Prefecture and at the army's General Headquarters occupied by MacMahon, Ladmirault, Salignac de Fénelon, and others; a ball, too, at the branch headquarters and at the General Treasury, not to mention parties at the homes of the great industrialists, businessmen, and rich property owners. How times have changed!"*

As president of the prefectural council in a *département* where wealth and poverty confronted each other more directly perhaps than anywhere else in France, Michel-Charles must have been aware of what was going on behind the scenes; but he remembers only the footlights and the chandeliers. The years of the empire pass by wearing tutus, like Degas' dancers. It doesn't occur to him to wonder if the disaster of 1870 might have had its seeds in those government policies based on dust in the eyes, fancy footwork, and the good life; on the contrary, he will always remember that he received his ribbon at the Tuileries from the hands of the emperor himself, and that he and Noémi and little Michel, sitting in a hired landau, saw the empress's caleche roll past on the avenue du Bois, surrounded by handsome officers on high-spirited horses and completely filled with the flounces of Eugénie and her ladies-in-waiting. Noémi herself likes to repeat an innocent witticism of Michel's, uttered in front of a fine bread bakery on the rue de Rivoli that proclaimed in gold letters on the window: *Purveyors to Their Majesties the Emperor and Empress.* "What!" exclaimed the boy. "Do the emperor and empress eat bread?"

Those memoirs, which devote so much space to the imperial gala, have not a word to say about the chaos of the Terrible Year and the grim period that followed. Michel-Charles notes only that he resigned his post after the fall of the government. But this morose retreat into private life was brief. Some of Lille's most prominent people, whose judgment he trusted, soon persuaded him to resume his duties. Likewise he does not say that in the *Journal Officiel* of March 12, 1871, a decree by the council president naming him prefect of Nord appeared next to a decree by the minister of the interior delegating the same powers to a Monsieur Baron, former secretary-general of the prefecture. After three weeks of bureaucratic skirmishes, a certain Monsieur Séguier, appointed with a greater degree of consensus, replaced both of them. My grandfather took up his former functions, which, he says, gave him great power over the affairs of the *département*. For ten more years he occupied the position of *éminence grise* (at least, it was perceived as such), trying to forget that he was now serving the Republic—which had been voted in, it's true, by a majority of only one vote.

But one day in 1880 he was surprised to read, likewise in the *Journal Officiel*, that he was being allowed to request retirement. Since he was still a few years short of the mandatory age, this was a disguised way of depriving him of his pension and of the money that had been accruing for his retirement over the course of more than three decades. This injustice created a stir: republicans themselves, he declares, came to the rue Marais to offer their condolences. Paul Cambon tried to placate the sacked official by offering him an honorary presidency with a full pension. Michel-Charles took credit for refusing.

We have two portraits of him from the 1870s—images that are almost as contradictory as the orders and counter-orders that came from above. One is the solemn type. The "Flemish patrician" has squared his shoulders and lost the gloomy air that made him so interesting around 1860. He wears the glittering outfit of his position and holds his cocked hat in his finely shaped hands. This is the portrait of a loyal civil servant, a man of complete integrity and authority, prepared to be nailed to the wall, if necessary, by the enemies of law and order. The other, a photograph that had doubtless been taken to eliminate the need for lengthy sittings (the pose and the attire duplicate those of the painting point for point), shows a personage who is just as official but whose features and side-whiskers are a bit less perfectly aligned. The mocking eye, almost like a sorcerer's, too handsome for its possessor, is the eye of a Celtic peasant indicating to a Roman legion the wrong path through a swamp, or of a Jean Cleenewerck maneuvering with utmost subtlety against Thomas Looten. Such a man was not merely a worthy victim: on many occasions he must have outwitted his republican prefect.

For Michel, who was at this time completing what was known as "his philosophy," his father's bureaucratic woes were, of course, virtually nonexistent. The débacle of 1870 affected him even less than it did Rimbaud, his contemporary from Charleville (which, one must admit, was closer to the sites of the disaster). Still, he would remember all his life, with mocking disdain, the disorder and the strident deceptions of that period—the historic words, true or false, that sum up a state of mind: the empress' assertion "It's my war"; the French soldiers, "prepared to the last gaiter-button," whom Bismarck would knock down ruthlessly like a mass of bowling pins; the Parisian onlookers' cries of "To Berlin!" (which sounded much like the opera chorus' "March on!") and all that patriotism for streetwalkers and café waiters; the defiant words "Not an inch of our territories, not a stone of our fortresses!" shouted just when everyone knew it must come to that. Later, Michel would hear male choirs bawling, "You will never have Alsace and Lorraine!" just when the Germans already had them—and he would find such gestures ridiculous.

But the true awakening came in May 1871, during the repression of the Commune. Was he aware of the numbers? Did he take note of the ninety-six hostages shot by the insurgents and the twenty thousand or so poor devils liquidated by the powers at Versailles? (On both sides, one does what one can.) Did he see the horrible photograph, one of the first photographic pieces of historical evidence, that shows six or seven Communards recently sent before the firing squad? Lined up in their coffins of unfinished wood, an inventory number at their feet, the scoundrels look as if they were slightly rachitic, a bit consumptive, nourished on pork butcher's meat and steeped in the pure air of the Faubourg Saint-Antoine. In any case, Michel witnessed the Great Fear that shook the well-off, who ended up sympathizing with the Prussians—viewed as upholders of

Michel-Charles Cleenewerck de Crayencour, 1870s

law and order, except when they stole clocks. A regular guest at those Tuesday dinners (less elegant, alas, than they used to be) arrived in Versailles to find himself, so to speak, in a front-row seat. He watched the sisters and wives of the right-thinking legislators line the edges of the sidewalks; as the Communard prisoners passed by, they poked the faces and eyes of those wretched men with the tips of their parasols. ("But after all, they didn't steal anything!") This account, which would haunt Michel his entire life, did not make him a man of the Left; it prevented him from becoming a man of the Right. At school, the worthy priests confiscated from his desk an "Ode to the

Commune's Dead," in which genuine outrage was expressed in clichés reminiscent of Hugo, without the grand afflatus of the old man of Guernsey. They threatened him with expulsion; but on the eve of his examinations they would scarcely expel this undisciplined yet brilliant student, who was, moreover, a young man of good family. Michel passed his baccalaureate in triumph.

His university years, first in Louvain and then in Lille (unless it's the other way around), are nothing but a somewhat wild horseback ride. When he attends balls, Michel sports shoes with red heels and shirts with cascades of lace at the throat. He finds young women in his milieu—sisters of his classmates, daughters of his professors—who share his craving for experience. His life evokes the *Loves of the Chevalier de Faublas* or the very early years of Casanova before he met Henriette: something rapid, simple, and a bit clumsy. A frolicking of dogs on the grass. In Louvain especially, where Michel-Charles has doubtless sent his son because he has confidence in the Catholic university there, the eternal Flemish bacchanal continues on the sly. Those young women so closely chaperoned play tricks with duplicate keys, and keep corners well prepared in the stable, on the straw, or in the laundry house, on the piles of linen; the good-hearted servants speak like Juliet's nurse and have the same compliant ways. This exuberance sometimes had consequences. One pretty girl who had a wealth of admirers gave birth to a child in secret; it was taken to the foundlings' home in a hatbox. But little of this appears to have made any

227

lasting impression on our student. He quickly forgot the names of his dance partners.

Nor did he remember the name of the schoolmate whom he persuaded to go with him to Saxon-les-Bains in Switzerland, a town notorious in those days for its gambling halls. The two boys, convinced in advance that they would break the bank, were on the contrary obliged to leave their hotel surreptitiously, abandoning their suitcases. Michel made his way on foot to Lausanne. There, at the general-delivery office, he found a money order that had been sent by his father and that just covered the cost of a third-class train ticket. This time Michel-Charles didn't bother to respond to his son's appeal in person. It was the young man's first encounter with the devil of the gaming table, but he had doubtless been a passionate gambler since the days when he'd played marbles.

These distractions left little time for serious things. The student had inherited his father's excellent memory: the examinations for his licentiate did not frighten him. Although there is a tradition that says he became a doctor of law, I doubt that his ambition or his eagerness to please ever went that far. One day I asked him where he had found the necessary zeal to write his essay for the licentiate and, if he'd ever undertaken it, his dissertation. He replied that it was never difficult to find professors who were in need of money. When we think of the countless sons of good families who in the nineteenth century obtained their doctor of law degree without any real motivation or aptitude, and without the slightest intention of ever making use of their diploma, we come to the conclusion that this type of expedient must have been fairly common. But Michel's airy indifference shows the great distance that separates him from his father, who was so proud of the fact that he'd graduated with highest honors.

A profound disgust takes hold of the young Hamlet. Gambling, the pleasures of vanity, pleasure pure and simple, sheepskins earned through noble or ignoble means—not one of these things has brought him all that he thought it would. As for familial institutions, he has already developed the habit of sarcastically quoting the catchphrase of the day: *Where is one better off than in the bosom of one's family?* His emphatic response: "Anywhere!" The "family" means Noémi and Grandfather Dufresne, as well as Michel-Charles, whom his son persists in seeing, rightly or wrongly, as nothing but one of those downtrodden and conciliatory husbands that he himself vows never to become. He is often sent to Bailleul to have Sunday dinner with his grandmother. He is quite fond of that attractive octogenarian and his two aunts, who seem to him scarcely less ancient than their mother. Still, he's not sufficiently interested in their lives to get them to talk about their youth, which passed during the reign of Louis-Philippe, or to collect the reminiscences of Reine, whose earliest memories go back to the Directory. The insipid guests spoil the exquisite dinners for him. In thirty years not a single new idea has made its way into those narrow heads or behind those wrinkled faces; legacies, genealogies, and the crimes of the Republic are the only topics of conversation. He is not, however, so foolish as not to appreciate certain Spanish touches that are now quite outmoded. The devout Aunt P., widow of the Orleanist deputy, had a son who died while a consul in China; she keeps his heart in a vase made of crystal and gold, and has turned her boudoir into a mortuary chapel aglow with candles. Even more striking is a sense of decency, courtesy, and integrity that seems to have come directly from the Golden Age and to have survived amid all the base, selfish quarrels like a healthful herb amid poisonous weeds. Every Sunday a certain cousin of modest means was invited to dinner but seated quite far from the mistress of the house. A few years previously, when an extremely wealthy relative had died intestate, the fortune had devolved on him and Michel-Charles. They had decided to divide the silver and knickknacks into bundles and then draw lots for them. Michel-Charles and Noémi busied themselves in the drawing room; the slightly infirm cousin was seated in the dining room, near the heating stove, and was sorting silver into drawers that had been placed within arm's reach. All of a sudden he called out to them. Michel-Charles came running and saw him holding a piece of paper that he'd found folded up under a silver ladle.

"The will! It says that the entire fortune is yours!"

In telling this story to his son, Michel-Charles emphasized the fact that a good fire was burning in the stove. In Michel's eyes, the legacy ought to have been divided as if nothing had happened. His father and Noémi were of a different opinion.

The worthy Henri died while all this was taking place. The family hastened to examine the closets and cabinets in which his secrets had been hidden. They expected to find lascivious prints and books regarded as "light." What they unearthed were old liberal pamphlets inveighing against Badinguet and a few odd volumes by Pierre Leroux and Proudhon. In a locked drawer lay a student notebook, every page of which was covered with the furiously written words "Long live the Republic!" Only Michel, who was no doubt romanticizing that scatterbrained fellow, saw him as a man who'd been buried alive.

Lille, for Michel, remained above all the city of nightmares. He hated its soot-blackened walls; its greasy pavements; its dirty skies; the frowning iron grilles and carriage gates of its rich neighborhoods; the stale odor of its poor alleyways and the coughing that could be heard in their basements; the wan little girls, often pregnant by the time they were twelve, selling matches while eyeing gentlemen who were so starved for young flesh that they would take their chances in those wretched neighborhoods; the hatless women fetching their drunken husbands from the taverns—all the things that respectable folk, in their starched shirtfronts and decorated lapels, were either unaware of or refused to believe existed. The town had lugubrious secrets: Michel had been about thirteen when the door of a local convent had opened and a nun had run out to throw herself into a canal. What despair had been burning beneath that habit? Young or old, beautiful or plain, victim of the petty spite of the cloister, perhaps mad, perhaps pregnant—that unknown woman, who might have come straight out of Diderot's novel *The Nun*, haunted his imagination like a sultan's wife drowned in the Bosporus.

But the supreme drop of bitterness will be distilled in the dining room of 26 rue Marais one evening during a Christmas dinner. Again it concerns an impecunious cousin, but this time from the Dufresne side. The family is sitting around the table. The stuffed turkey has just been sent down to the servants' hall, half dissected and eaten, when Cousin X is suddenly announced—an ordinary gentleman, unlucky in business, who at the moment is managing a Catholic dairy. He is not one of those relatives who get invited at Christmastime, not even the sort of person for whom one sets a place when he appears at the door unexpectedly. It's Judge Dufresne whom he wishes to see. Amable orders that he be shown into Michel-Charles's study, and leaves the table with the expression he wears on days when he sees petitioners.

The oak doors are thick; though the study is right next to the dining room, no one can hear a word. But then the door opens. The cousin, who has chosen the wrong way out and who staggers as if he's been drinking, crosses the dining room without looking at anyone. Amable takes his place again at the table and begins eating the plum pudding imported from England. As soon as the valet has left, he gives a brief account of his conversation with the importunate man. As everyone knows, that imbecile X has a son who is a lieutenant in Algeria, and the young good-for-nothing has gotten himself into debt. The father, in order to help his son, has dipped into the funds of the Catholic dairy.

"I have no money for people of that sort," Amable concludes.

Everyone approves his decision, and no one except Michel is very troubled when it is learned a few days later that the cousin, doubtless suffering from a toothache, has taken an overdose of laudanum.

The rue Marais is a prison. And the world is likewise one, as Shakespeare said long before Michel. But it's already an advantage if a man can change his cell. When he's gotten to that point, several avenues of escape open up. One is the religious life, but the philistine Christianity of the family was part of the very context that Michel was fleeing; he didn't think of La Trappe until thirty years later, and even then not very seriously. Art, with a capital A whenever possible, is another way out, but he didn't think he had it in him to be either a great poet or a great painter. The most convenient avenue, generally speaking, is adventure. This would come, but the chance event which at that time would have pushed Michel toward it had not yet occurred, and the escapade in Antwerp had discouraged him from trying his luck aboard a freighter bound for the colonies. What burst of feeling or what caprice propelled him toward the army? A trifle, perhaps: a soldier strolling near the Citadel, men marching beneath his windows, a bit of music in his head, as in the days of the little English governess. In any case, what I know of his later life assures me that once he had made the decision, he didn't think twice about it. In January 1873 a letter written from a Parisian café, on lined paper and with the establishment's muddy ink, informed Michel-Charles and Noémi that their son had enlisted.

PART III

How many roads must a man walk down
Before they call him a man? . . .
How many years can a mountain exist,
Before it's washed to the sea? . . .

The answer, my friend, is blowin' in the wind,
The answer is blowin' in the wind.

— BOB DYLAN

ANANKĒ

Michel-Charles, shocked and dismayed, catches the first train for Paris. As we have seen, military service has not been traditional in the family (at least not since the return from exile); Reine's brother, who died fighting for Napoleon, is merely a forgotten exception. If only Michel had attended one of the prestigious academies! His father is angry at himself for not having urged him toward Saint-Cyr or Saumur. An officer, perhaps someday a general, even at the beck and call of that harlot the Republic, would be acceptable if worst came to worst; but everything in Michel-Charles rebels at the thought of his son's entering the ranks. As soon as he reaches Paris, he goes to see MacMahon. The marshal was once a regular guest at the Thursday dinners in Lille and remembers his host with pleasure. Both men are Catholics, their Catholicism being the sort that consists of political conviction welded to religious tradition, and both are reactionaries; the marshal, who in three months will become president of the Republic, is scarcely any more of a republican than the president of the prefectural council. Michel-Charles is cordially received, but when he mentions his son's decision (striving to make it seem as if he takes the matter lightly) and hints that Michel's education and abilities ought to advance him soon to a rank that befits his family's position, the marshal adopts a Roman tone: "He'll be treated better than others if he conducts himself well, and more severely than others if he conducts himself badly." However much Michel-Charles admires the austere style of Plutarch's statesmen, he would have welcomed a less imperious reply. But it would be useless for him to persist.

My grandfather paces sadly up and down the rue de Vaugirard, wishing that his son were a diligent, docile student willing to follow the family's suggestions. How the world has changed! And not only governments . . . But you never know —perhaps the army will help his prodigal son settle down; in seven years Michel will still be only twenty-six. The young volunteer has been assigned to the Seventh Cuirassiers' Regiment and sent to Niort. Michel-Charles feels the urge to go there and embrace his son, but such a demonstration of affection would be inappropriate. This gentleman from the provinces usually regards visits to Paris as opportunities for indulging in private pleasures. But on this occasion neither the theater nor the Café Riche nor the attractive women he sees on the boulevards arouse any desire in him. He buys a doll for little Marie and returns to Lille.

Michel takes to the army immediately. We have seen that patriotism is not one of his more ardent passions; if war broke out, he would see it as nothing but an exciting game of chance in which his life was at stake. While he waits, military routine relieves him of all but the most basic responsibilities. He likes the uniform—the boots, the gauntlets, and the helmet and cuirass that blaze in the sun like flaming mirrors; indeed, on one Bastille Day he will fall fainting from his horse while marching in review in the midday heat. He excels at grooming and training the horses, and takes great delight in the early-morning trot to the parade ground. He likes his fellow soldiers—likes their peasant shrewdness and banter or, if they come from the outskirts of Paris, their quickwittedness; their way of life, which consists of taking things as they come; and the extravagant obscenity and scatology of their marching songs. He has fond memories of going boating with these comrades and of eating freshly caught fish on the riverbank.

Other soldierly amusements are less appealing to him. He dislikes sitting in cafés, playing with greasy decks of cards and watching the saucers pile up, dislikes the tiresome smutty jokes repeated every time a pretty girl passes by, dislikes the insipid conversations punctuated by silences and yawns. Often he will pull a volume of Théophile Gautier or Musset from his pocket and read lines to his comrades after buying them a round of drinks. The young men listen to him with the good-natured politeness of the common people, but they are all aware that the prologue to *Rolla* has nothing to say to them. Michel has suffered throughout his life from the fact that enthusiasm cannot be communicated like fire on a trail of gunpowder, the way candles are lit on Easter eve in the Orthodox churches he will later enjoy visiting in Paris. He has learned, to his cost, that gunpowder soon sputters out, and that you can't simply put people face to face with a lovely landscape or a fine book and expect them to appreciate it. He goes to sit on the grass with his favorite poets and leafs through them while watching the water flow by.

A corporal who has taken this wellborn young man under his wing suggests that he accompany him to the town's best brothel. Michel has a horror of prostitutes, and what he sees in the drawing room of this establishment does nothing to change his mind: the perpetually jovial fat woman, the simpering beauty who is somewhat over the hill and who has seen better days, the robust gossip who is a prostitute the way a man would be a stevedore, the impulsive, reckless drinker, puffy from taking too many little nips, the dark-haired Andalusian who actually hails from Perpignan. While the corporal slips out with one of the women, Michel confesses somewhat awkwardly to the assistant madam that he hasn't seen anyone who quite suits him.

"If only one of them looked like you," he says gallantly.

The assistant madam, a brunette of thirty, takes him at his word. If he really wants to, Madame will gladly take her place for an hour or two; the rest of her time is her own. Michel would think it ungracious to refuse. Besides, he finds her attractive. He spends a pleasant night with her. At dawn the young man, who is as unlike Don José as anyone could possibly be, gets dressed in a hurry so as not to miss roll call, and before leaving places two louis on a small table. The clink of metal against marble wakes the sleeping beauty; she sees the gold coins next to the empty champagne glasses, sits up, and assails her partner with abuse mingled with sobs. He takes her for a whore, a woman to be had for money; he doesn't understand that she's taken a fancy to him; he's nothing but a filthy beast, just like all men. And that's what she gets for being nicer to him than she's ever been to anyone.

He leaves the house distressed at having offended her. Out in the street, the gold louis fall on the pavement at his feet; he doesn't pick them up. Much later in his life he will remember the insult he unwittingly inflicted on that affectionate woman. Who knows? Perhaps she cared for him more than other women he lived with for years. He never returns to that house.

The visit that Michel-Charles paid to MacMahon has doubtless not been as useless as he thought. Promoted from corporal to sergeant, the young man quickly exchanges Niort for Versailles. The good life begins. His father gives him a decent allowance; most of his fellow soldiers are of a different caliber from the ones back in Deux-Sèvres. The son of the Salignac de

Fénelon who was a frequent guest at the house on the rue Marais in Lille becomes a brother in arms to Michel. A generation later, a Bernard de Salignac de Fénelon will apparently be the model for Proust's Saint-Loup. I wonder if Michel's young companion mightn't be recognizable as the father of that character in *A la recherche du temps perdu*. According to Saint-Loup, his father was a man of exquisite taste but had had the misfortune to be born in the age of *La Belle Hélène* rather than that of *The Valkyrie*; he was a likable rake who for some reason jumped the wall of clan and caste and allied himself in Nice with Monsieur Nissim Bernard. Whatever the truth may be, Michel and his elegant friend feel like Princes of Youth. They share a taste for fine horses, gourmet dinners, fashionable plays, and fashionable women—those whom one can (with a bit of effort) assume are interested in things other than money. Both of them are fond of gambling, Michel to a ruinous degree. The brilliant junior officer introduces the newcomer to his friends in Parisian society, just as Saint-Loup will introduce Marcel. When they return to the barracks at night, they save time by taking a shortcut through the Bois de Boulogne, having earlier hidden two decorated caps under the seat of their cart, so that they can put them on at the proper moment and thus be allowed through a gate reserved only for officers.

Salignac de Fénelon takes Michel to visit two of his relatives, who live in Versailles. The young wife has a somewhat spare elegance; the husband, who is middle-aged, is passionately fond of photography. He spends his days in his darkroom amid basins and drip pans. The lady bestows her favors on Michel, but there is something hard and tense in this half-mistress that makes the young man uneasy. One day when he has been invited to lunch, he finds Monsieur de X in the garden, his foot swathed in bandages. Just a sprain—a mere accident. Madame receives word that her milliner has brought a hat for her to try on; she leaves the two men for a few minutes. Monsieur de X says with a smile: "My darkroom is in the basement. The stairs are treacherous, and I usually walk down them with my hands full of fragile things. Fortunately, I watch my step. But yesterday I stumbled. By the greatest good luck my left hand was free, or I wouldn't have been able to catch hold of the banister and break my fall. I escaped with nothing more than this sprain. But while I was getting up as best I could, I noticed that someone had stretched a fine wire ankle-high across one of the steps. No, don't think that she cares for you to that extent. She has a lover; you're merely serving as a screen for him."

The lady of the house reappears. Walking next to her husband, who is leaning on a cane, she helps him to the dining room. The atmosphere during the meal is polite. Michel comes to visit less often.

At the gaming tables he has occasionally lost small sums, which Michel-Charles has covered. But in August 1874 he plunges in far over his head. With time growing short for paying this so-called debt of honor, Michel sends a telegram to the rue Marais, taking the risk that the message might be intercepted by his mother. In any case, the amount is too large to keep secret—she's bound to find out about this new folly. That very evening the young man receives a terse reply: "Impossible."

No further help can be expected. Salignac de Fénelon is as short of money as he is. That night—the seventeenth of August 1874, a mere seven days after his twenty-first birthday—Michel carefully dresses in civilian clothes, and kisses his cuirass and helmet the way a monk on the verge of leaving his order would kiss his cowl. He heads for the Versailles station to catch the train for Paris—the same one that nearly proved fatal to his father. Since the end of the war, passports have ceased to be a problem. At Saint-Lazare station he boards a train for Dieppe, and there embarks for England.

Michel is of such a mercurial temperament that the many new things he sees—the tall policemen on the docks at Southampton, the green countryside his train passes through, and soon the vast city of London itself—make his worries evaporate. Not for long, however. His most immediate concern is lack of money. He takes a room in a rather shabby hotel in Charing Cross which he has heard mentioned by traveling salesmen in Lille who "do" England. Lille has accustomed him to soot and damp black filth, but the fuliginous chaos of London defies all comparison.

For the first time in his life he is alone. Alone as even the most unhappy and rebellious young man cannot be within his family, his school, his regiment, where his name and face are known and where he can expect something from those around him—if not help, at least a reproach, a mocking comment (perhaps inoffensive, perhaps not), a gesture of friendship, or, on the contrary, a sign of one of those hatreds that are the inverse of affection. In Lille even the strangers are more or less known, or at least can be classified in familiar categories. Bailleul has no strangers. In Louvain he was defined by his status as a student; in Niort and Paris, by his uniform. During the escapades of his adolescent years, he experienced loneliness and want, but only briefly, and his father was always there, at the other end of a telegraph wire. Now it seems as if Michel-Charles no longer exists, and the loneliness of London is multiplied by several million people. No one cares whether he manages to survive or whether he drowns himself in the Thames, like that half-legendary nun who threw herself into a canal in Lille when he was a boy.

Ever since he deserted his regiment, the name of a respected English firm specializing in imported fabrics has sustained him like a talisman. This company does business with a number of spinning mills in Nord; the owner of one of them is related to Aunt P. Until now nothing has interested Michel less than textile manufacture, but the imposing W. Company is the only establishment he knows in this enormous city, apart from the Tower of London and the Bank of England. It is also his first opportunity to try his luck.

He obtains the address from a city directory and asks a café waiter for directions. His English, which seemed excellent in college, leaves him at a loss when he encounters the cockney that people speak on the streets. This plunge into London is as exhausting as a trek through a dense forest. In order to save money he declined the hotel's copious English breakfast, and now he is hungry. He loses his way several times before reaching his destination. The director of the W. Company is not seeing anyone. Michel stubbornly takes a seat in the waiting room, prepared to stay as long as necessary. On the stroke of noon, the director (whom Michel recognizes by the discreet bows of the employees) leaves the office to eat lunch at a nearby restaurant. Both on his way out and on his return, he notices the young stranger, who seems rooted to the spot. Out of curiosity, he at last decides to see him.

Michel's university English serves him better in the office than it did in the street. The young man mentions the name of his cousin the factory owner (whom he has actually met only twice in his life) and suggests that he could be of service in a clerical capacity, helping with the firm's French correspondence. The director toys with his watch chain and listens with half an ear. He soon shows the importunate fellow the door.

The wellborn young man who has just been politely thrown out sits for a while in the waiting room to collect his thoughts, wondering if it wouldn't be better to look immediately for a position as a waiter or dishwasher in some French restaurant. As he is musing, a man with gentle, intelligent eyes comes up to him and asks him a few questions. The kindness of this dusky-skinned little fellow, who speaks English with a strong Central European accent, is irresistible. Michel confides everything to him, except perhaps his true name. The little man puts down the fabric samples he is holding and ushers him into an office that is less imposing than the first and that turns out to be the shipping manager's. The young man is hired at a quite modest salary to affix labels and help package the fabrics. Michel feels as if he has been rescued. But he discovers with surprise that when a man at last finds employment, it's rarely in a field in which he believes himself trained and in which he thought he could be of service. A bell rings to signal the end of the workday. Out on the street Michel once again encounters his benefactor, who refuses to accept any thanks and who asks Mr. Michel Michel where he is planning to stay. The young man has no idea.

"Why don't you stay with us? We've just bought a house and we've already agreed that by taking a lodger we'll be able to pay off the mortgage more quickly. We won't overcharge you on the rent."

They stop at the hotel to pick up the Frenchman's slender

suitcase. Even as he is reiterating his thanks, which are once again brushed aside, Michel is sizing up this somewhat portly little man, who is to him what the Archangel Raphael was for young Tobias in the Bible. The house is in Putney. On the way, Rolf Nagel (he has told Michel his name) talks freely about himself. His father, a Jew born in Budapest and exiled in the aftermath of some insurrection or other, owned a Hungarian restaurant in Soho for many years. But Rolf preferred textiles to cooking, and he has succeeded quite respectably. To this gentle anarchist who has found the best niche he can in the commercial life of London, the fact that Michel is a deserter is one more reason to like him.

The modest brick house covered with ivy seems idyllic after the noise and crowds of the business district. Rolf introduces Mr. Michel to his young wife—whom I'll call Maud, since my father never told me her first name. (The husband's first and last names are likewise my own invention.) Maud is beautiful, with creamy skin, rosy cheeks, and dark red hair. This delicate Englishwoman has the somewhat disquieting charm of some of the subjects painted by Rossetti and Burne-Jones, whose work Michel will soon become familiar with in color lithographs and art museums. After the meal they go into the drawing room, which is decorated with cheap furniture and knickknacks. Rolf sits down at the piano. Though he can't read a note of music, he gives spirited renditions of popular operetta tunes and music-hall songs, humming along and mangling the words. Michel, out of politeness, requests a Hungarian air—and then a different man comes to the surface. Rolf launches into an old song with a sort of concentrated passion, but ends with a bit of clowning. The rent he asks of Michel will scarcely hasten the payment of his mortgage. When it comes to his guest, this refugee from a Central European ghetto displays the generosity of a prince.

I won't keep my readers on tenterhooks: it's clear where

things are heading. Less than three months later, Michel and Maud are entwined on the mattress of the large chintz-curtained bed, which Rolf bought at an auction and which is one of his cherished possessions. The shy young wife turns out to be a Bacchante. Every Saturday Rolf goes to visit his father in a Jewish rest home at the other end of London, thus giving the two lovers pleasant hours to themselves. As soon as he leaves, the conjugal bedroom turns into the Venusberg. The mirrored armoire and the looking glass on the dresser witness scenes that Rolf has no inkling of when he returns in the evening. From time to time this passionate music lover will attend a concert by himself, since neither Maud nor his tenant ever feels like going with him. On Sundays the three take a stroll on the Putney Common or go as far as Richmond Park, where Maud likes to pet the tame deer. Rolf introduces Michel to what he considers the poetry of London: streets offering an array of semi-luxurious pleasures and goods and brilliantly lit by their gleaming display windows, prostitutes on the lookout for clients beneath the pale light of the streetlamps, little theaters where he invariably knows the manager or the ticket seller, good but moderately priced restaurants, Madame Tussaud's wax museum, and the outer walls of the prisons. From time to time he treats his wife and tenant to a musical comedy. The show, which they see for a reduced price, is followed by a modest private dinner; the gentlemen share the cost.

The trust that Rolf places in him seems both touching and slightly grotesque to Michel, but the reproaches he heaps on himself are purely for convention's sake: there's no possibility that he'll renounce the delights of the bedroom. If only the husband whose honor has been wounded would demand satisfaction by the sword! But Rolf, even if he suspects something, thinks no more about challenging his tenant to a duel than he does about jousting in the lists. At the dinner table, on walks, and around the inevitable piano in the evening, Maud is always completely at ease, and lavishes kind attentions on the two men.

At the end of several months, however, Michel has had enough of this living as a threesome. Through the *Times* classifieds, he eventually finds a job teaching horseback riding and French conversation in a boys' school. A cottage is put at the disposal of Mr. and Mrs. Michel. He persuades Maud to come away with him.

One Saturday, Mr. Michel Michel says a final good-bye to mailing labels and bales of fabric. Much later he will learn that Maud, in order to obtain some ready money, sold the few modest pieces of jewelry that Rolf had given her, as well as some of the unattractive knickknacks in the drawing room. But tonight he can't help feeling sorry for the poor man returning to his deserted house. Maud is less tenderhearted. But she does not, like so many women, take advantage of the intimacies of adultery to disparage her husband. Rolf is a good fellow who has always treated her well. She was an apprentice milliner when they came to know each other; a few more years of that sort of work and she probably would have died of consumption. No, Rolf is considerably better than that; he's neither unpleasant nor extremely demanding in love. Does she think he's suspected something for a while? Well, when it comes to things like that, you never know.

They enjoy happy months in that cottage in Surrey, which is covered with woodbine that turns ruddy in the fall. The thoroughbreds in Michel's care satisfy his need to be near horses, which he has missed deeply since his desertion from the army. He likes to teach riding and to speak French with those of his students who know the language; with the others, he immediately falls back into English, since he has little desire to hear their gibberish. Maud has that very English type of imagination which consists in making a fairy tale out of the adventures of a mouse searching for crumbs and turning a chipped teapot into a whimsical character. She takes pleasure in sitting outdoors and letting the wind play in her hair; part water nymph and part salamander, she goes hatless in the rain and then has to dry herself later in front of the kitchen stove. Everything is delightful to them: a late colchicum under the leaves, rabbits in the grass, the half-frozen stream that diverges behind the house, forming a little island which has become a nesting place for birds. At Christmastime the scent of freshly cut pine boughs blends with the aroma of roast turkey. If happiness were phosphorescent, the little house under the trees would glow with a thousand lights.

Yet Maud sometimes feels as if she has landed in a bed of nettles. In the eyes of the proper spouses of the other instructors, this young woman is too pretty and not entirely a lady. The suspicion that the couple's union has not been blessed by the church floats vaguely around them. Michel merely laughs at those dowdy prudes, and on some days Maud laughs with him. But at the end of the term, when the diplomas are handed out, the administration declines to request Mr. Michel's services for another year.

With the bit of money they have left, they settle for the summer on a farm in Devonshire that takes boarders for a small fee. The food is a disappointment. The milk, cream, eggs, and fruit are sent to London every morning; to consume them, the owners say, would be to "eat money." The lovers help with the haying and the apple picking; they stroll through the open countryside, which is traversed by narrow valleys winding between stretches of woods. A sensual stupor, a moist warmth, emanates from the high grass. But one day in a little neighboring town, where they have come to visit the market, the music of a regiment in the main square suddenly hits Michel like a slap. Since his anguish often expresses itself as anger, he tries to start a quarrel with Maud. They return home along the main road without speaking.

The next day, as they are talking about the months they lived in Surrey, Maud describes how the boldest of the youths at the school, having heard some whispered rumors concerning her at one of the headmaster's teas, made a bet that he could easily win the favors of the unconventional Mrs. Michel. He took advantage of the riding instructor's absence to come to the cottage and pay the most ardent court to her; she fended him off, but not without difficulty. Michel exclaims that she is lying. They reconcile with tears and mutual assurances of fidelity.

When night comes, however, Michel is once more assailed by doubts. Why would this woman who is so fond of lovemaking have rejected the advances of that handsome blond boy? The quarrel is renewed the next day, on the subject of a postal money order that Maud has received. She claims it was sent by an aunt, her only relative, who is fond of her; in reality, the small sum comes from Rolf. Michel packs his valise and returns to France and his regiment.

He is demoted, and the ceremony in which his stripes are torn off (later he casually compares it to the extraction of a tooth) is doubtless more painful than he will admit. A comrade who has returned to the military fold at the same time endures the ritual at his side, which makes things easier; they joke about it afterward. Despite this ordeal, Michel feels a sort of animal contentment at returning to his barracks, and the companionship of men his own age distracts his thoughts from the languorous pleasures of a mistress. Far from disgracing him in the eyes of these simple youths, his adventures make him a romantic figure. Thanks to the favors that his father obtained for him on the rue Saint-Dominique and from the old man in the Elysée palace, the prodigal sergeant quickly wins back his lost stripes.

A family portrait, ca. 1873:
the young Michel; his father, Michel-Charles;
his mother, Noémi; and his younger sister, Marie

He must have gone to Lille to make peace with his relatives, since we have a surprising family portrait that dates from about this time. It was no doubt taken in a photographer's studio, but the drawing room on the rue Marais certainly contained similar furniture, as well as palms in identical pots. Michel-Charles has aged a great deal. He's seated uncomfortably on the edge of a chair, with his legs stretched out before him (perhaps they're a bit stiff) and his round head framed in gray side-whiskers. He appears ill at ease in this proper and convincing image, which was probably commissioned in order to silence the rumors that were circulating concerning the couple's break with their only son. Noémi—very erect, closely confined in her black dress with its whalebone and shirring, wearing her hair as Princess Mathilde did in those days—is sitting in an armchair. But she reminds us less of Napoleon III's cousin than of her contemporary from the other side of the world: the dowager empress Tz'u-hsi. She has the same solid, indestructible air and the same rigidity of a carved idol. She gazes with distrust through her half-closed eyelids, as if through a slit in a fortress wall. The photographer, when he arranged his subjects, had her place her arm over the shoulders of little Marie, who is seated on the rug with her legs folded under her, and who reveals her long black stockings and little black boots with a child's unaffected grace. The girl turns to look at her father; her fair face is that of a well-behaved daughter. Her hair is gathered in a charming ponytail and tied with a ribbon. Michel is leaning on the back of Michel-Charles's chair; thin, pale, and a bit haggard, he appears to be somewhere else. His troubled, gloomy eyes seem to be looking toward distant lands, toward "anywhere at all"— that is (for the moment), toward England.

As soon as the group is no longer under the photographer's eye, it relaxes. Noémi does not deprive herself of the satisfaction of telling her son that he will end up on the scaffold, a prediction that she has been repeating tirelessly since he was a boy. The Byronic young man makes no reply; he can put up with a lot when he has only a few days' furlough in Lille. Michel-Charles remains kind and taciturn. Something in him—which he does not discuss, so as not to shock those around him—refuses to accept that a thinking man belongs in uniform. His son's desertion in peacetime has always seemed to him a rash impulse rather than a crime. Besides, the incident is closed.

Michel spends his nights in London. He writes to Maud nearly every day—letters studded with quotations from English poetry, which he has been reading avidly ever since English became, for him, the language of love. He mails these letters in two envelopes, addressing the outer one to the owner of the shop where the young woman buys her groceries. This precaution, recommended by Maud, is perhaps unnecessary: there's no evidence that Rolf might have intercepted any of their correspondence. Maud replies sometimes with brief notes that reveal nothing, and sometimes with gay and affectionate effusions, full of references to their shared life and embellished with X's and O's signifying hugs and kisses.

A day comes, finally, when Michel can't bear it any longer. He and Maud decide that she will leave Rolf for good and will rejoin her lover on an agreed-upon date in a little hotel in Piccadilly. (This must have been in March 1878.) For the second time, the young junior officer lays his carefully folded uniform in a drawer, takes a last look at his cuirass gleaming on a closet shelf, puts on civilian clothes, and discreetly leaves the barracks. He is quite aware that he is thus making a definitive break not only with the army but also with his family and his country. Unless there is an amnesty, he will not be able to return to France until he is forty-five years old.

After Michel and Maud have exchanged their first caresses, she tells him a bit of good news. One of her friends who owns a shop in Liverpool has gone to Ireland to collect a small inheritance and is thinking of settling there. She has asked Maud to manage her business for one year. It's a convenient way to make a living, until Michel can find something better. The shop, which specializes in toilette articles, cosmetics, and perfumes, turns out to be located on a gloomy little street near the theater. The clientele seems to consist chiefly of ladies of doubtful virtue and actresses on tour. An inspection of the stock sends them into gales of laughter. The labels and promotional brochures promise eternal youth, voluptuous but not excessively rounded figures, the thirty-six charms of the odalisques of the seraglio, glossy lips, sweet breath. There are personal toilette articles as well. Michel, who hates perfumes ("A woman who smells good is a woman who doesn't smell at all"), finds it difficult to bear the vague stale odors of oil of Macassar and rosewater. He soon discovers that the little shop is a sort of advertising center for those who provide and those who need certain services: the procuress and the abortionist come there almost as often as the traveling salesmen who deal in perfumes. The young man's suspicions are aroused when he comes upon a blackish paste with a disturbing odor; Maud explains that the owner gave her strict orders not to sell this dangerous preparation to anyone but a select group of people, whose names she wrote down for her.

A crisis erupts when an actress besotted with gin comes in to buy some pomade for her breasts. Unhooking her bodice, she insists that Mr. Michel apply it himself to her sagging torso.

Despite the objections of Maud, who is less ill at ease than he
is in this shady atmosphere, he decides to close up shop and
slip the key under the door.

During their brief sojourn in Liverpool, the young Frenchman spends a good deal of time strolling around the docks and
the city streets. I myself saw the harbor only after the bombardments of World War II and know little about how it must
have looked in 1878. But I found it pervaded by the haughty
presence of the large maritime companies, the wheeling and
dealing of international trade, the excitement of departures,
and the commotion of arrivals. As a boy, Michel had wandered
about the docks in Antwerp; some of that teenager now comes
to life again in this young exile, who will not admit to himself
that he may have chosen the wrong path in life. He never tires
of the welter of masts and smokestacks, of those hulls corroded
and encrusted by the sea, of the bustling men of all nationalities
and races, sometimes turbaned and barefoot (no doubt it's one
of them who furnishes Maud's shop with that black preparation), weaving through the dense mass of locals with their red,
beige, or dark complexions. Michel likes to spend a quarter of
an hour here and there in friendly conversation with some of
these people, the ones who are going away perhaps never to
return. If only he could do what they're doing; if only he could
leave that woman . . . He listens to Australians boast of Melbourne and Yankees praise New York. Melbourne is so far away
. . . Michel thinks he knows a few things about New York:
he's sure that people there die on the spot if they don't win
their fortune at a single stroke; and everything over there is so
ugly that rich Americans have only one passion, namely Europe.
Nevertheless, he's haunted by vague romantic notions, bits of
information that hover in his memory and beckon to him: he
could teach horseback riding to the heirs of Wall Street nabobs,
could buy a ranch in that mysterious West that he would have

trouble locating on a map, could wander from state to state in a broad-brimmed felt hat, winning and losing fortunes at poker and righting occasional wrongs . . . If necessary, Maud could always find work in Manhattan as a milliner or a maidservant, and he himself could go, like so many others, to mine guano in South America or smuggle arms in Mexico. This seeker of adventure isn't extremely short of money at the moment, so naturally he buys first-class tickets for the voyage. And since evening gowns will be indispensable on board ship, Maud purchases some at a secondhand shop.

The crossing is gloomy. Maud's demimondaine dresses, as well as her beauty, attract the attention of certain passengers, and Michel is offended. Perhaps she hoped that he would react otherwise. Far from winning a fortune at poker, he manages to lose, in just a few games, part of the money his father has been secretly sending him in small amounts; in those days cardsharps were the bane of transatlantic passengers. When Michel and Maud arrive in the United States, the only thing they see is Ellis Island; their uncertain marital status proves objectionable to the authorities. On the trip back to England, their room is between decks.

Maud and Michel view the whole misadventure as a lark. Their infatuation with America has cooled considerably. The fiasco seems to them a farce that they all but staged for themselves. Michel finds a position as an instructor in a boys' school that has a somewhat lower reputation than the preceding one. The headmaster, a clergyman by profession, has built his school's success by ensuring that the students receive both good food and good monthly grades; the families are delighted with their sons' round cheeks and academic prizes. Again, Michel is provided with a cottage, this time draped in clematis but not quite as comfortable as the one in Surrey; the horses, likewise, aren't quite so spirited. The charm of the English countryside once more transforms the life of the two lovers. The beautiful, indolent Maud resumes her strolls around the meadows or through the woods. Their existence is enlivened by a magnificent flame-colored setter that Michel bought from a rustic who was neglecting it. Red (I've made up this commonplace name and would give a great deal to know his real one) accompanies the riding instructor on his jaunts and sleeps at the foot of the bed that habit has made a conjugal bed for Maud and Michel.

But the anguish that persists deep within the young man rises to the surface in his physical ailments. He suffers from insomnia; his pulse is irregular; and although he is supremely steady in the saddle, he has attacks of dizziness when he looks out of a second-storey window. He consults a doctor in the little town nearby. This practitioner is in favor of telling the truth at all costs—which, as a professional creed, is certainly preferable to well-intentioned lies but troublesome when the person who subscribes to it is a poor diagnostician. He asks about the sort of work Michel does, and frowns as he listens to the response.

"You must give up horseback riding. Where are your parents?"

Michel's parents live in France.

"Alert them immediately. You suffer from a heart ailment that could be fatal at any moment. Only constant rest and care can improve your chances of living a few more years. And be wary of sexual activity, which could aggravate your condition."

Having duly paid the bill for his death sentence, Michel walks the two or three miles back to his house. He does not tell Maud what the oracle said. Many years ago he came to the conclusion that the phenomenon we call "living" is like the brief effervescence from a chemical reaction: before long, the fizzing stops. It's hardly worth worrying about, and it's certainly not something with which to alarm his father. The doctor's diagnosis gradually fades from his memory, but sometimes I wonder whether Michel's absurd generosity, his readiness to relinquish things, his passion for seizing the moment, and his disdain for the future weren't reinforced by this idea of sudden death—an idea that remained more or less beneath the surface for nearly fifty years.

Michel and Maud have reached the point where lovers take vacations from each other. Maud often spends weekends visiting her aunt, a vague individual who seems part alibi and part phantom. During one of these absences, Michel, who has always seen certain attractions in the headmaster's plump little wife, engages in more than mere conversation with her. Just like Maud, the clergyman's wife loves to make love. In order to enjoy some complete freedom with the young Frenchman, she comes up with the idea of spending twenty-four hours with him in the attic of her house. The husband devotes every Sunday to his sermons and to meetings with those of his students' mothers who occupy themselves with good works. It is also the day that he regularly dines with Lord X. The maid is off until Monday morning. Very early, at an hour when the windows in the village are still shuttered, the ardent woman lets Michel in by the service door. Well hidden in the attic, he listens as the deceived husband goes downstairs and says a tender goodbye to his faithless wife. She then forbids Michel to walk about the empty house, for fear that the neighbors might glimpse a man's form through the window. As in the libertine novels of the eighteenth century, he experiences the somewhat humiliating pleasure of receiving his food and having his humble needs taken care of by his passionate but prudent lover. The clergyman comes home at a late hour and retires early, allowing this Anglican Messalina to rejoin her captive almost immediately, though he would perhaps prefer to go to sleep. At dawn she discreetly lets him out of the house.

But this debauch puts a distance between them. Whether from fear or from satiety, the headmaster's wife henceforth merely nods to the riding instructor from afar, and he returns her greeting in the same style. This licentious little bourgeoise (such is his characterization of her, which is perhaps too summary a judgment) seems to him less worthy of respect than a prostitute—and, when all is said and done, endowed with fewer charms.

That evening he waits for Maud at the train station with renewed tenderness. She springs down onto the platform, her arms full of packages. A helpful fellow passenger hands her the bulkier boxes through the door; the smile she gives him as thanks irritates Michel. Yes, her aunt is well; they did their Christmas shopping together, very economically. The rest, if there was a rest, consists of things she doesn't mention. This period of Maud and Michel's life is full of unpleasant scenes. Maud objects to the lessons that Michel gives to some young ladies living nearby, girls with aristocratic names and close-fitting riding habits. On days when the weather is bad and the lowering sky seems to do nothing but produce rain, Mrs. Michel lies on the couch reading romantic novels. When Michel comes home, wanting above all to have his boots dried and to change his socks, Red is the only one who gives him a warm welcome. Bitter reproaches flavor his cup of tea. Didn't she leave her husband for him—a man who danced attendance on her and who someday might well become department head or assistant director? People can live comfortably only in London, after all; she's ruining her hands cooking on the cottage's old stove; Michel is unfaithful, like all Frenchmen; he wouldn't sacrifice so much as a fingertip for her. One day he takes up her challenge:

"That's what you think, my little Maud."

Ananké

Immersed once again in her book, a novel by Ouida, she doesn't hear him go upstairs to their room, fetch something, and go out through the half-open door. This time it's a mild, cloudy afternoon. Making use of a bit of loose rope he finds somewhere, he ties his own left hand to the back of a garden chair. At the sound of the gunshot Maud comes running out, terrified. His middle finger is dangling, attached by only a few scraps of flesh at the first joint. Blood is trickling through the perforations in the metal chair, as if through a sieve. She bandages his hand as best she can. With his arm in a sling across his chest, he walks the two leagues or so to the doctor's office.

The doctor amputates his finger and sends him on his way, his arm still in a sling, his stump well daubed with iodine and swathed in bandages. The doctor accepts his story about an accident. Seeing that he is very pale, he insists that the wounded man lie down for a moment on the couch in his office. But Michel doesn't stay there for long. He asks if he can take the severed finger with him wrapped in his handkerchief, as an odd sort of keepsake. At the last moment, however, he uses it for what he thinks is a very funny joke: he drops it down the neck of the little housemaid who opens the street door for him. The young woman faints. Michel hails a cart that is going in his direction and climbs up onto the seat next to the farmer. Just in time: he's feeling a bit faint himself.

Such a gesture is the equal of any of the most extravagant episodes in Ouida's novels. It temporarily revives Maud and Michel's love. But Michel, contemplating his scarred stump, says to himself that although it's splendid to kill oneself for a woman, it's perhaps idiotic to sacrifice two-thirds of a finger for her. Then affection gets the better of him. The little cottage is haunted by the memory of too many scenes. The couple decide to make a fresh start somewhere else.

Michel, who is now receiving money regularly from his

father, suggests to Maud that they move closer to the big city. About twenty miles from their current residence, they find a place to rent—a little house near a suburban station, where, whenever they feel like it, they can catch a train for London and be there in an hour. It's a pleasure to say goodbye to the boys' school; and it's another to see the few possessions they've accumulated piled onto a farmer's cart and transported to their new home. Since a mere three weeks remain until the end of the academic term, Michel, accompanied only by Red, returns to oversee the equestrian exercises of his too-well-fed students. At the last minute he does something that costs him great effort: he decides to leave Red with his neighbor, a kindly farmer. The handsome animal is used to roaming freely through the fields and woods, and Michel can't imagine him confined within the walls of a suburban garden. But the day after his return to his new home, he hears a scratching and barking at the door. The big flame-colored dog launches himself joyfully at his master's breast, then falls to the floor, too exhausted even to drink from the bowl of water he's offered, thumping his tail feebly against the floor. Red has left the farmer's house and has found his way, the Lord knows how, over some twenty miles. Michel swears he will keep the dog with him as long as the animal lives.

Maud and Michel's new life is as pleasant as they hoped it would be. They make frequent trips to London. Maud visits the shops; he buys books and attends the theater, developing a passion for Irving and for Ellen Terry. He has found a job in the mornings at a local riding school. To occupy herself and to augment their slender resources, Maud once again begins working as a milliner, out of her home. In the evenings it's a pleasure for Michel to see her lovely hands, of which she is very proud, busy themselves with ribbons and plaited straw. But except for the books, and the fact that there is no piano and no one humming operetta tunes, their life is scarcely different from the one that Rolf and Maud led in Putney.

Meanwhile, Michel receives a letter from his father. It's cordial and brief, as always, and sealed with the family crest. Michel-Charles is not in the best of health; he has always wanted to see London and has decided to do so while he still has the desire and the strength. He will stay eight days, and would like to have his son with him as much as possible. Since he doesn't speak English, he also hopes that Michel will be there to meet him when he arrives at the wharf in Dover.

Soon after the steamer has docked, Michel spies a tall, somewhat portly old man coming down the gangway with the first-class passengers. In one hand he holds a suitcase and in the other a travel rug that is carefully rolled up and bound with a strap; an umbrella protrudes from the bundle at either end. On the train, father and son begin conversing as if nothing unusual has happened in the interim. Yes, the crossing from Calais to Dover was smooth. Michel-Charles's health is far from perfect; he's once again suffering from stomach ulcers, after a respite of almost thirty years; with every passing winter, the damp weather in Lille is aggravating his rheumatism. The traveler accepts with pleasure the hot cup of tea that a waiter brings him; when the train stops at Canterbury he puts his head out the door, trying to get a glimpse of the cathedral. In the tone of a man returning to one of his harmless obsessions, he reminds his son that in olden times several members of the family were christened Thomas Becket, either because the martyred prelate was extremely popular throughout medieval Europe or because certain Flemish families had close ties to England in those days. A bit farther on, he admires the green hop fields that extend into the distance, bordering the train's path just as they do at the foot of Mont-Noir.

In London Michel-Charles puts up at an excellent hotel, one of those sober establishments that avoid ostentatious luxury and that provide all the comforts of home. He has reserved a room next to his for Michel. He requests that dinner be brought up to them and orders some English dishes that he has always wanted to try. The meal is served by the fire, in a handsome room whose red curtains are tightly drawn so as to muffle the noise from the street. The evening will be entirely devoted to an emotion that is rarely treated in literature but that, whenever it happens to exist, is one of the strongest and most fulfilling there is—namely, the mutual affection of a father and son.

Michel-Charles discreetly leads Michel toward confidential matters. It's been a long time since the young man has been with someone he can talk to without constraint. However much he perfects his English, there will always be ideas and feelings that he can express only in his own tongue and to an understanding ear. A long-submerged part of himself rises to the surface that evening. He even tells his father about his transatlantic escapade (making light of it, so as not to appear to have taken it too much to heart); but concerning his amputated finger he gives the version that ascribes it to an accident—a story which he has had time to embellish with some invented details. Still, his account of the events of the preceding seven years seems to him as insubstantial as a dream. As soon as he explains his actions, he no longer understands them. He can't think of a great deal to say about Maud—perhaps because the young woman remains an enigma to him, despite all the time they have lived together; perhaps because the emotions she inspires in him are difficult to express in words; perhaps also because in speaking about her he realizes that deep down he has ceased to love her. He shows his father a photograph of her, with the usual disclaimer that the snapshot doesn't do her justice. Michel-Charles becomes pensive when he sees the beautiful face; he gazes at the image for a long time and returns it to his son without a word.

When they've lit up their cigars, the father coughs to clear his voice.

"You can see for yourself that I'm far from well . . . I'd like you to be properly established and settled not far from me, before it's too late . . . I've given a lot of thought to the problem of your marriage, which is of course complicated by your military situation. Certain families would be shocked by it. The young woman I have in mind for you comes from Artois, daughter of a fine old family which, to tell the truth, is of modest means. The negotiations with her parents are taking their normal course. I've met her once. Dark, attractive—even more than attractive: she's really quite stunning. Twenty-three years old. She rides like a daredevil; you'll have that in common, at least. And then," he adds, returning to his favorite topic, that of genealogy, "her family and ours have already been linked by marriage, in the eighteenth century."

Restraining himself from saying that this detail is of little interest to him, Michel mentions that unless the government grants an amnesty, he can't return to France for another fifteen years.

"Of course," says his father. "Of course. But let's not exaggerate the difficulty. Mont-Noir is two steps from the border. Everyone in the area knows us, including the customs officers. People will close their eyes to visits lasting only a few hours. And the de L. family is almost in the same situation: their estate in Artois is not far from Tournai. We'll solve the problem by finding you a house on Belgian soil."

These plans, which seem sensible to his father, reawaken in Michel all his old distaste for those well-cushioned and proper

circles in which everything can always be worked out. That
world immune to misfortune is precisely what he was fleeing
when he joined the army and then went to England. But Michel-
Charles's hand trembles slightly when the young man passes
him a glass of grog, which a solemn waiter has just brought.
First the elderly gentleman takes from his waistcoat pocket a
folded square of tissue paper, holds it to his lips, and pours a
digestive powder down his throat.

"This isn't a decision you can make right away," he says,
stirring his steaming drink. "But I have the impression that the
best of your adventure is already behind you. I wouldn't want
you to become bogged down . . . All the same, you're thirty
years old . . . And I've no time to lose if I want to see your first
child with my own eyes."

Michel is tempted to say that marriage, too, can bog you
down. But something whispers to him that his life with Maud
is likewise a dead end. Michel-Charles, moreover, does not
insist; he changes the subject. The son helps his father
straighten things up and retires to his room next door.

The next day they are concerned only with seeing the sights
and tasting the pleasures of London. Before anything else
Michel-Charles wants to have himself measured for a suit at
one of the city's finest tailors; Michel takes him to Bond Street.
The father uses this opportunity to add some new items to his
son's wardrobe. Michel-Charles has long dreamed of owning a
stopwatch by a certain famous English maker; after much hesitation, he chooses the most expensive one in the shop. The
extra-thin double case opens first to a dial on which a minuscule
hand ticks off the seconds; the motto, *Tempus fugit irreparabile*,
pleases this man who has always been an admirer of Horace.
A second gold disk, even thinner than the first and released by
a spring, reveals the entire complex mechanism designed to
pulverize time. The old man spends a long while gazing at it,

doubtless wondering how many days, months, and years those wheels and escapements will toil for him. This purchase, made at such a late date, is perhaps a form of defiance, or of propitiation.

At the typically English restaurant where Michel-Charles has wanted to dine, his son smilingly puts a five-pound note on the table; it's the commission that the jeweler discreetly handed him, taking him for a guide who was showing the wealthy foreigner around the city. With a kindly gesture, Michel-Charles pushes this windfall back toward his son. Later, the traveler has to buy a good suitcase to hold his new clothes. Another purchase and another commission. In the display window of a shop in Piccadilly, Michel-Charles sees a jet-embroidered shawl that he wants to buy for Noémi; and here the knowledge that Michel has acquired from Rolf concerning the tricks of London merchants proves quite useful. Michel knows that the item displayed in the window is sometimes of better quality than the supposedly identical one presented to the customer in the dimly lit shop. He is firm in his request: it's the shawl in the window that will envelop Noémi's well-corseted form.

The rest of the eight days are spent seeing London. Michel is afraid that his father will find a visit to the Tower too exhausting, but neither the spiral staircases nor the vast courtyards are beyond the strength of this tourist who is so interested in Anne Boleyn and Thomas More. Together they admire the gardens at Hampton Court and eat thin slices of cucumber and buttered bread in a teahouse on the Thames. At Westminster Michel-Charles pauses thoughtfully before each recumbent effigy, and his son marvels at his detailed knowledge of even the most minor Plantagenets and Tudors. In the British Museum, the old man respectfully contemplates the fragments from the Parthenon, but pauses longest at the Greco-Roman antiquities, which remind him of the works he loved so much as a young man when he saw them in Italy and in the Louvre. So far as painting goes, with the exception of a few eighteenth-century portraitists, he admires only the Dutch and Flemish schools, and Michel recalls the visits he and his father made long ago to the art museum in Amsterdam, where the father held his little son by the hand and tried to explain *The Night Watch.* Although neither of them is a passionate lover of music, Michel-Charles wants to attend a performance at Covent Garden. The evening they decide to go, an Italian opera troupe is singing *Norma.*

On the day of Michel-Charles's departure, the weather is rainy. He's a bit concerned about his handsome new suitcase. The two men embrace on the wharf. The father says that as soon as he gets back to Lille, he will write concerning the plans they discussed. In the meantime, Michel needn't make any decision but should continue to think the matter over. While waiting, does he perhaps need some money?

Michel does need money, but says nothing, out of delicacy. Michel-Charles ventures hesitantly:

"The young woman . . . If things work out the way your parents would like them to . . . Perhaps a sum by way of compensation . . ."

"No," says Michel a bit coldly. "I don't think that would be appropriate."

Michel-Charles senses that he has wounded his son by seeming to slight the absent woman. Michel disguises his withdrawal by busying himself with the luggage. The traveler disappears in the crowd, then reappears; he taps little farewell gestures on one of the windows of the dining room for first-class passengers. He is old and ill—two conditions that the young man has given scarcely any thought to until now.

In the suburban train that takes him back to Maud, Michel realizes that he has already come to a decision without ever needing to think much about the lovely brown-haired woman from the old and respected family. But how is he to broach the subject to Maud? She's one of those women with whom you can laugh, cry, and make love, but not discuss things. The little house is dark when he arrives. Red is the only one waiting for him in the unlit hallway. Maud's armoire is open and empty; a letter is pinned to the pillow. She is quite aware of what this long visit by Michel's father means. She has returned to Rolf, who is only too happy to have her back. She and Michel have had good times together, but everything must come to an end. If Michel doesn't come home right away, the housekeeper will look after the dog. And out of habit, she puts a row of circles under her signature, to signify kisses.

Michel spends the next day paying. Paying the rent on their lease, which still has two months left to run; paying the butcher, the fruit seller, the fishmonger, the grocer; paying the housekeeper. Since Maud has never kept any sort of account book, there is no means of verifying the amounts. Short of money, especially since he sent two dozen roses to Putney via a London florist, Michel takes a room in town while waiting to hear from his father. To save money, he eats cheap fried fish (which Jewish shops in this poor neighborhood sell wrapped in newspaper) or cooks himself an egg over the little gas flame that lights his room. Red's food costs more than his own.

The letter arrives after a delay of three weeks. Michel-Charles fell ill immediately upon his arrival in Lille and was unable to write sooner. Doubtless he was paying the price of his strenuous activities during his stay in London, which, he declares, was one of the high points of his life. Everything is ready for the prodigal son's return. He should take the steamer to Ostend and then have himself driven to Ypres, where a trustworthy person will help him across the border. Michel-Charles encloses a sum large enough to pay for the journey.

On his last evening, Michel cannot resist prowling about the house in Putney. The curtains are carefully closed. Rolf, who comes out in a smoking jacket to mail a letter, spies the young Frenchman and greets him cordially. Michel tells him he's leaving England the next day. The irrepressible Rolf proposes that the three of them go out for supper to a restaurant in Richmond that serves excellent oysters. Feeling that he really ought to refuse, Michel says yes. Rolf goes upstairs to change, leaving him to wait in the drawing room for a few interminable minutes. Maud appears at last, dressed as if she's going to a private party. She says little at dinner, and Michel isn't very talkative either, but Rolf succeeds in creating a gay and noisy atmosphere all by himself. He mentions that he will become assistant director on January 1, 1884—that is, in a little more than three months. He tells stories about the office that make him laugh till he cries, and even comes out with an amusing reference to Michel and Maud's American fiasco. Michel clenches his fists; Maud shouldn't have talked about that. But Rolf doesn't harp on the subject. His large, kind eyes gaze benevolently in turn on his wife, on Michel, on the diners at the table next to them, on the waiter in his white apron, on a young rosy-cheeked woman who is collecting money for the Salvation Army. Over dinner, Maud has removed her veil. I imagine her (since Michel didn't give me any description of how she looked on this last occasion) dressed in green, a color that Englishwomen are fond of; I see her holding an oyster shell with two fingers and lifting it to her lips like a tiny version of Venus' half-shell.

Michel feels vaguely as if he has been manipulated—as if Rolf has been pulling the strings of two marionettes. Did he perhaps have a mistress, and was he happy to have been temporarily relieved of his young wife? Is his love for Maud almost paternal (he's fifteen years older than she is), and has he successfully completed a dangerous experiment? Namely, has he given his wife, once and for all, a thorough dose of passion and romance, knowing that she's the type who in the long run will always prefer a house in Putney and a husband who's an assistant director? The young man remembers the postal money order Maud received in Devonshire and her visits to her aunt in London. What if it had been Rolf and not some friends moving to Ireland who'd suggested that they take over the management of the perfume shop in Liverpool? Michel sinks lower and lower, toward abysses of perdition that he can only vaguely imagine— abysses that are as rank and dangerous as sulfur pits. What if Rolf were more or less impotent and had intended from the very first to offer Maud some harmless pleasure by means of the young foreigner? What if Rolf had a core of vice in him—or a masochistic streak, like so many others of his persecuted people? Amid these explanations, which after all explain nothing, Michel does not hit on the rarest, which is also the simplest: that Rolf was just immensely, incorrigibly kind.

After a polite altercation on the subject of who is to pay the bill, the gentlemen each pay half. The three of them drink to Michel's journey and to Rolf's promotion. They bid each other farewell by the light of a streetlamp.

Monsieur Michel Michel, who had once again become Michel de C. (though in the future, when he felt like it, he would often call himself simply Michel Michel), followed his father's instructions. Two or three secret visits to Mont-Noir took place in the fall of 1883. Michel would walk the fifteen or so kilometers from Ypres, variously greeted or ignored by the customs officers. But it was a risky game; if the deserter was recognized and arrested, he would be sentenced to at least two years in prison. The more prudent Michel-Charles occasionally had his own carriage take him to Ypres or Courtrai to see his son. Only once, out of bravado, did the young man slip into Lille, the tiresome city of his birth, which had acquired the charm of a forbidden place. Around the feast of Saint-Sylvester, Michel-Charles, accompanied this time by Noémi, met his son in Tournai, at the Noble Rose Hotel, where the other guests from France included Baron Loys de L.; his wife, Marie-Athénaïs; and their daughter, who was going to marry Michel. This official meeting put the seal on the engagement. Marie-Athénaïs had in fact been born in Tournai, where her ancestors had emigrated during the Revolution; this energetic mother-in-law soon located a friend or relative in the town who agreed to rent a house to the young couple until Michel could officially return to France. Michel-Charles filled the dwelling with fine old furniture that Noémi had relegated to their attic. Michel married Berthe de L. in Tournai in April 1884.

Shortly before this he had an experience that remained more vivid in his mind than the wedding ceremony, about which he seemed to have nothing to say. One evening in March he was returning to Mont-Noir for the last time prior to his marriage, and was taking the usual precautions. That year Michel-Charles had gone to the country early in the season, perhaps to be closer to his son. As always, Michel was making the trip on foot. A dusting of late snow covered the bare branches and the dry brown fields. Red was accompanying his master as usual, bounding along the road, prowling among the thickets, disappearing suddenly, then flying back with the swiftness of a meteor, as dogs do when they want to make sure you're still there. Along that border a number of smugglers would hang little bundles of prohibited goods from the necks of their dogs; the well-trained animals would shuttle across the frontier by themselves. That evening a customs officer saw the shape of an apparently unaccompanied dog silhouetted against the pale layer of snow; he fired at the animal. The detonation and the yelp that followed brought Michel running to the next curve in the road. Red, mortally wounded, scarcely had the strength to lick his young master's hand. Michel threw himself on the ground and wept. He picked up the body and carried it in his arms to Mont-Noir, where he buried it honorably beneath a tree. The swift, graceful dog was as heavy as stone. He had been the most precious thing that Michel had brought back from his years in England. But Red was more to him than merely a memento of Maud: he was an animal comrade with whom he had made a pact, especially since the day Red had searched for him to the point of exhaustion and found him at last. He was also the victim of a crime that we have all committed—the crime of persuading an innocent creature to trust us, but then being unable to protect him and save him. If Michel had been superstitious, he would have seen that heartbreaking event as a sign.

My grandfather's wishes were promptly fulfilled. One year after the wedding the couple's only child was born. He was named Michel-Fernand-Marie-Joseph; we'll call him Michel-Joseph for short. I don't intend to refer very often to this half brother who was eighteen years my senior, but unless I significantly truncate my account, I can't eliminate him from it altogether. It seems a bit early to be describing someone who at this point is still wailing in the arms of a nursemaid. Yet one quotation is essential. It comes from Michel-Joseph himself—namely, from the brief memoirs that he wrote some sixty years later and that I've spoken of elsewhere. He begins by evoking his birth, with a sentence whose like is perhaps not to be found in any other autobiography: "I was born in Tournai, in a mansion whose furnishings (according to a document preserved in the town's archives) cost twenty-six thousand francs."

I've described the affection that persisted between Michel-Charles and his son even after the latter's many scrapes. With the next generation, things were different. Michel-Joseph's upbringing had something to do with this. Since the boy couldn't very well accompany his parents on their endless round of resorts and horse shows, he spent part of his youth in the affectionate but haphazard care of his grandmother Marie-Athénaïs on the family estate of Fées (I've changed the name), and part at Mont-Noir, where the sullen child didn't get along too badly with the prickly Noémi, his other grandmother. In the winter Michel-Joseph was put under the thumb of a surly old military officer and his wife, a little woman who painted on porcelain and passed off her works as artifacts from historic Lille; the unpleasant events that resulted from this chicanery no doubt traumatized the couple's young lodger. Later Michel's devout sister Marie de S., who was dismayed by her teenage nephew's churlishness, asked her brother to remove him from the couple's care. In rapid succession he went from a religious institution to a lay institution, from the Jesuits on the rue de Vaugirard to the lycée in Douai, and from there to a boardinghouse for wellborn boys on the Riviera. There were no differences worth noting in these establishments, other than minor variations in the poor quality of the food and the dirtiness of the premises. Michel was always an extravagantly generous man; whenever he thought of his son (which was rarely), he would shower him with presents, ranging from his first toy soldiers, to his first motorcycle, to his first racing car. When his son was still an adolescent, he offered him long trips abroad accompanied by a friend of his choosing, who would serve as escort. I've said elsewhere that he sometimes invited his son to join him during vacations, or even took him out of school arbitrarily so that the boy could spend some time with him and his second wife or one of his mistresses. These episodes often turned out badly.

As a result, the two men conceived a mutual dislike that lasted all their lives. When the son attained his majority in 1906, he opted for Belgian citizenship, a choice made available to him by the fact that he'd been born in Tournai. Michel was annoyed by this; it didn't occur to him that it was his own status as a deserter that had caused Michel-Joseph to be born outside France and had thus made such a choice possible. Like others in the same situation, the boy thought only of evading the mandatory three years of French military service, an attitude that ought not to have shocked his father, who was anything but a flag-waving patriot. But logic is not the strong point of passionate natures. Michel felt vaguely that, in changing nationalities, his son was also renouncing Montaigne, Racine, the pastels of La Tour, and *La Légende des siècles*. He was not entirely wrong. In a predictable reaction, the son went counter to his father in just about everything. Michel, despite three wives and numerous mistresses, had a total of two children; Michel-Joseph would be the father of a large family. Michel was a great book lover; his son would pride himself on being an ignoramus. Though Michel felt deeply drawn to certain aspects of the religious life, he would live and die free of any faith; Michel-Joseph assiduously attended eleven o'clock Mass. Michel, a patrician who didn't give a damn about his ancestors, never even knew the name of his paternal great-grandmother; Michel-Joseph had a taste for genealogy. The father was indifferent and easygoing toward his son; the son would be severe with his own children. In his brief memoirs, Michel-Joseph speaks as little as possible of the father he perpetually resisted; Berthe, referred to as "my dear mama," appears only once—namely, at her death, which was precisely the event that Michel would reproach the teenager for not having mourned.

But they were most at odds over their attitudes toward the Golden Calf. Michel liked money only because he could spend it; Michel-Joseph liked it because he knew that all the things dear to him—the respect of society, good marriages, worldly success—needed a substantial bank account as their foundation. Throughout my childhood, I heard hate-filled words fly back and forth between the two men like bullets. "You sold the estates that were in the family for generations! Crayencour, Dranoutre, Mont-Noir . . ." "You're a fine one to talk about the estates of our ancestors! . . . You aren't even a citizen of the country they're a part of!" On at least one occasion, I saw those arguments—which seemed especially foolish in Nord, whose borders were so fluid—turn into a fistfight. Today, at such a distance, I find it impossible to tell whether the son's hatred for his father (which was perhaps nourished by a good deal of frustrated affection) resulted from the fact that Michel had disparaged everything his son wanted to believe in, or whether the presumptive heir simply could not forgive the reigning monarch for having squandered a fortune. To a person who considers devolutions of inheritance as a type of investiture, the two attitudes are one.

I see quite well how it would be possible to compose a hagiographic portrait of my half brother depicting him as a restorationist succeeding a dissipator. Having married and settled in Belgium in 1911, Michel-Joseph took up residence in that worldly and business-oriented city of Brussels, where acquisitiveness and the snobbery of name and title are more prevalent than anywhere else. But let's not forget that we regard this taste for commercial enterprise with respect, even downright lyricism, when we're speaking of Amsterdam in the Golden Age; and that we find the sentimental fondness for heraldry and small noble coteries charming in the outmoded courts of eighteenth-century Germany. A person can almost always get what he wants if he strives for it over the course of forty years. My half brother succeeded in making his way into those circles which were largely unfamiliar to him but in which he wanted to live; he enabled his children to make excellent and solid marriages. In 1957, after a silence between us lasting twenty-five years, he sent me a letter announcing that he had obtained, or had had confirmed for himself and his descendants, the title of "chevalier," which his grandfather in Lille had declined to use because it was out of fashion in France. I all but smiled at this, yet today I think differently: when a man is a citizen of a small nation that still has a royal court and a living, active nobility, even though their activities are utterly superficial, it is no more absurd for him to take pleasure in obtaining a parchment that proclaims him a chevalier than for a Frenchman to polish up his Legion of Honor medal.

I'm trying to paint this man with a single stroke—this character who is of secondary importance here but who has nevertheless played a part in my life. When I was a child, his way of suddenly appearing out of nowhere used to frighten me. As a young man he carried himself well and had a curious ability to slip into a room without making a sound; his gliding, dance-like gait, which I rediscovered later in certain professional flamenco dancers, gave the impression that the bit of gypsy blood he was supposed to have inherited from a maternal ancestor was not merely a family legend. But although in his youth he loved to act like a hooligan, he soon caught hold of the proprieties and clung to them as if they were a buoy. He was irritated that his half sister, who in his eyes was already flawed merely because she existed, should be more thoughtful, more serious, more tranquil than the conventional image he had formed of little girls—and was irritated all the more since the child with the wide laughing mouth (which I also was) never laughed in his presence. I remember one afternoon at the seaside. I was sitting on a dune, contemplating the waves as they swelled, hollowed out, and broke on the sand in a single, long, endlessly re-emerging line. The sentence that I've just written is, of course, a creation of the present; but the vague perceptions of the little girl of seven, though she didn't express them in words, were as intense as or stronger than those of the elderly woman. My half brother approached with his noiseless tread. A grave voice

admonished me: "What are you doing there? A child ought to
be playing and not daydreaming. Where's your doll? A little girl
should never be without her doll." With the contemptuous
indifference of childhood, I put this young adult in the category
labeled "imbeciles": he was uttering what I already recognized
as commonplaces. Actually, though, he had his quirks and mysteries like everyone else.

The smallest gesture of kindness—a flower left for him on
a day when he was bedridden with the flu—moved the high-
strung fellow to tears. It was a long time before I understood
that this form of emotionalism is often found in impoverished
natures who give nothing in return and are surprised that other
people should give something to them. But I've also seen him
act with unbelievable harshness toward those who are supposedly dear to him. He believed in the "unquiet dead," and feared
them, thinking that there were some in his family line. Such
notions were surprising in a man who always claimed to have
little imagination; perhaps he got them from his grandmother
Marie-Athénaïs, who allegedly encountered ghosts from time to
time. Like many boys who have been educated by morally ex-
acting priests, he played with ambiguities that could not be
called out-and-out lies. When he was questioned by Noémi,
who was sure in advance that the De Dion–Bouton hadn't been
able to climb Mont-des-Cats, he answered that he'd gotten to
the summit in the "vehicle"; he meant the hay cart that had
picked him up after his car broke down at the foot of the mountain. Later, he boasted of the fact that he never paid his bills
until the last possible moment, so as not to lose the interest on
the sums in question; it never occurred to him that such delays
might have caused problems for the shopkeepers. Other times
he was capable of acting as a man of honor, almost a chevalier:
once he defended the rights of an illegitimate daughter who had
been left destitute by her father—a man whose fortune he

counted on inheriting and who subsequently, of course, disinherited him. I'm sorry to say that on this occasion Michel made fun of him. We're all made of odd bits and pieces, as Montaigne said.

I lost sight of my half brother when I was twelve, and had no further contact with him until I was twenty-five. In January 1929, in Lausanne, I wrote him a letter asking him to come to the bedside of his dying father. I shouldn't have done this; Michel had told me not to. But two years and two or three months previously, when Michel was already ailing, he had taken a third wife, an Englishwoman. She was sentimental and conventional as only someone from the British middle class can be, but she cared for him devotedly. She thought it natural—as indeed it was—that her stepson be informed of his father's condition. Michel-Joseph replied that since he was just then building himself a house on the outskirts of Brussels, he didn't have any money to spare for the trip. Moreover, the winter was proving to be harsh; a snowstorm had hit the city only that morning, and his wife had had a nervous attack at the thought of him traveling to Switzerland. Actually, this defender of solid family traditions feared that he would have to help defray the cost of the lengthy illness and the funeral of a man who was dying in poverty and who he thought had wronged him.

I should have stopped there. But my stepmother, that Englishwoman who thought Dickens common and revered the upright families in Galsworthy's novels, believed in reconciliations between close relatives. Like many Britishers of modest means in those days, she had recently spent a number of years living in family boardinghouses on the Continent, primarily in Belgium. A small factory that she had just inherited in London allowed her to indulge in a few fantasies: she saw herself returning to her native country adorned with the title of viscountess. Neither my father (who, as I've said, eventually let

Christine Hovelt (or Brown-Hovelt), later Christine de
Crayencour, Michel's third wife, 1920s

tradespeople address him as "count") nor I (more rigorous on this point) had ever succeeded in persuading her that the owner of former viscontial lands was not necessarily a viscount, and I'm quite convinced that even Michel failed to appreciate the importance of this fact. Moreover, the inheritance from my mother, which consisted entirely of properties in Hainaut and which Michel had left in the hands of estate managers, needed attention. Over the course of about eighteen months—until Christine de C., disappointed by Brussels, came back to settle in Switzerland, where her husband had lived the last two years of his life—I made intermittent visits to Belgium. I dined fairly often at my half brother's newly built house, which was decorated from top to bottom with furniture and portraits from the families of Bailleul and Lille—objects that Michel, who didn't know what to do with them after Mont-Noir was sold, had allowed his son to take. When it came to dividing the estate after his father's death, Michel-Joseph adhered to the simple notion of primogeniture. But let's be fair: he continued to believe that Michel had not died utterly ruined and that he had enhanced the fortunes of his daughter by mysterious means. For me, in any case, those ornate cabinets and ancestors in wigs had no appeal.

We often speak of the way society, in certain periods near our own (when it's not our own, despite appearances), deliberately leaves young people ignorant when it comes to sexual matters. But we don't speak enough of the extraordinary ignorance of financial and legal matters that afflicts us all. The most perspicacious and best educated among us often know virtually nothing about these fields of knowledge, which are essential to our independence and sometimes even our lives. I knew just enough about them to realize that in these domains I could not manage by myself. In those days I was based in Paris, where my first book had just been published, and I was always sorry when I had to leave that city for Brussels, which seemed to me then the capital of tedium. Eventually I began telling myself that a half brother who was living on the scene and involved in the real-estate business would be more capable than I when it came to selling those lands and investing the proceeds. No wise person had yet taught me that in such cases it's always a mistake to rely on a family member, especially when tensions have existed between him and us. In matters that concern us, the most scrupulous person must feel a touch of hostility or indifference. Indifference was enough. I was present at one of the discussions between my agent and a prospective buyer. On every point, the hard-bargaining peasant got the better of the city dweller, who knew nothing about the properties. I should have intervened; I knew I couldn't. Perhaps I also felt some vague embarrassment at the thought of profiting from lands that my mother and I had more or less received income from, without ever taking the trouble to stroll through those fields or among those trees. Michel-Joseph sold off those farms one by one and invested the proceeds. Half went into the real-estate firm that he directed, and half (he had obviously not given much thought to distributing the risk) into a large mortgage given to the owners of a hotel for the purposes of expansion and renovation. The people were named Monsieur and Madame Rombaut. Their names came back to me thirty-five years later when I needed to baptize two characters in *The Abyss*, a married couple from Bruges. You take whatever profits you can.

The wind from the American economic crisis was already causing the European house of cards to tremble. The real-estate firm went under, and since it was not a limited-liability company (I didn't yet know the meaning of this phrase), I lost more than I had invested in it. The hotel, too, collapsed—at least metaphorically. The mortgage was merely a second mortgage, and supposedly irrecoverable. I did what I should have done two years earlier: I requested the help of an elderly French lawyer who had extricated Michel from difficult situations in days gone by. With the aid of one of his Belgian colleagues, he recovered about half the money loaned to the bankrupt hoteliers. I decided that this sum, if spent prudently a little at a time, would be enough to give me ten to twelve years of sumptuous freedom. Afterward, I'd take stock again. I didn't notice that I was thus repeating, in a different era, the type of risky calculations that my two maternal uncles had made around 1900. This decision, which I congratulate myself for having made, took me up to September 1939, with a slender margin of security. Had I lived on the income from funds invested in Belgium and managed by my half brother, I would have remained more or less connected to a family with which I had no affinities and to the country of my birth and my mother, which, at least in its current aspect, was completely foreign to me. That three-fourths bankruptcy restored me to myself.

But if I took the loss fairly well (more from inexperience than from magnanimity), the way it was announced to me was a shock. Michel-Joseph had always made a game of sending impudent postcards. On the back of a card showing a view of Brussels' main square, he informed me straight out that everything remaining from my maternal inheritance had been lost. To hear him tell it, I had no choice but to sell apples on street corners (there are, of course, more foolish occupations). I didn't get the point of this jest, which was inspired by stories of the chaos on Wall Street; the crisis was being reported widely, but I hadn't read the newspapers. The joke seemed in bad taste, coming from the man who had proposed himself as the manager of those funds so easily lost. I didn't reply to the postcard. I never saw Michel-Joseph again, and all communication between us ceased, except for the heraldic announcement I mentioned above, which he sent to me a quarter of a century later.

Ananke

Shortly before that minor financial catastrophe, I saw him again; it would be our last meeting, though I didn't know this. I had come to Brussels to visit my stepmother, and during my stay I went to his house to sign some papers. He gave me and my suitcase a lift to the Gare du Midi; I was going back to Paris, and from there to Vienna. It was a hot, humid, stormy summer evening, and the rain was falling quite heavily at times. As always, Brussels looked like a vast demolition yard: everywhere something was being torn down, rebuilt, or modified. What with barricaded streets and oceans of mud, our progress was slow. When we arrived at the station, the train I had intended to take was long gone, and the next one didn't leave for an hour. Seated side by side, waiting for the downpour to let up so we could leave the car, imprisoned in that box of metal and glass furrowed by streams of water, we chatted like two strangers who have met by chance in a bar. He envied me my freedom (which he overestimated); he mused over the fact that life swiftly creates new ties which take the place of those we thought we had cut ourselves loose from; whatever we do and wherever we go, walls go up around us as a result of our efforts, initially a shelter but soon a prison. Yet these truths weren't clear to me either in those days. Michel-Joseph, who wanted to be the opposite of his father in everything, felt that he had exhausted his allotted choices in a single stroke. "What can you do? Once you've acquired a circle of dependents, you can't simply strangle them all." We agreed that this sort of housecleaning would have been suitable only for the likes of Sultan Murad. For the first time, though, I realized that this man felt a yearning for freedom that was not very different from my own, just as his taste for genealogy corresponded to my interest in history. There were similarities between us that went beyond the arched line of our brows and the color of our eyes.

Let's return to the present—that is, to 1886—and pay another visit to Michel-Charles. My grandfather was at Mont-Noir during the autumn of 1885, which would prove to be his last. The days of long walks were over. He spent his time copying the letters he had written in Italy forty years earlier; he then destroyed the originals, perhaps after correcting and improving them here and there. He also wrote a brief summary of his life for the benefit of his children. Permeated by a not overly rigorous sincerity, it is the chronicle of a kindly man who is determined to see everything in a favorable light, if not through rose-colored glasses. He praises Noémi's intelligence, and even her admirable worldly graces. His daughter Marie, who has replaced the deceased Gabrielle (already dead for nearly twenty years), has become, as he hoped, the angel of his old age. He has no doubt that when she makes her debut in Lille society this winter, she will enjoy the greatest success. A photograph of Marie taken the same year shows that this doting father is right: the pretty girl in her satin dress, with a serious expression but a gay light in her clear eyes, is seduction itself. As for her brother Michel, his father tells us he has "a fiery temperament and a heart of gold." Michel-Charles says nothing about the two desertions from the army and the seven years spent in England, or about the sorrow that the expatriate's father must have felt; but he does mention the marriage with Berthe. "Michel adores her, and she is equally fond of him. They've just given us a fine big boy." Michel-Charles doubtless did not have the joy of seeing this fervently wished-for child very often: Tournai was too far away for an invalid, and the government's proscription still curtailed Michel's visits to France. Did he really believe that the young couple had settled into a honeymoon that would last all their lives? It's possible; this judicious man could sometimes be quite naïve. I don't know whether he had already received his terminal diagnosis from the doctor, but his ulcers, an old ailment that he had grown used to, had given way to cancer of the stomach, which was inoperable back then. His days were numbered. But there are silent verdicts that our bodies pronounce on themselves and that something records within us. I imagine that in leaving Mont-Noir and its lovely woods, decimated after the war and in our own day by developers, Michel-Charles gazed at the trees with the eye of a man who has put some of his immortality into those tall green creatures. Of course, I doubt that such a thought ever consciously occurred to my grandfather, much less that he ever expressed it. Still, it floats, unformulated, from century to century, from millennium to millennium, in the minds of all those who love their land and their trees.

In Lille, Michel-Charles takes to his room and will never again leave it. The lace curtains on its windows must be washed every week, since the soot of Lille doesn't spare even the finest houses. Despite the servants' best efforts, a dirty film that drifts down from the sky, a foul by-product of the factories and coal works in the vicinity, sticks to the gilded frames, clouds the mirror, coats the black marble of the chimneypiece. As in the case of my other grandfather, I could speculate about what's going through his mind—whether he's caressing in his imagination a smooth fragment of classical marble abandoned in the Roman *campagna* or stroking the dusky breast of a beautiful *contadina* who gives herself readily to the stranger from abroad—and its pink tip trembles and stands erect, the pliancy of the flesh contrasting with the immobility of the marble. Does he still think of his companions on that fatal evening in May and of the grisettes who accompanied them on their excursion to Versailles? Perhaps he's not thinking of anything, except the dull pain in his stomach, where death has come to lodge. Furthermore, his weary body is afflicted with rheumatism.

He is all alone in the spacious conjugal bedchamber, since Noémi has moved to the room next to it, partly so that the invalid will have more peace and quiet, and partly because there's nothing pleasant about being near a body that is breaking down. The lovely room smells like a stable. Michel-Charles has let his coachman persuade him that horse urine is a sovereign remedy for rheumatism. He's had a basin of the ammoniac liquid placed by his bed, and now and then, almost surreptitiously, he dips his right arm in it, hoping it will relieve its pain and stiffness.

These days Noémi is extremely busy. Isn't it essential that she send for the pharmacist or the herbalist at all hours; send for the doctor if the invalid suddenly takes a turn for the worse; summon other physicians for consultations; pay a visit to her old friend the notary, or have him admitted discreetly into the drawing room downstairs, to make sure everything is in order; receive, likewise discreetly, the dressmaker who will be sewing mourning clothes for her and everyone else in the house? But her main concern is to keep an eye on the worthy nuns who are serving as nurses. She has to make sure they don't spend all their time telling their rosaries or reading their missals at

Marie de Crayencour, Michel's younger sister, 1886

the invalid's bedside, thus leaving most of the nursing to the already overtaxed maidservants. (Those peasant women in their white headdresses have an annoying tendency to let the servants wait on them.) On other occasions, in contrast, it's the collusion between the convent and the servants' hall that worries Noémi. Under the pretext of fetching or returning a tray, one of the good sisters will sometimes go to the kitchen and stuff tidbits into the large basket that ostensibly holds her eyeglasses, her knitting, and her prayer book; Noémi is positive she's detected this maneuver more than once. Starched headdresses and metal crosses worn as pendants do not diminish her mistrust of the "help" in the slightest, and these days the good sisters are part of the help. She forgets to dye her hair, or (to use her own words) to "rinse" it, as she does every week with the aid of a strong solution of coffee.

Marie, who is a born nurse, enlivens the room with some of her gaiety and the vigor of her eighteen years. She knows better than anyone how to plump up a pillow and how to persuade the sick man to take a sip of milk. Toward the end, Michel risks a visit to Lille. It is tacitly understood that the authorities will look the other way; no one is going to arrest the deserter at the deathbed of such a respected father. But the visitor prudently keeps to the invalid's room. On his last day Michel-Charles painfully pulls from his swollen fingers the signet ring engraved on precious stone, which he inherited from Michel-Donatien, and the beautiful classical cameo bearing an image of the aged Augustus. He gives them to his son. With a movement of his head, he also indicates the dresser-top tray, where Michel finds the precious stopwatch purchased in England. *Tempus fugit irreparabile.*

Early in the morning on the day after his father's death, Michel hears the doorbell ring. He leans over the banister on the second floor and looks down, half hidden by the folds of a door curtain. Perhaps it's someone from the funeral home who has come to take measurements. No, it's a lady from Lille's fashionable set, who lives on the same street and has come early to offer her condolences. Noémi crosses the vestibule to receive her.

"But my poor Noémi, your hair's gone all gray!"

"It's the grief, my good Adeline, it's the grief."

Michel leaves before the funeral in Bailleul has taken place. A legend transmitted by my half brother, who perhaps invented the whole thing, claims that Michel-Charles, in his will, endowed a bed for ailing paupers in one of the hospitals in Lille, on one condition: that his son, if ever the need arose, be taken in and cared for there until his death. Described in these terms, such a bequest evokes the seventeenth century rather than the nineteenth. However that may be, Michel will never have to avail himself of this provision. He is destined to die amid the luxury of a Swiss clinic. Notwithstanding Michel-Charles's love and concern, the share of the inheritance he has left to his prodigal son is placed under the trusteeship of a family council, presided over by Noémi with the aid of her notaries. The excuse given is that it is impossible for Michel to return to his country for long periods, and hence impossible for him to manage his fortune. This difficulty is resolved sooner than anyone thought it would be: in 1889 an unexpected amnesty officially reopens France to him. But neither Lille nor Mont-Noir, where Noémi holds sway, attracts him. And Tournai is a hole where he settled only to please a man who is no longer among the living. One season has been enough to exhaust the charms of the people one meets in châteaus and fine hotels. The money that Noémi dispatches to her son three times a year, along with an acrimonious letter, is enough to enable the young couple to gratify their passion for ever-changing scenery. During the thirteen years that come between the death of his father and that of Berthe, Michel, whether he likes it or not, keeps heading for adventure.

Berthe's family—extremely old, as Michel-Charles had said—had its origins in the antiquity of legend. Baron Loys de L. took pride in his parchments; he also derived comfort from them when he needed it, which is to say often. People smiled to hear him claim that he descended, on the women's side, from Charlemagne, and thus from Bertha of the Big Foot. Such smiles are perhaps born of an exaggerated respect for the great figures of history; we find it difficult to believe that the descendants of the descendants of those figures could be as ordinary as the gentleman who's speaking to us. The great-granddaughter of that first Charles the Great, Judith of France, who married a count of Flanders and was buried at Saint-Omer, left traces of her blood in obscure feudal families throughout the region. Some, like the baron's, remained in possession of their archival documents, while others in the course of time doubtless became submerged in the masses of the peasantry. It was the same with Ethelrude, the daughter of Alfred, King of Wessex: she, too, married a count of Flanders, this one a contemporary of the Norman invasions and an ancestor of Baron Loys at a distance of twenty-seven generations. This fact shows above all how ancient the links between Flanders and England are.

A man endowed with imagination—and the baron was not lacking in this quality—takes pleasure in feeling the very axis of history pass through him. Judith and Ethelrude sustained him in times of trouble. Michel, in his frequent moments of irritation amid the family, would reproach his father-in-law for declining from his ancestors rather than descending from them; but he was being quite unfair. The baron wasn't declining from anything. On the contrary, his greatest virtue was a sort of immovability. In times more recent than the Carolingian past, his great-grandfather had died while an émigré in Holland; his great-aunt had been incarcerated in Douai at the age of four with the rest of her family, on the charge of having participated in the royalist plot against the Republic. His legitimism had ancestral roots. A well-appointed stable was the sole luxury of this man who allowed himself few luxuries. His fine horses, always kept at the ready, would have the honor of serving as the first relay of mounts for Henri V when he re-entered France, after making up his mind to reconquer his kingdom. But the history of France in the nineteenth century is so complicated that the baron's passion for the white flag had long been combined with loyalty to the government of Napoleon III. He had been a midshipman in the imperial navy, then a captain in the 48th *de marche*, then a battalion leader in the territorial infantry. Wounded in the thigh at Gravelotte by a piece of shrapnel, he limped with dignity. The advent of the Republic exasperated his legitimist sympathies. At Fées the annual cleaning of the cesspool took place on the fourteenth of July, and he would have scowled at any servants or farmhands capable of abandoning this scatological task for the attractions of taverns adorned with tricolor lanterns on the village square.

Next to this little man, who held himself somewhat stiffly

so as not to lose an inch of his height, Marie-Athénaïs was dazzling. I've remarked elsewhere on the Spanish strain in the families of Nord, and the way in which it gave rise to numerous legends. But the *sangre azul* was clearly evident in this tall, thin woman with the handsome profile of a falcon. Her great-great-great-grandfather had fought on the Iberian peninsula in the seventeenth century, in the days when Chamilly was repeatedly seducing and abandoning his Portuguese Nun. More faithful than the lover of Mariana Alcoforado, the baroness's ancestor brought back a certain María-Josefa Rebacq y Barca from Seville as his legitimate wife. Some of the baroness's admirers, looking farther to the south, toward Granada and the caves of Sacromonte, claimed that their idol had gypsy ancestors. Her temperament justified this hypothesis. A century earlier another forebear, a bourgeois from Douai, called himself simply Lespagnol ("The Spaniard"), which meant that you could imagine him as having been a former soldier under Charles V or Philippe II, or, if you preferred, the descendant of one of those foreign merchants who settled in ancient Flanders in the days when trade in linen and wool was flourishing.

All those Spains blazing beneath the ashes gave Marie-Athénaïs not beauty, strictly speaking, but a sort of animal splendor. Michel liked to say that, from time immemorial, certain places have been imbued with characteristic influences. To him Mont-Noir appeared to be devoted to discord and family hatreds; in contrast, Venus reigned at Fées. The austere baron himself made sacrifices to the goddess. Marie-Athénaïs was fiercely jealous when it came to her husband, who seemed to count for little in her eyes, despite seven children. One summer they invited a cousin from Arras to stay with them—a young widow whom they were hoping to distract from her grief. She'd been there only a short time when the baroness, entering the guest's room unannounced, found her husband in the blond woman's arms. Without deigning to give the lovers a second glance, Marie-Athénaïs went to the armoire, opened it wide, seized armfuls of dresses, shoes, and hats, and threw them into the wanton cousin's open trunk. While the baron discreetly made himself scarce, the beauty rushed to the defense of her possessions. In the fracas that followed, some of the guest's toilette articles flew out the window. Marie-Athénaïs summoned the valet to fasten the trunk, had the horses hitched up, and led the cousin by the arm to the footboard of the carriage, allowing her just enough time to gather up a comb and a silver-handled mirror that had landed on the grass.

Michel recalled seeing her slap a manservant who was waiting at table with dirty hands; a moment later, though, the fellow was called back and presented with the remains of a bottle of brandy to share with his comrades in the servants' hall. The children of this Fury loved her without having any illusions about her. One fine evening when a country neighbor had been invited to the house, Baudouin, the eldest son, took the visitor's overcoat and hat from their pegs, put them on, and, slipping onto the terrace where Marie-Athénaïs had gone as usual to finish her cigar, put his arm tenderly about her waist. She didn't slap him until he'd revealed who he was.

The baroness's two eldest daughters were likewise dazzling, though their Spanish heritage wasn't so visible in them. The two younger ones, Madeleine and Claudine, were of a more rustic type. As if her name had brought her bad luck, Claudine *claudiquait* (limped). Finally, the youngest daughter—who broke the assembly-line pattern, so to speak—was still in bibs and diapers.

The baron had failed to shape his sons in his own image. The rough-mannered, good-hearted Baudouin shared none of his father's political passions—except, of course, the ones arising from the inevitable stubborn prejudices against Jews, Prot-

estants, republicans, and foreigners, on which everyone was in
agreement. A good man in all senses of the term, he would
doubtless have distinguished himself at Bouvines or, in more
recent times, in the 48th *de marche*, but his life as a country
gentleman bogged him down little by little in hunting, drinking
beer at the local tavern, and bedding farm girls, though he never
went to unpleasant extremes. The spiciness of his language was
celebrated. He was one of those men who define themselves by
telling anecdotes, so that when you try to describe him you wind
up turning a chapter into a kind of mini-anthology.

I won't give more than a sampling here of the stories that
were told and retold within the family. The count of X was a
deputy of the Right, a member of the recent and perhaps papal
nobility but one whose social standing was undisputed, and a
member of the governing boards of various mines and textile
firms. He owned an estate not far from Fées that was, as the
local newspaper put it, the jewel of the region. The count would
not have been displeased to be able to marry his daughter into
this family, whose means were modest but whose venerable
history would, as it were, reflect back on him. He invited Baudouin to call. His opulent residence had, among other luxuries,
an abbé who performed Mass in a brand-new Gothic chapel and
who was said to be teaching the son of the house his ABC's.
The abbé was not lacking in shrewdness, and the family thought
it would be wise to let him sound out the ideas, plans, and
feelings of their intended son-in-law. Baudouin and the abbé
were sitting by themselves one evening before a flask of old
cognac, which the churchman did not dole out stingily to his
guest. After a few glassfuls, the abbé thought the moment had
come to sing the praises of the young lady—to extol her education, her moral qualities, and (more discreetly) her charms.

"Oh, I don't really care, Abbé," said Baudouin, draining
his glass yet again, "so long as she's got plenty of dough . . ."

Michel thought his brother-in-law's crudeness was the affectation of a country gentleman who swears, curses, and bellows partly out of shyness and partly out of pride, to make it very clear that he is a certain kind of person and no other. He rightly saw that this man, who asked nothing more of life than what he had and took his pleasures from day to day, was something of a cynic. Moreover, Baudouin had some fine devil-may-care types in his family tree. His uncle Idesbald, an eccentric lost in the mists of the preceding generation, had lived in harmony for twenty years with a village woman. Eventually he was persuaded to make an honest woman of her. One fine morning the bells rang for the wedding. Idesbald appeared, clothed and booted as if intending to take a stroll along the muddy paths of his estate, a flower in the buttonhole of his old jacket, escorting his heart's desire, who sported a new dress made in Lille. Around the groom's left wrist was wound a triple leash, on which he was leading his three favorite dogs. At the threshold of the church, he scanned the crowd of bystanders for someone to look after Azor, Flambeau, and Duchesse, spotted an urchin he knew, and handed him the leash, which he retrieved after the ceremony.

Recalling his happy days as a midshipman in the imperial navy, the baron had sent his younger son Fernand to Borda, in part to wean him from his life of ease. Since the young man's nearsightedness precluded a military career, he fell back on the merchant marine. But the spirit of Venus that reigned at Fées followed him to Bordeaux, where his unit was stationed. Having assumed command of his first ship, and on the verge of embarking for Brazil, Fernand brought on board a "cabin boy"— a young woman who was quite convincing dressed as a man. As a result of this escapade worthy of a Shakespearean comedy, he lost his post and for a long time afterward remained in a subordinate rank. Restored to grace, he commanded a transport of troops during the First World War. He used to say that his comings and goings among the islands and reefs of the Aegean made him feel as if he were "tickling Death's tits." But Death proved to be a good-hearted girl. In 1916, in Paris, where he came to be treated for a lingering case of malaria, I often saw that gloomy, thickset fellow, with his cold—or rather closed— expression, who described the horrors of Gallipoli in an even-toned voice. He retired after the Armistice, and settled in a little town in the southwest of France with the young woman who for a long time had been the delight of his furloughs.

In the years when Michel came to Fées only in secret, he enjoyed his visits to the estate, where no one thought to resurface the façade of the house and where the baron was the only one who liked gardening; he tended the scanty flower beds with love but no taste. The house had nothing feudal about it but nevertheless was like a fortified castle whose inhabitants were constantly repelling attackers. A telescope was mounted on the veranda; when the carriage of some tiresome acquaintance was spotted at the far end of the lane, everyone scattered until the intruder had left his or her calling card and departed. And it was fortunate if the inconvenient visitor didn't hear insulting remarks coming from behind a door or laughter erupting from the depths of a closet. Mornings were devoted to exercising the horses destined for Henri V; in the evening the family played innocent games. When it was a question of finding some hidden object, the baroness inevitably won: "someone," she maintained, always guided her unerringly toward it. She told fortunes with cards, and cheated expertly when she had to foil some scheme on the part of her opponents.

In London Michel had enthusiastically attended a number of displays of hypnotism. One evening when the famous Pittman was performing on the stage of a large music hall, the hypnotist, as usual, called for volunteers from the audience. Michel saw that powerful gaze come to rest on him and mounted the steps to the stage with an almost mechanical tread. But what followed was a duel. The young man was on the verge of yielding to that incomprehensible force; he wanted to give in, but resisted despite himself, returning every fixed gaze the man trained on him. He claimed that never until that evening had he so well understood the magical force of eyes, which not only refract light and reflect objects but attest to the secret powers of the soul, which reveal themselves nowhere else. For ten minutes Pittman kept at it, then dismissed the unknown fellow with a gesture.

"Unsatisfactory subject. Is there another volunteer . . . ?"

Afterward, Michel found out that he, too, had some talent for sorcery. During the family's evening sessions at Fées, he hypnotized everyone except the baron, who never participated. Marie-Athénaïs refused to believe that she had succumbed. To prove it to her, Michel hypnotized her again and forced her to remove her sixteen-button boots and her woolen stockings. When she came to, the scarcely prudish baroness, embarrassed at the sight of her bare feet, fled from the room with cries of dismay.

It seems that the powers inherited from Sacromonte also allowed Marie-Athénaïs to see ghosts. At night, wandering about the grounds of the estate, she several times encountered two specters. Phantoms of the past, as she believed, or phantoms of the future, as I now think more probable? Whatever the case may be, those two ghosts strolling arm in arm down the lane, revenants who might well have inspired fear, only made people smile, just as the baron's genealogies (though these were authentic) likewise made people smile. Most people's imaginations refuse to be led that far.

Nevertheless, it was at Monte Carlo, where in 1889 Michel and Berthe rented a small villa, that the baroness gave the most

The château of Fées, home of Baron Loys de L. and his family

impressive demonstration of her clairvoyance. She had come there for several weeks to visit her son-in-law and eldest daughter. Gabrielle, her second daughter, was causing her serious concern at the time. The young woman was about to divorce her husband, a rich and stingy man from Lille who owned some celebrated hothouses and who preferred flowers to women. Like her sister, Gabrielle was beautiful, athletic, elegant, and fond of living in style. She had no use for a husband who spent on heating fuel the money she wanted to spend on clothes. The news of the divorce cast a pall over Fées. The baron never mentioned it; Marie-Athénaïs, who viewed love's whims with indulgence, was nonetheless a devout Catholic who was scandalized by divorce, a form of rebellion that was completely new in those days. Whether Gabrielle was unfaithful to her husband was relatively unimportant, but that Monsieur M. (I've changed the initial) and his wife should cease living together and using the same name outraged this mother, who was to end her days wearing the robes of a Franciscan tertiary. Marie-Athénaïs thought of Gabrielle with a mixture of anguish and exasperation.

Toward one o'clock in the morning, in the villa at Monte Carlo, Berthe and Michel were sleeping in their room on the second floor. Marie-Athénaïs was on the third floor, directly above them. The couple were awakened by a creaking on the stairs. Before Michel could light a candle, a pale gleam appeared under the door. The door opened, and the baroness appeared in her long white nightdress, holding a candlestick on which a small flame was flickering. Michel thought of Lady Macbeth. The sleepwalker sat on the foot of the bed and declared in a hollow voice:

"Gabrielle is very sick. I must return home to take care of her."

"You're dreaming, Baroness. Go back upstairs to bed."

Slowly, without seeming to have heard him, she rose and

went toward the door. The mirrored armoire and the looking glass over the fireplace reflected her tall figure and the light from her candle. She carefully closed the door of the room behind her; again Michel and Berthe heard creaking on the stairs. Then, just above them, came the sound of something heavy being dragged gratingly across the floor; they heard water being poured into a basin and, shortly afterward, emptied all at once into the refuse pail. Then silence. Berthe and Michel decided to go back to sleep. At dawn he went up to the third floor; everything seemed calm. Marie-Athénaïs' door was wide open. Her trunk was half packed and standing in the middle of the room, surrounded by various objects; the refuse pail was full of soapy water. On the bed, which had been hastily made and covered with its quilt, Marie-Athénaïs was sleeping, fully clothed and holding her umbrella in her hands. While they were all at breakfast that morning, a message arrived informing them that Gabrielle had come down with typhoid fever.

The anecdote would be more striking if the young woman had died. She did no such thing. Restored to health and freedom, the blond Gabrielle rejoined Berthe and her brother-in-law, either in the wake of her recent divorce or in anticipation of it. Ten years later the two sisters would die within four days of each other.

Like the seven-year period Michel spent with Maud, this new phase in his life, which lasted thirteen years (fifteen if we begin counting from the wedding in Tournai), is familiar to me only from Michel's own accounts. He provided abundant details on certain points, but left enormous gaps, and never supplied motives or dates for those incidents and sudden changes, so that the life he recounted in this way appears to lack intention and to resist any inquiry into original causes. In a sense, this impression is correct. Those years seem to have dissipated at random like the water of a stream that sometimes flows swiftly and brightly and sometimes lies stagnant, here and there forming ponds and swamps, and everywhere being absorbed into the earth.

We could explain his exile in England, if we had to, by referring to his submission to a demanding love, his desire to flee far from his family, or simply the attractions of English life, which are so powerful once you come to know them. During the period that follows, in contrast, Michel is merely idling, like an engine in neutral. To begin with, the marriage that he made to please his father has not given him a fixed residence; neither is there any question of his "founding a family," to the extent that this expression (which implies the existence of a solid social edifice, or one that still believes itself so) means anything to him. There is no possibility that he will establish himself in any profession or useful employment. And activities of the mind, which will occupy such an important place in Michel's late-middle years and old age, have no appeal at this point. For a whole ten years Michel, Berthe, and Gabrielle seem to be gliding on a skating rink in time to fashionable waltzes, under lighting that evokes scenes by Toulouse-Lautrec. From Ostend to Scheveningen, from Bad Homburg to Wiesbaden and the wedding-cake façades of Monte Carlo, they do not miss a single public dance, a single flower festival, a single performance by a Parisian theater company in a resort town, a single gala dinner, a single one of those horse shows in which Berthe and Gabrielle often win prizes for their equestrian skill, or (above all) a single one of those evening parties, graced by chandeliers and croupiers, where one has the pleasure of sitting next to the Prince of Wales as he bets on his favorite number and watching Felix Krull play banker at baccarat.

At least until the still far-off and perhaps already gloomy day when the glacial beauty of a winter in Ukraine will penetrate Michel like a sharp knife, the landscapes that have served as backdrops for these escapades have left no traces in his memory. For the two sisters, living abroad seems to be nothing but a long string of pleasantries on the clumsiness of the local people, the women's clothes, and the outlandishness of the food and other customs. They trot out all the relevant clichés they've picked up in small theaters and cabarets ("There's no such thing in Germany"). The annual cruises in their two sailboats, first the *Péri* and then the *Banshee*, are always an occasion for reveling in the water and air out on the open sea, but the trio seem to have been oblivious to the wild beauty of the Dutch, German, and Danish islands, a seasonal refuge for birds, or to the old-fashioned charm of the antiquated little ports of Friesland. One Sunday the three inseparable companions, whom Baudouin has joined this year, disembark at Leeuwarden. Berthe and Gabrielle immediately take pleasure in shocking the locals, whether by wearing frilly Parisian gowns and padding out their figures to exaggerated proportions or, at the opposite extreme, by pretending to be sailors' wives and going about in slovenly disarray. On this particular day a collection is being taken up on behalf of a rest home for old seafarers. They are asked to participate in this charity. Baudouin persuades or challenges his brother-in-law to stand with him on either side of the main door of the Protestant church during the service, holding a chamber pot; he's sure that this clownishness will make the good Dutch people laugh and will loosen their purse strings. And indeed, copper sous and even some florins fill the two receptacles to the brim. Other times, Baudouin's challenges are gastronomic. On one occasion each gentleman does his best to consume his share of an omelette made of thirty eggs, and the contest is held to the applause of the captain of their boat, a deckhand, a ship's boy, a band of rustics, and the two ladies.

In the shady world of casinos, where those who gamble from idleness and those who gamble from vice gather seasonally around tables that are always green, hierarchies are established: society people recognize and bow to one another in the crowd. But under that artificial light the most authentic coats of arms are worth scarcely more than cotillion accessories; gold turns to brass and diamonds to rhinestones. Berthe and Gabrielle know every single piece of diamond jewelry, whether real or fake, that the other women own. They've seen them sparkle at

Bad Homburg; they will see them again at Monte Carlo, sometimes on other wrists and throats. The regulars at the Hôtel de
Paris and the private room at the casino form an aristocracy in
this throng of many castes. The women engage in a kind of war
of dresses, but the legitimate ladies are forced to surrender in
the face of that showy variety of kept woman, the grand courtesan, who is maintained by princes and presidents. One evening La Belle Otero fought a battle with Emilienne d'Alençon;
each was trying to prove that in the course of her career she
had amassed more jewels than her competitor. The ample Otero
sailed majestically amid the gaming tables, rings on every finger,
bracelets stacked from wrist to shoulder, necklaces clinking on
her pink breast; and the small bit of bust that remained under
her low-cut bodice was covered so thickly with brooches that it
was impossible to see the fabric. Since she couldn't very well
wear diamonds on her backside, her chambermaid accompanied
her, in a high-necked dress and a little lace apron, decked out
with all the diamonds that Madame couldn't manage to wear.

The spice of this life consists of the whims of chance, the
delays in the mail, the pangs that come every week or every
trimester and that precede the arrival of the sealed envelope
from the notary. "Fluctuations" at the gaming table sometimes
have the effect of a ride on a roller coaster. Berthe and Gabrielle
may have to sell their evening gowns to the dress vendor, but
will order new ones, or retrieve the former ones, when pockets
and reticules are once again full. In Wiesbaden, on a day when
they are flat broke, the trio decide to pull off one great coup.
The two ladies, before returning to France, sew numerous little
packets beneath the flounces of their dresses; the packets contain a white powder that is worth its weight in gold on the other
side of the border. Michel's heart beats wildly all night.

When it comes time to determine how to get rid of the

magic powder, they consult three ancient sisters living in Lille (but perhaps originally from Douai or Armentières), who take care of the entire business.

These Buzzards, prosaic Fates who pull the strings of a fair number of schemes and who sever them if necessary, are three old women, of whom at least one was married back in the dim dark past. They began quite innocently. Former housemaids, they got their start on one of the beaches in the north of France, where they sold cheap toys, ships in glass bottles, bathing caps, and postcards. Now they own a small luxury-goods shop in Ostend and another in Monte Carlo, and have invested money in a third, similar business in Wiesbaden. They rent rooms above their shops. I suspect that formerly, in their spare moments, they sometimes devoted themselves to the profitable business that around the same time was enriching Bernard Shaw's Mrs. Warren, and that they, like their English model, sensibly calculated the advantages and disadvantages of the profession. They migrate annually from one shop to another, traveling third class at night to save on the cost of a hotel room; or, if they decide to splurge on one, they make do with a single bed and sleep crosswise on the mattress, their legs and feet resting on three chairs placed side by side. As ugly as sin, they are frugal, temperate, honest in their own way, and utterly unscrupulous. They are also unhypocritical. "You see, sir," the most talkative of the three old ladies once said to Michel, "to make a living, you have to work for the gullet or for the crotch. That's all there is." In their company Michel gets a whiff of the atmosphere of the shady shop in Liverpool, but transformed by the keen lucidity characteristic of French peasants. As the need arises, they also lend him money, which he repays tenfold.

Some of the schemes that the three old women devise are almost innocent, apparently engineered for love of the art, since they could hardly bring much of a return. But no profit is too small for the Buzzards. One trick is to fill a box with fine lingerie, each piece carefully wrapped in tissue paper, and deliver it to the people occupying the best room at the best hotel. Madame, who hasn't purchased anything from the store in question, tells the concierge there's been a mistake. One of the old women, forewarned, goes up to the room to make apologies (the concierge is in on the scheme) and takes advantage of the opportunity to extol the merchandise. It's rare that the contents of the box, in whole or in part, do not remain with the supposed client. The Buzzards have quickly perceived that Gabrielle, who is young and pretty and marvelously adept at playing a dressmaker's apprentice down on her luck, is more successful than they are with the ladies, and sometimes also with the gentlemen who control the purchases of these ladies. Gabrielle lets stray locks of hair hang down the back of her neck, adopts a drawling mode of speech that is as loose as her hair, and pretends to be a weary seamstress whom the Buzzards are overworking and who moreover has been deserted by her lover. Nothing is missing, not even the pins in the bodice and the badly applied makeup. To persuade the clients, she agrees to try on the filmy peignoirs and the finely pleated shifts, on which the Buzzards give her a commission. And if perchance that very evening she dines at a restaurant with Madame X, whom Michel and Berthe have just met, Gabrielle—beautifully powdered, coiffed, and corseted, attired in a low-cut gown, and wearing on her fingers, neck, and ears the remaining diamonds from the amateur horticulturist of Lille—looks so different that at the very most Madame X finds that her elegant and aristocratic acquaintance reminds her of someone, but for the life of her she can't think whom.

This man who has always preferred to live with women and for women has few male friends. Except for some ecclesiastics with whom he will become close and who are something between confidants and mentors, every man who penetrates his life seems to him an intruder or a rival. Salignac de Fénelon, at Versailles, was a comrade more than a friend, and Rolf was little more than a nuisance. It's curious that the principal (and last) exception to this deliberate rejection of the male presence was again a Hungarian; but the son of the humble Jewish restaurant-owner exiled to London had nothing in common with the sumptuous Magyar who now joins the inseparable threesome.

The baron of Galay (I've invented this name) used to be one of the dashing young men of Budapest society; prominent at the court of Vienna, he is said to have worn the uniform of a regiment of hussars and to have fought his share of saber duels. This conventional reputation was long ago replaced by a more satanic legend: Galay the gambler. He stakes his money with the same élan that his forebears displayed when attacking a company of Janissaries. He's been seen in every gambling den and casino in Europe, his pockets stuffed with gold and bank notes, tossing crumpled bills to the doormen who summon carriages for him, not at all out of ostentation and scarcely out of generosity but because he prefers the louis to paper money, which always looks dirty to him. People have also seen him lose at a single stroke the equivalent of one or two small farms in the Carpathians. He is not known to have any vices but this one, which must have devoured all the others, if he ever had any. This man who knows how to drink like a Hungarian and a gentleman is never drunk; and he's the ultimate cavalier, who treats society women and prostitutes with the same ceremonial scorn. Michel admires his casualness, that of the great lord and the wicked man, but a basic decency prevents him from emulating the baron. At Baden a German woman, a châtelaine of the vicinity and a lady devoted to good works, learned that Galay, whom she knew slightly, had broken the bank the day before. She said to herself that now was the time to persuade him to donate money to a school or a hospital. She came to the Grand Hotel and asked to see him; the baron's servant let her into his master's little drawing room. Monsieur was sleeping, drinking his coffee, taking a bath, but if Madame would care to wait . . . A furious voice burst out in Hungarian on the other side of the wall. Suddenly a door opened and Galay entered, dripping water and completely nude; he bowed and kissed the hand of the *gnädige Frau* from Germany: "How may I be of service to you, gracious lady?" She fled with all possible speed.

These two men who enjoy alienating people quickly establish a bond. Galay's way of life, centered on a single passion and completely detached from everything else, floating in midair, cannot but enchant Michel. For his part, the Hungarian sees that the Frenchman has a bit of his own violence and perhaps also some of his fondness for solitude. They form a tacit alliance. At the gaming table, one bails out the other in the event of losses. They also share a love for horses. Galay scorns those that are trained to compete in the ring, but the inseparable threesome travel with their own mounts. One day, in a German railway station, a shipping employee refuses to let the three animals ride in a car attached to the train in which Michel himself is going to be a passenger. The hotheaded young man seizes the fellow by the collar, drags him over the counter, and hurls him to the floor. Galay sometimes accompanies Michel and one or the other of the women on horseback rides along forest trails or on the beaches. The two sisters find him extremely attractive, but Berthe's equestrian feats evoke nothing from him but cold disdain.

"Madame, the Empress of Austria behaves badly on horseback. She's beautiful, everyone says. And everyone says she rides well. In England one can scarcely find an escort for her who is as bold as she is on the obstacle course. Don't imitate her. A woman has no right to risk the life of a man, or that of a horse, because she feels like breaking her own neck."

Berthe is incensed, all the more so since Michel agrees with the Hungarian; but she allows this sharp-voiced man to say things to her that she would never tolerate from anyone else.

One fine October day, Michel confesses to his friend that he's completely broke for the current four months, and that furthermore he owes the moneylenders his income for the trimester to come. Never mind: Galay has an estate in Ukraine that he inherited from his mother's family and that by some fluke he hasn't yet sold. Next to the main house is a stud farm run by an Englishman, a former jockey whom the Hungarian feels he can no longer trust. The trio can stay there for a few months until Michel has shored up his finances. Galay himself will join them at the end of the winter, during his annual round of visits to relatives who he still hopes will leave him some money. (He boasts that he's already consumed the fortunes of two of his aunts.) This exciting plan enchants Michel and the two sisters. The three of them embark on an interminable train ride through a rainy Germany and an already frozen Poland. In Ukraine, where the cars are heated by wood stoves, at every stop a cloud of snow swirls in through the half-open doors. Muzhiks, who appear to Michel as if they've just stepped out of a novel by Tolstoy, help keep the tracks clear.

In Kiev, where they spend several days in one of those luxurious little French-style hotels (which were usually run by the former majordomo of some grand duke and which were common in Russia in those days), the travelers are completely won over. The two women come out now and then with remarks about the locals—pleasantries they've gleaned from little Paris newspapers; but life has changed its pattern and no longer trips along in time to the popular tunes of the cabarets. In these glimpses of Russia, Michel sees an ancient Christian world that here burns like a lamp but that in western Europe has been extinguished for centuries. He's also touching the fringes of Asia. Like a swimmer going with the tide, he yields to the powerful waves of the religious chants. Feeling as if he's rediscovering forgotten gestures and modes of life, he gazes at the pilgrims who kiss the ground before the icons, cross themselves while murmuring unintelligibly, press their lips, weeping, to those faces painted on gold backgrounds or to the thin mummified hands of saints displayed in the cathedral's crypts, before whom the faithful file by, just as one day their children will file by the embalmed corpse of Lenin. Michel never wearies of those great gilded domes, apparently dilated by the warmth of prayer, swollen like captive balloons or elongated like breasts. Heavily laden carts cross the river on its thick ice; at the market held on its banks, he watches a merchant hawking his wares, holding up his stiffly frozen fish, and a milk seller who slices a white block with blows of his ax. He will never forget the opulent beauty of the Jewish women, or the luxurious appearance of the ladies dressed in European-style clothes, riding in their sleighs driven by coachmen in fur hats. For the first and only time during those long years, he seems to have noticed and retained more of the world than merely fashionable beaches and gambling halls.

Galay's estate, a few versts from Kiev, likewise has its enchantments and surprises. Except for the horses, which are well cared for, everything is dirty; the French threesome discover the weight of Russian inertia. They take up residence in the comparatively sumptuous apartments of the owner (sabers, divans, Turkish carpets) on the second floor of a sort of long *isba*, whose caretaker occupies the other wing. This scoundrel is polite and reserved. Michel is sure that the veterinarian who has come from Kiev is working hand-in-glove with the former jockey to steal foals that they will sell on the sly to farmers in the vicinity; the Englishman cheats the peasants who sell him their oats and swindles the master in his absence. But the scheming of the locals and the impossibility of getting any information from the servants, whose language he doesn't even understand, prevents Michel from making an investigation, which in any case would lead nowhere. Besides, the jockey, who lived for many years in Chantilly, is an amusing fellow. The brief daylight hours are spent exercising the horses in the open fields, whose size makes even the most enormous of the great cornfields in northern France seem insignificant. In the evening, in the huge empty rooms where the candles flicker in the drafts, the caretaker's son strums away on a guitar. The former jockey engages Michel in artfully played games of écarté.

People eat succulent and heavy foods, to which the steward's wife occasionally adds a British dish, assuaging Michel's eternal nostalgia for England. At night, when going to the privy, they stumble over the servants lying on the floor and snoring in the corridors. The French guests try the saunas but soon leave, repelled by the hot steam, the gloomy half-light, the reddened bodies of the men and women who lash themselves with birch switches, and the hissing of the cold water on the white-hot stones. The wretchedness of the few *isbas* they happen to enter frightens them; the vermin-invested peasants are scarcely human. (Michel would perhaps soften his judgment if he had clearer memories of the slums of London and the squalid basements of Lille.) The isolation and monotony of this life oppress the two women, who can console themselves only by paying occasional visits to the shops in Kiev.

When Galay arrives, everything changes. The Hungarian is at home in all the pleasure spots in the town; he turns the nights into revels filled with gypsy music. The gypsies themselves—prophetic people who nevertheless have no inkling that in about fifty years they will be engulfed in the crematoria—sing and dance for the rich landowners, who likewise have no inkling that their children will end up as taxi drivers in Paris or working in the mines. Playing poker with country neighbors takes the place of roulette.

At first I thought that the sojourn in Ukraine had immediately preceded that of Galay and his guests in Budapest. But Michel's chronology was vague. Nothing proves that the two episodes weren't separated by a few months in western Europe. The visit to Hungary was in any case brief. Galay and his guests stayed for some days on the immense plain, in an isolated mansion that the baron was trying to sell.

He had arranged a meeting there with an estate buyer. On

the appointed day, a carriage arrived from the station bringing a thin, shabby Jew whose manner was excessively courteous. One might have called him servile, if a kind of tranquil detachment hadn't been visible beneath the deference. Kaunitz (I've borrowed this name from an unjustly neglected novel by Stefan Zweig that contains a character of the same human type) took a tour of the house, the outbuildings, and the grounds, guided by the baron, who, in a sort of carefully orchestrated duet, set his dry and lordly politeness in counterpoint to the somewhat honeyed politeness of the buyer. Galay expected to be cheated. He doubtless was, but no more than any seller would have been by any buyer in an analogous situation. He was even cheated a bit less.

The Jew pointed out that the seller in such a case would do better if he sold everything separately and over a longer period of time. He would thus realize a greater profit from the silver, the paintings, and the antique furniture that adorned the house he was giving up. But the baron wouldn't listen to such advice. He wanted to sell everything all at once, and for cash. The sum that Kaunitz offered reflected these circumstances: it wasn't derisory, but it was low, and the dealer was the first to acknowledge this. The transaction concluded, Galay accompanied his visitor to the main gate. But the Jew couldn't help feeling a sort of hesitation before this man who was ruining himself; or perhaps, as the heir to an ancient tradition, he felt misgivings before this nobleman who was sacrificing his own tradition in every knickknack and portrait.

"All the same, Monsieur de Galay, if there's something in this house you're attached to—a family portrait, a clock, any object whatsoever . . . Without making the slightest adjustment in the price we've agreed on, I'd be happy to . . ."

"That will do, Monsieur Kaunitz," said Galay, bending over a flower bed and picking a carnation for his buttonhole.

To Michel, that gesture was the height of elegance. The timid proposition of the dealer also had its price.

If what I am writing here were a novel, I could easily imagine a certain coolness developing between the Hungarian and his French friends following these sojourns in eastern Europe, whether because the supposedly misogynistic baron was too attractive to one of the women, or to both of them, or at least had tried too hard to be attractive; or because, on the contrary, his arrogance offended them; or because those two equally violent men insulted each other for no good reason. It's more likely that the pride of the French threesome was wounded. In the pleasure spots of western Europe, Galay was their equal; here, whatever they might do, they were under obligation to a prince, even if a ruined one.

In any case, they returned to France alone. It seems that Galay, as he was tending to do more and more frequently, went to pursue his vice in one of the little casinos on the Dalmatian coast. A few months earlier, finding himself with Michel in Abbazia, he had taken Michel to a deserted spot on the shore to admire a rocky spur looking out over the sea. "The currents in this spot lead to the open ocean. If a man shot himself here and fell into the water, his body would never be found." Michel always wanted to believe that the Hungarian had come to his end in this way, perhaps because this would have been one of the possible exits for him as well.

But in Vienna the three travelers were once again short of money, all the more so since Michel hadn't wanted to be indebted to Galay for champagne and gypsy girls. They decided to head back west in the wake of a circus, in which they performed an act displaying their skill at dressage and helped out with the care of the horses. According to Michel it was their straitened circumstances that motivated this decision. I imagine, though, that other attractions had something to do with it: the sawdust, the red velvet seats, the chestnut horses flourishing their tails in time to the band's fanfares, the odor of sweat and of wild animals. Renoir, Degas, and Manet had loved those things, too.

Is that all? No one is more aware of the inanity of the foregoing pages than I am. It's possible that the distance separating me from those people, and the age I've reached at the time I'm writing this, have made me prone to forget the elements of gaiety, boldness, physical and carnal pleasure, unfettered caprice, and simple joie de vivre that were blended with all that commotion and tawdriness. Still, the fact remains that almost nothing of the Michel I would come to know some twenty years later was discernible in the Michel of those reckless years. The older one, nevertheless, was born of the younger one.

Indeed, it seems as if the greatest obstacle to complete truth here is propriety, which is not always located where one expects. Just as Proust's Swann would have found it indecent to speak of himself, except in passing or with a touch of the comic, and would have carefully denied himself a favorable part in his own story, Michel sometimes described almost picaresque episodes in his life or mentioned his role in unusual or curious circumstances that he, as a lover of the world's theater, took pleasure in recounting, but he never thought of depicting himself or explaining his actions at length. Whatever he felt, thought, suffered, or loved stayed deep within him. Those thirteen years were a stage nearly empty of supporting players, and we have no way of knowing what went on behind the scenes. I imagine that Michel read Saint-Simon or the cardinal de Retz while the women read Willy, or that he entrusted Berthe and her sister to Galay for an evening at the Olympia, so that he himself could go see Lugné-Poë in *Hedda Gabler*, which was of no interest to the women. But he never said so. Even less did he try to define his relations with Berthe and Gabrielle or explore the reasons for his infatuation with Galay. People who keep company with one another for a long time almost always end up taking all the possible configurations they can with respect to one another, like dancers in a quadrille. To use a metaphor that is less ambitious than one might think (since we're all made of the same matter as the heavenly bodies), such beings, as they move through time, invert their positions like the stars that revolve around Polaris during the night; or, like the constellations of the Zodiac, they appear to glide along an ecliptic that exists only in relation to ourselves, and are isolated or grouped otherwise than we imagine. But the course of the stars (or at least their apparent course) can be plotted in advance by an astronomer or astrologer, whereas even after the fact, nothing allows us to draw a map of the changes that must have taken place in the relations among those people during that period of their life.

Michel clearly reveals a taste for low company, or at least the habit of finding pleasure in circumstances that were beneath him, perhaps because he thought, rightly or wrongly, that hypocrisy was less prevalent there than anywhere else. Lowlife, too, has its poses and affectations, but Michel never became involved in it deeply enough to recognize them; he was by nature one of those people who never become deeply involved in anything. We must take into account the innocence of a man who is sure that nothing dubious can touch him or the people he has gathered into his immediate orbit. Even when his illusions are shattered, he will be somewhat naïvely surprised. He told me once that he had lived for a fairly long time with a woman whom he thought immune to the usual rogueries of loose-living people. "Of course, we went to gambling halls. Once there, we would always separate, so as not to bring bad luck to each other. At the end of the evening she would rejoin me, her reticule filled with the louis she had won. She won without fail. Later, I learned that she would leave the casino and go to a nearby hotel with an unknown man, who paid her. All women are liars," he would add, unwisely generalizing, as he usually did, "and there's no way of reading this in their eyes."

He spoke of Berthe and Gabrielle only when they figured in one of the anecdotes I've recounted above. He mentioned their innate elegance (he was sparing with the word "beauty"), their graceful walk, their skill as horsewomen. Nothing more. Yet on the subject of my mother, whom he might have been more inclined to speak of in my presence, Michel was almost as unforthcoming. It was not his way to speak nostalgically of the dead. There was only one woman, someone he would love and lose in my childhood, of whom he retained an unforgettable image—one that would impress itself upon me as a model for life. But we haven't yet gotten to that point.

I would be wrong if, perhaps out of a novelist's unconscious desire to enliven a subject, I were to describe the behavior of that pre-1900 Michel so as to bring out whatever elements of worry or gloom it may have expressed. At first glance there seem to be no such emotions in that pleasure-seeking man. Yet certain signs point in this direction. His enthusiasm for the Russia he glimpsed on his travels, analogous to the overwhelming feeling Rilke had while visiting Slavic lands a few years later, seems to bespeak an unfulfilled yearning that he himself perceived only when separated from the ordinary sites of his everyday routines. A stronger indication can be seen in the names he gave the sailboats that satisfied his need for outings on the sea. The first name, *Péri*, seems to have been inspired by nothing more than the artificial Orientalism of the musicians of those days, of a Massenet or a Léo Delibes, or perhaps an ode by the young Hugo, just as the name of the boat he later bought for my mother—*Valkyrie*—evokes only the contemporary vogue for Wagner. But *Banshee*, the name of his second boat, which took him sailing on the North Sea with Berthe and Gabrielle, leads the mind on more interesting journeys. In England Michel had surely heard people speak of those fairies the Irish believe in —fairies that, like ghostly old women, weep on the doorsteps of houses in which someone is about to die. It's strange, to say the least, that he should have named a pleasure boat, a frail and always endangered thing, after one of those mournful heralds.

But of all those slight indications, the most irrefutable are inevitably the photographs. I have only two from those years. They serve as antidotes to a particular ingredient in Belle Epoque elegance, something that is spicy and coarse and that betrays itself disagreeably in the women of Colette's early novels and the artificial young girls of Proust, in the studied romantic air of the princesse de Guermantes and the dry facetiousness of her cousin Oriane. Michel, Berthe, and Gabrielle, that impetuous threesome, must have more or less let the winds of their times blow over them, but photographs reveal no traces of this. I have no pictures of Gabrielle; her charm and her gaiety have vanished. There exists a photo of Berthe taken when she was about thirty. In her high-necked dress, which fits her body like a smooth skin, this slim, erect woman reminds us less of a houri of 1890 than of the queens carved on church portals. Her beautiful firm hands are the ones that hold the reins so

Berthe de L., Michel's first wife, ca. 1890

Michel in 1890, at the age of thirty-seven

well; her hair, crimped according to the current fashion, frames her face, in which the dark eyes look straight ahead, or perhaps see nothing, but only dream; the mouth, soft as a rose, gives no hint of a smile. The photo marked on the back *Michel at the age of thirty-seven* is also a surprise. Though he looks very young, he does not give the impression of vigor and alacrity that will characterize his portraits as an older man; he's still at that uncertain stage, showing the weakness that in so many young people mysteriously precedes and paves the way for force. Neither is it the portrait of the assiduous pleasure-seeker who liked to frolic at fashionable resorts. The eyes are dreamy; the long-fingered hand adorned with a signet ring negligently holds a cigarette and likewise seems to daydream. An inexplicable melancholy and hesitancy emanate from that face and body. It's the portrait of a Saint-Loup in the days when he was still troubled about Rachel, or about Monsieur d'Amercoeur.

I thought I hadn't seen anything Michel had written in those years that could tell us something about him. I was mistaken. Perhaps even before his marriage to Berthe, he had had six letters tattooed on the inside of his left arm: 'ΑΝΆΓΚΗ—Fate, Necessity.

That he should have chosen this word is almost as surprising as the tattoo itself. At least at the time I knew him, the classical notion of Fate had no echo in my father, any more than the vague popular notion that is subsumed in the same term. His own life seems rather to have been dominated by Luck, the god of the gambler, with all that this implies for inconsistency and accident. Moreover, this dull, sad word is ill-suited to the temperament of a man so eager to take pleasure in the passing moment. Everything I saw proves that within Michel there existed a happiness that was, so to speak, innate and that persisted even in moments when anguish and distress clearly submerged it, just as one senses in a flooded land the firm ground beneath the temporary incursion of the water. Did despair nevertheless seep into the spaces underground? The profound detachment, the calm disillusionment of the aged Michel could persuade us of this, and, if necessary, could be explained by it.

But if that's the case, at what date and for what reasons did he feel the inevitable weighing on him? Fate, 'ANÁГKH. One could imagine that the student in Lille or Louvain, after reading *Notre-Dame de Paris* and inventing in advance a tragic destiny for himself, had had his arm tattooed with those six letters so dear to the heart of Claude Frollo. George du Maurier, at about the same time, created the semiautobiographical character Peter Ibbetson, who is haunted by the gloomy Greek word that Hugo put in the mouth of his evil priest. But aside from the fact that around 1873 tattoos were reserved primarily for sailors and hardened criminals, and were probably found on very few students, this overly simple explanation explains nothing. Michel, who loved the great poems of Hugo and would love them even more in his later years (in his youth he preferred Musset), nevertheless disdained his novels to the point of injustice. Furthermore, if he had acted merely on a student whim, he would have readily and smilingly admitted this. He did nothing of the sort. Besides, I never asked him the meaning he attached to those six vaguely menacing letters. Our openness with each other had its limits. For him, the word evidently belonged to a domain of emotions that were over and done with, perhaps, but still private—a domain that it would have been both unwise and indiscreet to try to enter.

It's conceivable that he had the word tattooed on him during his second tour of duty with the Seventh Cuirassiers, in Versailles, at the point when, returning voluntarily to his regiment and accepting even the loss of his stripes in order to be readmitted to the army, he soon realized that he couldn't do without Maud and that he would forsake everything once again to find her. But I don't know whether there were any tattoo artists near the barracks in Versailles, or whether this type of ornament may have been one of those that the ground troops scornfully left to the navy.

Or Michel may have had it done at a later date in a sailors' bar in Liverpool, or even later, in the back of a tavern on the docks of Amsterdam in the days when the *Banshee* was taking him with Berthe and Gabrielle out on the North Sea. One can imagine him carefully writing those Greek letters on a piece of paper, to make a pattern for the artisan, and holding out his left arm. Ananké . . . There where a simple man would put a tattoo of a flower, a bird, a tricolor flag, a temporarily cherished name, or a pleasing feminine form, Michel had chosen to put those six letters that look like a convict's prison number. We would know him better if we knew what judgment on his own life they represented. But this isn't a novel. 'ANÁΓKH: Fate.

The episode of the touring circus would make a good finale for those thirteen years. It clearly belongs to the last stage of Michel's life with Berthe, but I have no firm evidence to show whether the flamboyant return from central Europe took place in 1899, which was disastrous for the trio, or two or three years earlier. Rarely does life announce catastrophes with a flourish of fife and drum.

In any case, Ostend, which played such an important role in this man's destiny, became a temporary residence for him. In 1889, after his amnesty, still avoiding Lille and Mont-Noir, he was persuaded to settle at Fées. But perhaps Gabrielle was less warmly received there after her divorce, and Berthe and Michel, who approved of her action, felt less welcome there. This is purely conjecture. It would be simpler to suppose that the charm of Fées diminished with time. After 1894, Michel, well versed now in the army's regulations, informed the military authorities that he was once again living abroad. He chose to live in Ostend, where he rented an apartment on the rue de Russie. He spent little time there. But at least this supposedly fixed domicile offered two attractions: gambling and the sea.

I don't know whether the threesome spent the entire winter of 1899 there, or whether it was during the preceding summer that Michel had a run of good luck at the gaming tables and indulged in some nautical excursions, either on the *Banshee*, if he still had it, or on trawlers. He often invited along Henry Arthur Jones, a mediocre English playwright who was very popular in those days and with whom he engaged in intoxicating reminiscences of London. He must also have sometimes gone from Ostend to Lille, where moneylenders willingly agreed to make loans that he could pay back on his mother's death (the high life made such transactions necessary). It was during one or the other of those two years that Berthe, seized with a dizzy spell while strolling on the beach, asked permission to sit on the front steps of a villa set apart on the dunes. There they struck up a friendship with its owner, Baroness V., an amiable old lady who was fond of music and books and who often invited the trio to accompany her on delightful excursions by landau into the countryside. The worldly parade on the seaside walk was particularly splendid at the height of the season, when the smart set from abroad blended with society people, financiers, and beautiful women from Leopold II's entourage. Berthe and Gabrielle would join the display at the fashionable times of day in their delicate white dresses, their scarves and skirts billowing in the sea breeze, their wide straw hats held on with raised arms that looked for all the world like pitcher handles. The two sisters enjoyed dressing alike, the only difference in their outfits being the colors of their belts and the stones in their buckles, rings, or brooches. One might wear a ruby, the other an emerald. It was in the apartment on the rue de Russie that Berthe would die on October 22, 1899, and that Gabrielle would follow four days later. They were, respectively, thirty-eight and thirty-three years old.

With the exception of two or three fairly insignificant remarks, which will appear further on, Michel never said anything to me about that grief-filled week. In a passage of my half brother's memoirs, published after his death in the *Notebooks* that his son brought out over the course of a year or two for the benefit of the family and a few friends, he says that Berthe and Gabrielle died in the aftermath of a "minor surgical procedure." Nothing indicates whether Michel knew about, much less approved, what seems from this distance to have been an unwise intervention, or whether he found himself suddenly confronted with the irreparable. The "season" had been over with for quite some time; perhaps they had stayed so late in Ostend because of Michel's fondness for the autumn breezes. We can thus imagine the atmosphere in which the death of the two sisters took place: in the background was a bitter wind gusting over a turbulent sea. Of course, those people who "knew everyone" in that fashionable vacation spot did not have any real friends. Only Baroness V., who liked to stay on into the off-season in her villa on the dunes, doubtless was present more or less intimately when the women died. I like to think she gave all the help she could to that desolate man, whose life she shortly afterward tried to rebuild by introducing him to Fernande de C. de M., who would become my mother.

In my mind's eye I see Michel as he comes and goes between the rooms in which Berthe and Gabrielle are dying separately; after the long years the sisters have spent together, they're being denied the poor comfort of caring for each other. The wife of a certain Dr. Hirsch, the cause of this disaster, seems to have served as nurse, perhaps to cover the traces of negligence on the part of the doctor, perhaps for the sake of the gratuities she could earn from her vigils by the bedside of the two dying women. Apparently some valuable objects disappeared, doubtless rings or earrings that had been left on dressing tables.

"Your mother didn't receive the care that a woman in her

condition should have received," I heard Michel say to his son one day, many years later, thus condemning Dr. and Madame Hirsch; but the fact remains that Michel does not seem to have summoned any other physicians. Afterward he reproached his son for having spent those mournful days playing the penny machines on the piers and frequenting the shooting galleries and rides at a fair. This shows he understood nothing about the way in which a boy of fourteen expresses grief. But he no doubt had enough sorrow of his own without having to be concerned with his son's.

As for the servants, they are nowhere to be seen in this drama. Perhaps they disappeared, making off with the silverware or the ladies' silk dresses. A certain silence, and utter disorder, seem to have surrounded the death of the two sisters. The furnished apartment that Michel rented by the year was probably located in one of those buildings where rich foreigners stayed in the summer. The house must have been almost empty in October, but the manager or owner surely feared any rumors of illness and death that may have alarmed the remaining tenants. Even in the off-season, dying is forced to take place behind the scenes at spas and seaside resorts.

One hopes that Gabrielle, so close to her own end, never knew that her sister had preceded her. From then on, Michel had only one death agony to occupy him. During her last hours, the young woman asked for the solace of religion. The curé and the vicar of the parish church, where Michel went to look for a priest, refused to take the trouble to come. It was common knowledge that Gabrielle was divorced, and this fact was enough to explain their severity, in an age when people of the Church were more intransigent than they are today. Michel never forgave those two priests for their barbaric refusal.

He also said to me (this is the third and last detail he provided) that Baron de L., who came in person to bring Gabrielle back to Fées for burial, seemed chiefly preoccupied with the unforeseen expense; but this was perhaps not surprising on the part of a man who was perpetually short of money. Berthe was interred in the crypt at Bailleul. Chance has preserved for me the two women's prayer cards, which came from a printer on the place Saint-Sulpice. That of Berthe, adorned with a *Mater Dolorosa* by Carlo Dolci, is banal: it's the one that the Catholic stationer of Lille must have offered to all the widowers that year to commemorate their dead wives. Its text praises the patience with which the deceased endured her final illness and assures us that she will continue to think of her loved ones in heaven. Gabrielle's prayer card is perhaps more remarkable. On the reverse side of a Christ by Guido Reni is a text that reads, "God made her pass through lengthy sufferings, and, having purified her, He found her worthy of Him." This bit of Scripture, with its implication of blame and its presumptuous certitude about what God does or does not do, was apparently not chosen by Michel, who would have found it inappropriate for the deceased and too assured in matters of divine justice. Neither of the cards makes a claim that was customary in those days even when it was untrue—namely, that the two women died provided with the sacraments of the Church. Whether it came from Michel or the baron, this truthfulness is honorable.

In this instance I'll burden the reader less than ever with my speculations. This is the second or third time that life has come to an end for Michel (the iron curtain is descending, and a new existence is about to begin); it verges too closely on the absurd and the unexplained to justify any comment. It would be necessary to know things we cannot know: the true nature of Michel's relations with each of the two women, the extent to which the spouses were faithful to each other, and the varying emotions, probably diverse and contradictory, that the survivor felt in the presence of the two dying women. Regarding the two sisters, we can assume a great deal of mutual affection; without it, we cannot account for that long shared existence, but it would not have precluded temporary rivalries and jealousies. We can also glimpse the pain and suffering of their last hours, but respect for two human beings forbids us to novelize any further. It seems as if we are watching the two equestriennes disappear into a ditch (and in both cases the rider is the soul, and her horse is the body), stumbling over an obstacle that we cannot see. Concerning all the incidents in this account beginning with his early childhood, Michel is my principal source, and most of the time my sole informant. In those places where he has chosen not to speak, I can do nothing but record his silence.

But as I write these lines, the idea suddenly occurs to me that it is Berthe's untimely death which made possible, one year later, Michel's marriage to Fernande and, less than four years after that, my own birth. Whatever the true nature of that disaster, it allowed me to exist. A sort of bond has thus formed between Berthe and me.

I've said elsewhere that Berthe's death shook Michel without leaving him heartbroken. After closely re-examining the few facts available to me, I assume he was at least profoundly distressed. In any case, he seems to have returned to Mont-Noir with the intention of settling there for good—an intention that, for him, was like an admission of defeat. He took up residence in Saint-Jans-Cappel, a little village located at the far end of the estate. He was still there at the time of my birth, and stayed quite a bit longer, until the sale of Mont-Noir in 1912, when shortly after Noémi's death he rid himself of those places that he had never been able to love. (I apologize for these banal bits of information. They're virtually the only ones that can help me fix a date or determine a location during those unsettled years.) That winter he went to stay with his mother in her old house in Lille.

I'd like to know more about Michel's life during those cold gray months: what he read, what he thought (or avoided thinking about), his excursions on foot or on horseback—all the things that, after a fashion, occupied this man who was at loose ends. From time to time he perhaps visited the art museum in Lille, since he liked the wax bust titled *Unknown Woman* that is in its collection; in those days it was thought to be the funerary portrait of a young Roman lady, but today it's considered, more plausibly, a fine work from the Renaissance. It was doubtless the only personification of feminine charm he encountered that winter. A fairly interesting fact is that Madame Noémi began trying to marry the widower to a wealthy heiress, the descendant of a man who had been notorious for his ferocity while a member of the Convention. It seems, in sum, that she was striving to reproduce in a more showy and conspicuous way what her own marriage to Michel-Charles had been. Her son flatly said no. Many years later, in Paris, in the dining room of the Lutétia Hotel, he pointed out to me with a glance a woman seated by a window. She looked like a typical rich widow and was dining under the attentive eye of a maître d'hôtel. Michel congratulated himself for having had the sense to discourage his mother. Life had offered him something better in Fernande.

In March he received from Baroness V. an invitation to spend the Easter vacation at her house in Ostend. The old lady was intending to introduce him to a young friend of hers, a Belgian woman of good family, aged twenty-seven, whose education and cast of mind pleased her. After those five lonely months, Michel was tempted and accepted her invitation. I'm surprised he did so: I should have thought that the town and its seaside promenade would have given him nightmares. But he wasn't a man of obsessions and phantoms. I'm not sure he even took the trouble to walk up and down the rue de Russie —to stand beneath the windows of a certain building and summon up thoughts of two elusive shades who perhaps took their leave without any explanation. He spent those few days in the baroness's villa or on the still-empty beach, in the company of a young woman whose appearance and sensibilities he found

Fernande de Cartier de Marchienne, Michel's second wife and
Marguerite Yourcenar's mother, 1899

agreeable. Michel and Fernande said goodbye to each other after promising to take an engagement trip together in Germany. They were married on November 8, 1900.

Among the handful of people who knew all about those painful days in October 1899, and the emotions as well as the facts, one must count my mother. Michel doubtless told her about it almost immediately, if the baroness hadn't already done so. I've reproduced elsewhere a letter that Fernande wrote to her future husband on October 21, 1900, the day before the Mass that marked the first anniversary of Berthe's death, a Mass that Michel had gone to Mont-Noir to attend. It's perhaps worth quoting those few lines once again. Fernande had her faults, which I've made no effort to hide, but everything that was most touching in her is expressed in this note. Her tender concern for a man who had undergone trials she was not unaware of is more apparent after one has tried to follow Michel through the course of that difficult year, just as faded handwriting becomes vivid again when dipped in acid.

> *My dear Michel,*
>
> *I would like you to receive a note from me tomorrow. The day will be a sad one for you. You will be so alone.*
>
> *See now: how stupid social conventions are! . . . It was utterly impossible for me to come with you, and yet what could be simpler than for two people to hold each other close and help each other when they are in love . . . Beginning with these last days of October, forget all that is past, dear Michel. You know what good Monsieur Fouillée* says about*

---

* The first time I quoted this letter from Fernande to Michel, in *Souvenirs Pieux* (*Dear Departed*), I misread the name and wrote "good Monsieur Feuillée," and wondered vainly what old friend or country neighbor he could have been, this Feuillée who was so preoccupied with the problem of time. An unknown woman wrote to me afterward to say that he was no doubt the professor of philosophy Alfred Fouillée, who is mostly forgotten today but

*the notion of time: that the past is truly past for us only
when it has been forgotten.*

*Also, have confidence in the promise of the future, and
in me. I think that this dull, gray month of October is
merely a cloud coming between two periods of sunshine, that
of our charming trip to Germany and that of our life to come
. . . Over there, traveling beneath a clearer sky, we shall
recover all our joyful lightheartedness—that all-embracing
tenderness and intimacy, free from disturbance and vexation,
which we found so pleasant.*

*It makes me very happy to think that only three weeks
remain . . . And during these two days I shall say not
"Don't be sad" but "Don't be too sad." I look forward to
seeing you in the evening when you come on Tuesday . . .*

There is something moving in these condolences and these
promises made by one fragile human being to another, whose
wounds were not yet scarred over. The promises were kept to
the extent that it was in Fernande's power to keep them. The
future she refers to lasted a bit more than three years, if one
counts the "down payment" already made in the course of their
engagement trip. Three years of a slow waltz across Europe,
which this time was a Europe of museums, royal estates, forest
walks, and mountain trails; three years of conversation and
reading, of love, and of a happiness surely crossed here and
there by misunderstandings and disputes between this man
quick to become impatient and this easily wounded woman. But
happiness nevertheless: when Fernande died, Michel had a text
printed on the back of her prayer card which said that instead
of weeping because she was no more, we should rejoice because

who was widely known at the time. To educated people in those days, he was in some
sense the equivalent of what an Alain or a Jean Grenier would become at a later date.
Obviously Fernande was doing some serious reading.

she had existed. He added a somewhat more dubious enco-
mium—namely, that she had "tried to do her best." The letter
written by Fernande the day before the Mass on the first anniversary of Berthe's death shows that she had indeed tried.
The past had been, if not abolished (it never is), at least temporarily effaced. Three years of near-happiness in the company
of a different young woman, under a changed light, in an intimacy that appears steeped in a melody by Schumann: this is
no inconsiderable thing for a man of forty-six who has lived an
eventful and turbulent life.

On two occasions separated by an interval of several days, I happened to see phantoms from the past. I was twenty-three. I was with Michel in the South of France, and as usual the gambling halls of Monte Carlo were waylaying him, if not every day, at least fairly frequently. One day I went to wait for him at the door of a casino. I was old enough to go inside, but I was filled with the puritanism of youth; I would have found it indecent to enter that cavern where pale men and heavily made-up women wagered their excess (and often necessary) money on the plastic tokens that had replaced the gold pieces of days gone by. (I really think it was this substitution, as much as his virtually complete ruin, that greatly diminished Michel's passion for gambling. The gold louis had been at once the symbol of Fortune and her actual presence, giving to the victories and defeats of the game the intensity of those of life itself. They had been melted in the crucible of the First World War, which had also done away with royal monarchs.) Moreover, I had a dog with me, as I almost always did, and dogs aren't allowed in sacred places, whatever these might be. I don't know the whereabouts of the Englishwoman Michel would marry six months later; I suppose she was in her room, suffering from one of her migraines.

Suddenly, from where I was standing on the front steps, I spied Michel in the sort of transparent cage which served as the antechamber to that Temple of Chance. On its exterior wall the chamber had glass doors leading to the outside; on the interior wall it had identical doors that afforded a glimpse of what lay beyond them: the central vestibule of the sanctuary, which in turn led to the gambling halls. My father was evidently preparing to leave when he met, and recognized, a woman who was just coming in. No one would have looked at her twice. She was old, heavy, a bit stooped, dressed in cheap clothes that bespoke poor taste—one of those crones who put aside a small part of their dividends or their pension to go to Monte Carlo from time to time, to try out a "system." Michel spoke to her, or rather shouted at her, blocking the door, oblivious to the scene he was causing with his barrage of words that resembled blows. An electric chandelier lit them as if they were on a stage. The startled woman clearly was thinking only of flight, and managed to escape, losing herself in the crowd of people entering through the glass doors leading to the interior.

The doormen, who doubtless had seen and heard similar altercations, set in motion the revolving door and Michel came out. He was scarcely even looked at by the few people who had vaguely noticed that dispute between a gentleman and a lady, both of them getting on in years. Actually, the quarrel had been one-sided: the lady had said nothing. Michel's appearance alarmed me—he was unsteady on his feet.

One of the hackney cabs that in those days still lent their charm to vacation spots (at least when the horses weren't too lean or unduly exposed to the sun and flies) was waiting for fares at the foot of the steps. We climbed in. I won't say that I helped him up, since I never played Antigone with him.

"What happened back there?"

"That was Madame Hirsch, the widow of the doctor who attended Berthe and Gabrielle. I don't want to talk about it."

Like a bad dream, the same scene, with a few variations, recurred about ten days later. We were strolling in Nice, along a street that was lined with numerous antique shops of varying quality, almost one next to the other. Michel was not a collector of curios; he wasn't settled enough in his ways—had no fixed residence and no town he called home. ("We're not from around here; we're leaving tomorrow.") But he liked to look at all sorts of objects, discuss their good and bad points, comment on their prices, try to imagine the circumstances that had brought them there. As for me, I found it delightful to play the game that consists of choosing the object we would buy if we were the acquisitive type, and the even more pleasant game that consists of scorning with a glance everything we wouldn't buy. Engravings by Landseer, photographs by Bouguereau, an ivory Ganymede that reproduced in trinket size the marble statue by Benvenuto Cellini, a chess set with pieces made of shell and ebony, broken Moustiers—all have remained branded in my memory by the incident that followed.

Part of the contents of the shops spilled out onto the pavement. A woman, bareheaded, was sitting in a chair by the door of her shop. She rose and went inside when she saw us approach. But Michel had recognized her immediately, just as he had a few days earlier, despite the changes in her appearance that must have taken place in twenty-seven years. He followed her into the shop, leaving the door open behind him; its slightest movement set off, almost grotesquely, a carillon of little bells.

Ananké

The narrow room was crowded with chairs stacked one on top of another, clocks all displaying different times and sitting on Louis XIII buffets, fake rococo and fake rustic. The woman had withdrawn to the back wall, where she found herself cornered between a table piled with dishes and a small stand topped with a lamp. In this auction-room atmosphere, Michel gesticulated, brandishing his fists as if he were threatening both the fragile objects and that pale, bloated woman, who was doubtless even more vulnerable than her china and chandeliers. I heard him shout, "Killer's wife! Thief! Murderess!" and, as if gusts of foul air were escaping suddenly from the cellar of a ruined house, "Dirty Jewess!"

I know that Michel—who had no more fondness than I did for the Old Testament, a book that is comforting to some and odious or repellent to others—had, in contrast, an instinctive sympathy for the Jews of the Diaspora, misunderstood and persecuted. He was biased in favor of them, rich or poor, bankers or humble tailors—a people endowed sometimes with genius and almost always with human warmth. But he was beside himself, and was appropriating the insults of a Drumont or of the anti-Dreyfus partisans whom he had reviled in his youth, just as a passerby seized with fury will pick up a knife lying in the mud.

His anger faded on the spot. I took him by the arm; his tall body seemed drained of every ounce of strength. Fortunately, our hotel was close by. Michel took the elevator and, as soon as he got to his room, collapsed into the only armchair. He pulled off his cravat, unbuttoned the neck of his shirt; great drops of sweat trickled down his livid face onto his bare breast. I was afraid. The previous year we had visited the convent of the Camaldules, at Baïes, and a little later, on a street in Geneva, he had suffered a spell of weakness that seemed to indicate

347

a heart condition. I alerted Christine H., whose room was next door; she came in, affectionately tended to him, and ordered some tea. As usual, that magic beverage revived and calmed him. Before long, Michel was sufficiently recovered to be able to unfold the copy of *Le Temps* that lay within reach on the table. The incident was never mentioned again.

In June 1903 a gentleman dressed all in black, whom the porters and the conductor readily recognize as Monsieur de C., gets off a train in Lille and takes the local for Bailleul, where Madame Noémi's horses and their coachman, Achille, are waiting for him. On this occasion Monsieur de C. is not bringing back a coffin: Fernande has remained in Belgium with her family. But it takes a considerable amount of time to gather all the trunks, valises, umbrella stands, shawls, and crates of books on the platform at Bailleul. Monsieur de C. is leading a dachshund named Trier—a reminder of Fernande, who bought him in Germany on the engagement trip. Behind the gentleman, objects of his solicitude, walk two ladies who are likewise in black and whom the employees in the little station soon perceive are domestic servants. One is Barbe, or Barbra, as I will later call her, a fresh-faced girl of twenty in a brand-new British nurse's outfit purchased in Old England. The other is the nurse, Madame Azélie, who with Barbra's help tended Fernande in her last days, and who has agreed to spend the summer months at Mont-Noir teaching the rudiments of child care to the young chambermaid recently promoted to children's nurse. Madame

Azélie carries the little newborn on a pillow that is covered with a white cloth; for safety's sake, the baby is tied to the pillow with large satin bows.

Monsieur de C. climbs into the carriage and takes the forward seat, leaving the places in back for the two women with their burden. He settles the dog between his legs; but Trier, who is unhappy at not being able to see anything, repeatedly leaves his refuge, puts his crooked paws and long nose up against one of the two doors, and barks at the farm dogs and the gentle cows.

They turn off the road bordered with rustic garlands of hops, which must often have made Michel-Charles (and at this moment perhaps Michel) think of the grapevines of Italy. This country road, beneath a sky that is still the vast sky of Nord as van der Meulen painted it, dotted with fleecy clouds, will in eleven years be lined along its entire length, from Bailleul to Cassel, with a double row of dead or dying horses that have been eviscerated by the shells of 1914 and dragged into the ditch to make way for the expected English reinforcements. Already the carriage is climbing the hill under the black shadow of the pine trees that give their name to the estate. In twelve years they will go up in smoke as a burnt offering to the gods of war; and the mill and the château itself, farther on, will go up in smoke as well. But that which does not yet exist is nonexistent. The carriage follows the drive bordered with rhododendrons that are long past their bloom. It comes to a stop on the gravel at the foot of the front steps. Madame Noémi, sarcastic as always, is waiting above, by the door. This homecoming doubtless reminds her of the even sadder homecoming of four years ago. Furthermore, these people are in mourning, and even though she is dressed in black and adorned with jet as befits a widow, Madame Noémi despises everything that reminds her of death. Quickly the two women and the baby are shown

Marguerite Yourcenar and her nurse Barbra, 1904

Mont-Noir before World War I

Mont-Noir after World War I

upstairs to take possession of the large bedroom in the tower: this is the first dwelling I will remember. Monsieur C. goes up to the third floor to settle into the rooms he occupied last summer with Fernande.

Michel will be fifty on the tenth of August; a third of his life lies ahead of him. The future still has his greatest love in store, for a woman eminently worthy of affection and the only one for whom he will write poetry—a handful of beautiful lines, which he kept. And the future holds other things as well: a curious attachment, perhaps without anything sexual about it, for an ailing, whimsical woman who will help Monsieur de C. spend what remains of his fortune; a few liaisons with agreeable women, of more or less loose morals, who will enchant him until the threshold of old age; a third wife, who will prove to be the efficient and slightly dull companion of his last days; a tame and prudent form of gambling—banal and methodical, like all old vices; automobiles, initially an art, a science, a new passion that for a time will bring him closer to his son—then suddenly abandoned, just as he will abandon in turn, and always suddenly, cigarettes and women.

But the years to come will also bring happiness. Michel will at last realize the old dream of a life lived exclusively in sun-drenched lands, far from people that one felt obliged to associate with without knowing why. In addition, there will be some trips abroad, and long walks on the roads of Provence in the company of a teenager who draws him into her plans and daydreams and who is his daughter: me. There will be evenings spent reading or rereading the great poets out loud, evenings that resemble delightful séances in which the spirits of the dead are summoned and speak. There will be poverty that retains the appearance of wealth, and that has the advantages of both.

Finally, there will be a slow, accepting, and almost serene death at Lausanne.

The girl is now about six weeks old. Like most human newborns, she looks like a very old creature that will gradually become younger. And indeed, she is very old: by means of her ancestral blood and genes, or perhaps by means of the un-analyzed element that, in a beautiful classical metaphor, we call the soul, she has traversed the centuries. But she knows nothing of this; so much the better. Her head is covered with black fur, like a mouse's back; the fingers of her fists, when they are uncurled, look like the delicate tendrils of a plant; her eyes gaze at things that no one has yet defined or named for her. For the moment she is nothing but being—essence and substance blended indissolubly into a unity that will endure in this form approximately three-quarters of a century, and per-haps longer.

The times that she will live in will be the worst in history. She will see at least two "world" wars, as well as their sequelae of other conflicts flaring up here and there. She will see national wars and civil wars, class wars and race wars, and even, at one or two points on the globe, through an anachronism which proves that nothing is ever finished, religious wars, each con-taining enough sparks to set off the conflagration that will de-stroy everything. Torture, thought to have been relegated to the picturesque Middle Ages, will once again become a reality; the pullulation of humanity will cause the individual to be devalued. Forms of mass communication in the service of more or less camouflaged interests will inundate the world with ghostly vi-sions and sounds, an opiate of the masses that is more insidious than anything religion has ever been accused of spreading. A false abundance, disguising the gradual depletion of resources, will dispense foods that are more and more adulterated and diversions that are more and more gregarious—the *panem et circenses* of societies that believe themselves free. The speed that annihilates distances will also annihilate the difference between places, everywhere drawing pilgrims of pleasure toward the same artificial sounds and lights, the same monuments that are nowadays just as threatened as the elephants and whales: a Parthenon that is crumbling away and that people have suggested be placed under glass, a Strasbourg Cathedral that is corroding, a Giralda beneath a sky that is no longer so blue, a Venice that is decaying from chemical residues. Hundreds of species of animals that have managed to survive since the world was young will in just a few years be wiped out by avarice and brutality. Mankind will tear out its own lungs—the vast green forests. The water, the air, and the protective ozone layer, virtually unique wonders that have made life on earth possible, will be polluted and wasted. In certain ages, it is said, Shiva dances on the world, annihilating forms. What is dancing on the world today is man's foolishness, violence, and greed.

I do not make an idol of the past. Our visit with a few obscure families from what is today France's Nord has shown us what we would have seen anywhere—namely, that unenlightened power and self-interest have almost always held sway. In every age, man has done some good and a great deal of harm. The mechanical and chemical means of action that he has recently given himself, and the almost geometric progression in their effects, have rendered this harm irreversible; moreover, the errors and crimes that were insignificant so long as humankind was merely a species like any other on the earth have become deadly ever since man, seized with madness, began to consider himself all-powerful. The Cleenewerck of the seventeenth century must have been worried when he saw rising around Cassel the smoke of the bombardments of Monsieur, the king's brother, battling the prince of Orange; the air that

Michel, his daughter, Marguerite, and her pet sheep at
Mont-Noir, ca. 1910

Michel and Fernande's daughter will breathe will contain the smoke of Auschwitz, Dresden, and Hiroshima. Michel-Daniel de Crayencour, an émigré, found refuge in Germany; there are no longer any secure refuges. Michel-Charles was indifferent to the wretchedness in the cellars of Lille; but it's the state of the whole world that will someday weigh on this new baby girl.

The child who has just arrived at Mont-Noir is socially privileged; she will remain so. She has never—at least up to the moment I'm writing these lines—experienced cold or hunger; she has never, at least so far, had to endure torture; she has never, except for seven or eight years at the most, had to "earn a living" in the monotonous and everyday sense of the term; she has never, like millions of people in her time, been interned in a concentration camp or, like other millions who believe themselves free, been placed in the service of machines that turn out unending streams of useless or destructive objects, gadgets or armaments. She will be scarcely at all hindered, as so many women still are nowadays, by her status as a woman, perhaps because it has never occurred to her that she must inevitably be hindered by it. Contacts, examples, heavenly dispensations (who knows?), or a chain of circumstances that extend far behind her will permit her to compose little by little an image of the world that is less incomplete than the one her little aunt Gabrielle wrote in her large notebook in 1866. She will take tumbles now and then, and will raise herself on her scraped knees; she will learn, not without effort, to make use of her own eyes, and then, like a diver, to keep them wide open. She will try to make her way somehow out of what her forebears called "the century" and what people today call "the times," the only times that count for them, an agitated surface under which lie hidden the immobile ocean and the currents that traverse it. She will strive to let herself be borne along by those currents. She will live her "personal life," insofar as this term has a meaning, as best she can in the midst of all this. The events of that life interest me above all as a means of access by which certain experiences have come to her. It is for this reason, and this reason only, that I shall set them down someday, if the time is granted me and if I feel the urge to do so.

But it's too soon to speak of her, even supposing it were possible to speak without complacency or error of someone who inexplicably touches us so closely. Let's let her sleep on Madame Azélie's lap, on the terrace shaded by linden trees. Let's let her new eyes follow the flight of a bird or a ray of sunlight flickering between two leaves. The rest is perhaps less important than we think.

Author's Note

Translator's Notes

Author's Note

Concerning the history of the C. de C. family prior to the Revolution, I have relied on documents from family archives and on a few genealogical works, almost all of which were privately published. Among these is the *Généalogie de la famille Cleenewerck de Crayencour* (1944), written by my half brother, Michel, and afterward supplemented thanks to the inquiries and researches of his son, Commander Georges de Crayencour, to whom I am deeply grateful for his inexhaustible kindness. Another work, *La Famille Bieswal* (1970), by Paul Bieswal, contains certain chapters that are much more interesting than the simple genealogical list and constitute a precious addition to the history of a small town in France's Nord under the ancien régime.

Beginning with the early years of my grandfather Michel-Charles, much of my information consists of the accounts he himself related to his son, Michel; but my effort to reconstruct my grandfather is based chiefly on his own writings. I must once again thank Georges de Crayencour for helping me obtain a photocopy of Michel-Charles's travel albums, as well as some notes concerning his family and describing certain incidents in his life (the accident on the Versailles train in 1842, the revolution of 1848 in Lille, the accident that caused the death of his

363

daughter Gabrielle in 1866). I am also indebted to Monsieur René Robinet, director of the Archives du Nord, for some important documents concerning Michel-Charles and his father-in-law, Amable Dufresne.

I am especially grateful to Madame Jeanne Carayon and the management of the Archives of Versailles for numerous official documents concerning the railway accident of 1842, which allowed me to flesh out my grandfather's memoirs.

What I know of my father's life prior to his second marriage comes almost exclusively from his own accounts, related in the course of our conversations during the closing years of his life. A handful of letters preserved by chance, the yellowed pages of a military record book, and inscriptions on the backs of old photographs have helped me pinpoint dates that he often left vague. Finally, I am again indebted to Georges de Crayencour for enabling me to acquire a complete set of photographs of family portraits—portraits that are today scattered among my half brother's descendants and that I have often mentioned or described in the course of this book. On occasion, though very rarely, I have changed the names of certain places and people.

Translator's Notes

Anyone who has ever undertaken a translation knows that the task involves agreeing to live with an author's voice in your head day and night, perhaps for years—in a word, agreeing to be haunted. It has been a rare pleasure to be haunted by Yourcenar's voice, even when the translation process was most frustrating. Her long, balanced sentences are notoriously difficult to render into English. As Mavis Gallant wrote in *The New York Review of Books* in December 1985, the Yourcenarian phrase tends to lose its poise and tension in the carrying over, winding up in English as "a length of frayed elastic."

Yourcenar was quite aware of the problem. She lived in the United States for many years and had a solid command of English. (Readers wishing to know more about her life may consult Josyane Savigneau's excellent biography, *Marguerite Yourcenar: Inventing a Life.*) Before she died, in 1987, she was able to make a number of improvements in the translation of *Souvenirs Pieux*, her first volume of memoirs, published in English as *Dear Departed*. The second volume, unfortunately, had to be prepared without her guidance. She did, however, choose the title *How Many Years* (knowing that "Archives of Nord" would mean nothing to Anglo-American readers), and took it from a thoroughly American source:

the lines by Bob Dylan that appear as the epigraph to Part III. As we would expect, the title is full of nuances—at once a question, an exclamation, a meditation.

It might be said that Yourcenar chose the photographs, too, since most are images she discusses in the book. The Gallimard Folio edition that served as the basis for this translation contains no illustrations. Readers will see for themselves how much the images add to Yourcenar's text and to our knowledge of her methods. A photograph, a portrait, a sculpted form was for her a link to the departed and a stimulus to the *sympathie imaginative* that enabled her to re-create vanished lives and times. Her technique might best be described as empathic reanimation.

The genealogical chart, which does not appear in the Gallimard Folio edition, is included here as a guide to the large cast of characters, some of whom have the same name. The notes, too, are offered as an aid to readers. Few people nowadays—perhaps in any day—are likely to have Yourcenar's range of literary and historical knowledge, and although it would be impractical to attempt to explain all of her allusions in this book, I thought a few explanations would be better than none at all.

During the many months I worked on this book, I relied on a number of people for help and advice. I'm deeply grateful to all of them for their generous assistance. David Perkins of Harvard University read the entire draft with incomparable sensitivity and did much to smooth its frayed edges. Judith Ryan, also of Harvard University, has supported my translation work from the beginning and given me many well-timed words of encouragement. The trustees of the Petite Plaisance Trust, including Yvon Bernier and Jean Lunt, granted me access to the Yourcenar Archives in Northeast Harbor, Maine, and allowed me to reproduce previously unpublished photographs. Georges de Crayencour kindly provided me with a photograph of Yourcenar's great-grandfather Charles-Augustin Cleenewerck. Annette Kawecki was my consultant on points relating to the fine arts. Paul Elie and Lynn Warshow of Farrar, Straus & Giroux were superb editors. And George Scialabba, essayist and critic, advised me on matters of history, philosophy, theology, and literature and generally furthered this project in ways too numerous to mention.

———

Page

6 *"L'Intimé"*: In Jean Racine's comedy *Les Plaideurs*, or *The Litigants* (1668), which is based on Aristophanes' *The Wasps*, L'Intimé is the secretary of the mad Judge Dandin. The climax of the play is a farcical trial in which a dog is tried for stealing a capon; L'Intimé is the attorney for the defense. His name, in fact, means "the defendant."

12 *"Pisanellos"*: The reference is to Antonio Pisano, called Pisanello (c. 1395–1455), Italian artist and draftsman. He is known for his religious frescoes and his portraits executed as classical-style medals.

13 *"Monsieur Homais"*: The apothecary in Gustave Flaubert's *Madame Bovary* (1857). The epitome of the self-satisfied country busybody, he prides himself on being an enlightened man of science and an opponent of the Church.

15 *"Vercingetorix"*: Hero of the Gauls, a chieftain of the Arverni people (inhabitants of what was later known as Auvergne), who led the great revolt against the Romans in 52 B.C. He was defeated by Julius Caesar at Alesia (near Dijon), taken captive, and eventually put to death (46 B.C.).

15 *"Eponine"*: Gallic heroine who lived in the first century. She was the wife of Julius Sabinus, a Gallic chieftain who claimed to be descended from Caesar and who led a rebellion against Rome during the reign of Vespasian. After Sabinus was defeated, Eponine accompanied him into hiding. They lived in an underground cavern for nine years, but were betrayed to Vespasian and put to death in A.D. 78 or 79.

15 *"Cassel"*: Town in the northernmost part of France, near Dunkirk. Not to be confused with the city of Kassel in Hesse, Germany.

16 *"Atrebatian"*: Relating to the Atrebates, a tribe living in the region of Gaul that came to be known as Artois (today part of the French *département* of Pas-de-Calais).

17 *"D'Hozier"*: A work actually entitled *Généalogies des principales familles de France*, compiled by Pierre d'Hozier (1592–1660), Louis XIV's genealogist and historiographer. He was the first to make genealogical history a science, and was responsible not only for registering but also for verifying titles and coats of arms. Working with his son Charles-René, he spent half a century on the *Généalogies*, which consists of 150 volumes. Louis XIV honored him with titles and a great deal of money. Voltaire once wrote of him: "De véritablement grands hommes ont été bien moins récompensés. Leurs travaux n'étaient pas si nécessaires à la vanité humaine." ("Some truly great men were much less richly rewarded. Their labors were not so necessary to human vanity.")

17 *"Gueux"*: A name that in the sixteenth century was applied to the Huguenots of Flanders, who rebelled against the repressive religious policies of the ruling Spaniards.

The word, meaning "scoundrels" or "beggars," was first used in this connection by Margaret of Parma, Spanish governor of the Netherlands from 1559 to 1567.

17 *"Commius"*: Chieftain of the Atrebates, a Gallic tribe. Caesar thought highly of him and made him an ambassador to the Britons, but in the Gallic uprising of 52 B.C. Commius deserted Rome to fight with his countrymen. In 51 B.C. he surrendered to Marc Antony, commander of the Romans in Belgian Gaul. He retired to Britain and acquired sovereign power over the tribes of Hampshire, Sussex, Kent, and Surrey.

17 *"Claudius Civilis"*: Also known as Julius Civilis. Chieftain of the Batavii (a Germanic tribe living in what is today Holland), he led a revolt against Rome in A.D. 69–70. The rebellion spread rapidly throughout the Gallic and Germanic territories, and Civilis envisioned the founding of an independent kingdom of Gaul, but he was defeated by the Romans at Trier. He succeeded in negotiating a favorable treaty.

18 *"Rembrandt"*: Yourcenar is here referring to *The Conspiracy of Claudius Civilis: The Oath*, which Rembrandt executed in 1661–62 and which is now in the National Museum in Stockholm. The painting shows a strikingly lit scene, rendered in tones of red and gold, in which a group of Gallic warriors of the Batavi tribe swears to fight to the death against the Romans.

22 *"Isis"*: Egyptian goddess of motherhood and fertility, often represented as cow-headed. Her cult was one of the chief religions of the Roman empire.

22 *"Harpocrates"*: Greek name for the Egyptian sun god, Horus, who was worshipped widely in the late Roman empire. He was depicted as a young boy holding a finger to his lips, and came to be considered the god of silence.

22 *"Mithra"*: Persian god of light and wisdom, and opponent of the powers of darkness. He was often depicted as slaying a divine bull. The cult of Mithra was introduced into Rome during the reign of Trajan and was extremely popular among soldiers.

27 *"Patinir"*: Joachim de Patinir (d. 1524), Flemish painter known for his carefully detailed landscapes depicting immense vistas (though he also painted religious subjects). He was a friend of Albrecht Dürer's.

28 *"Poetry Society"*: The French term is *Chambre de Rhétorique*, which has been variously translated as "Chamber of Rhetoric," "Poetry Society," and "Literary Union." The best rendering might be a phrase taken from the title of a work by the seventeenth-century English rhetorician Thomas Blount: "Academy of Eloquence." Such societies flourished in the fifteenth and sixteenth centuries in Flanders. Some towns had more than one (Ghent had four), often with fanciful names: La Fontaine, Les Amis de Joie, Alpha et Omega, Les Boutons de la Rose, Les Ignorans, La Branche d'Olivier. The members competed in regional competitions, composing poems on agreed-upon topics; prizes were awarded for the best entries in French and in Flemish. Poetry societies declined in the late sixteenth century, when the country came under Spanish rule; they were revived on a small scale in the nineteenth century.

34 *"Salic law"*: Rule of succession among many noble families of Europe, prohibiting

women and those descended in the female line from inheriting titles and offices. In France, the rule was observed especially by the houses of Valois and Bourbon.

34 *"Year II of the Revolution"*: Under the Revolutionary calendar, Year II ran from September 22, 1793, to September 22, 1794. Louis XIV lived from 1638 to 1715; François I reigned 1515–47; Saint Louis (Louis IX) died in 1270.

36 *"Mechlin"*: In French, "Malines." City that today is in north-central Belgium. Originally a fortified town under the prince-bishops of Liège, it later passed to the dukes of Burgundy (1356), who made it the administrative capital of the Netherlands. Margaret of Austria, governor of the country from 1506 to 1530, built a palace in Mechlin that became one of the great centers of European humanism in the mid-sixteenth century. The town was brutally sacked by the duke of Alba's forces in 1572.

36 *"duke of Alba"*: Fernando Alvarez de Toledo, duque de Alba (1507–82), Spanish general and administrator. In 1567 he was appointed head of Spanish forces in the Netherlands, where he advocated ruthless treatment of the insurgents (the Protestants, or Gueux). The governor of the Netherlands, Margaret of Parma, resigned in protest of his policies and he succeeded her. Under his harsh regime, which lasted until 1573, approximately 18,000 people were executed.

36 *"Alessandro Farnese"*: 1545–92; duke of Parma, general and diplomat serving under Philip II of Spain. In the Netherlands he helped defeat the Protestants who rebelled against Spanish control, and in 1578 was appointed governor. He was the son of Margaret of Parma.

36 *"Marignano"*: Town southeast of Milan, site of one of the bloodiest battles of the Italian Wars, where in 1515 François I and his Venetian allies defeated the Swiss.

36 *"Cerignola"*: Town in southern Italy where, in 1503, during the Italian Wars, Spanish forces under Gonzalo Fernández de Córdoba defeated the French forces of Louis XII.

38 *"Charles the Bold"*: 1433–77; last reigning duke of Burgundy. He opposed the growing power of King Louis XI of France, and dreamed of re-establishing the kingdom of Lotharingia, which would have included territories now in Holland, Belgium, Luxembourg, Alsace, Lorraine, Burgundy, and northern France. In battles at the Swiss towns of Grandson and Murten (French: Morat) in 1476, he fought to consolidate his possessions. In 1477, at Nancy, Charles was defeated and killed by forces from Switzerland and Lorraine.

39 *"Louis the Well-Beloved"*: Sobriquet for Louis XV (1710–74); in French, "Louis le Bien-Aimé."

41 *"Chouans"*: Rebels who took part in the *Chouannerie*, the Royalist insurrections in Brittany and Normandy during the French Revolution. *Chouan* in Breton dialect means "owl." The name alludes to the fact that the rebels signaled to each other at night with birdlike cries. Balzac's novel *Les Chouans* (1829) tells of their exploits.

42 *"Sébastien Castalion"*: 1515–63; French Protestant theologian, known for his defense of religious toleration—a defense he put forward in the preface to his Latin translation of the Bible (1551).

46 *"Saint-Simon"*: Louis de Rouvroy, duc de Saint-Simon (1675–1755), courtier and diplomat during the reigns of Louis XIV and Louis XV. His *Mémoires* vividly portray the events, society, and manners of his day.

47 *"Condé"*: Louis II de Bourbon, prince de Condé (1621–86), French general known as the Great Condé. He won many battles for France during the Thirty Years War, but during the uprising known as the Fronde he fought with the nobles against Cardinal Mazarin and the court. After peace was declared, he was pardoned.

48 *"Fénelon"*: François de Salignac de la Mothe Fénelon (1651–1715), French theologian and writer, archbishop of Cambrai. His religious works were condemned by the pope for their mysticism, but his *Télémaque* (1699) was long considered exemplary moral reading for the young.

49 *"Villeroy"*: François de Neufville, duc de Villeroy (1644–1730), marshal of France. In 1695 Louis XIV made him commander of the army in Flanders.

49 *"Malbrouck"*: Nickname for John Churchill, first duke of Marlborough (1650–1722), English general and statesman. The sobriquet comes from an old French song, "Malbrouck s'en va-t-en guerre" ("va-t-en guerre" is a sarcastic gibe, meaning he wages war by fanfare instead of deed). During Louis XIV's campaigns, French people began applying the song to Marlborough, the king's chief enemy.

49 *"Frederick II"*: Frederick the Great (1712–86), King of Prussia. In the War of the Austrian Succession (1740–48), the Seven Years War (1756–63), and the War of the Bavarian Succession (1778–79) he expanded his country's borders and made Prussia into Europe's strongest military power.

49 *"Pangloss"*: A character in Voltaire's tale *Candide* (1759). He is a philosopher and an incurable optimist who believes that all is for the best in this best of all possible worlds.

49 *"nobility of the gown"*: Patricians who used their status as magistrates and professionals to join the aristocracy.

49 *"L'Ambacht"*: The name of the suburb actually means "trade" or "craft" in Flemish. In medieval times *ambacht* (from the Latin *ambactus*, a word of Germanic origin meaning "servant") stood for the area under the jurisdiction of a feudal lord and came to signify an administrative district.

51 *"Nattier"*: Jean-Marc Nattier (1685–1766), French painter, known especially for his portraits of Peter the Great and Catherine I of Russia and members of the French court.

51 *"Cana"*: Ancient town of Galilee and site of Jesus' first miracle: at a wedding celebration, He turned water into wine. The event has been represented in numerous paintings.

52 *"Embarkation for Cythera"*: Painting by Jean-Antoine Watteau (1684–1721), French artist of Flemish descent who is known for his lyrical, sensuous images. It depicts a group of elegantly dressed couples setting out in an ornate pleasure boat for Cythera, the legendary isle of love.

52 *"Primaticcio"*: Francesco Primaticcio (1504–70), Italian painter who worked on the

frescoes and ornamentation at Fontainebleau and other royal châteaus and monuments in France. Known in French as Le Primatice.

53 *"Jansenius"*: Cornelius Jansen (1585–1638), Dutch Roman Catholic theologian and bishop of Ypres. His writings, which advocated a return to the teachings of Saint Augustine, gave rise to the great movement known as Jansenism. Jansenists believed in predestination; they repudiated the role of human will and the doctrine of salvation by works, believing that divine grace alone was the means to salvation. Their influence derived from their moral austerity. The convent of Port-Royal was the most famous Jansenist center, and Blaise Pascal was the movement's greatest exponent. Jansenism was strongly opposed by the Jesuits, suppressed by Louis XIV, and condemned by several popes.

53 *"Jesuits"*: Members of the Society of Jesus, a Roman Catholic religious order founded by Saint Ignatius of Loyola in 1540. The Jesuits were particularly interested in foreign missions, the education of young people, and studies in the sciences and humanities. They were a major force in the Catholic Reformation and established schools in nearly every important European city. The Jesuits eventually became the object of criticism from vested Catholic interests; the Jansenists accused them of casuistry and of laxity in confessional practice. In 1773 Pope Clement XIV dissolved the order, but in 1814 Pius VII re-established it.

53 *"Expulsion"*: In 1656 the prominent Jansenist Antoine Arnauld was expelled from the Sorbonne, a major blow to the movement. In 1705 and 1713 papal bulls put the Jansenists out of the Roman Catholic Church, and in 1704 Port-Royal was closed.

53 *"Convulsionaries"*: Devout individuals who were subject to physical spasms resulting from intense religious emotion. There were many such individuals among the Jansenists, notably the Convulsionaries of the abbey of Saint-Médard.

54 *"Antoine Arnauld"*: 1612–94; Jansenist priest and theologian noted for his attacks on Calvinists and Jesuits; the latter are the target of his best-known work, *De la fréquente communion* (1643). He was a member of the faculty of theology at the Sorbonne, but was expelled in 1656 and eventually went to live in Belgium.

54 *"historiographer"*: Jean Racine (1639–99), French poet and playwright, who also served as official historiographer under Louis XIV.

55 *"Saint Cunegonde"*: Wife of the Holy Roman emperor Henry II. Henry accused her of infidelity and forced her to undergo trial by fire; it is said she came through the ordeal unscathed. After Henry's death in 1024 she established a convent near Cassel. She spent her entire fortune on good works, took holy orders, and lived the last fifteen years of her life as a nun. She died in 1040 and was canonized in 1200.

55 *"Saint Cucuphas"*: Spanish martyr tortured and decapitated by the Moors in Barcelona in the year 304; also known as Cucufat, Qoquofas, and Cugat. His relics (some say these consisted of his head) were brought to Paris by the monks of the abbey of Saint-Denis.

59 *"King of the Wood"*: According to a legend that goes back to the Greeks and that spread

to Europe via Italy (recounted by J. G. Frazer in *The Golden Bough*), the sacred grove of Diana Nemorensis ("Diana of the Wood") was located in ancient times near the Italian village of Nemi. In this sacred grove stood a sacred oak tree, guarded by a priest with a drawn sword. Anyone wishing to succeed the priest had to break off a bough from the sacred tree. He was then entitled to fight the priest in single combat, and if he slew him he reigned in his stead with the title "King of the Wood" (*Rex Nemorensis*). As a personification of the oak-god Jupiter, he mated with the oak-goddess; their union was deemed essential to the fertility of earth, humans, and animals.

59 *"The Hammer of Witches"*: The *Malleus maleficarum*, by Jakob Sprenger and Henricus Institorus (Heinrich Krämer), published in Germany in 1484. A large and detailed compendium by two inquisitors, it was the first systematic presentation of the doctrine of witchcraft. It discussed the nature, motivations, and methods of demons; the use of countercharms and exorcisms; and the proper means of exposing, trying, and punishing witches. For more than a century it guided the tribunals of the Inquisition, and it gave rise to a long series of "Hammers" *(Mallei)*—manuals designed to help inquisitors detect and punish witches.

61 *"hellebore"*: A plant that was long used for medicinal purposes. The Greeks and Romans believed it was an effective treatment for insanity.

61 *"Agrippa of Nettesheim"*: 1486–1533 or 1534; physician and philosopher, born Henri Corneille in Cologne. An enlightened man but quarrelsome and unstable, he lived and taught in many cities across Europe (London, Pavia, Turin, Metz, Geneva, Lyon, Brussels, Grenoble). In Metz he was vilified because he defended a peasant girl against charges of witchcraft. Among his works is *De occulta philosophia*, a treatise against superstition and the occult.

61 *"Théophraste Renaudot"*: 1586–1653; founder of the first French newspaper, *La Gazette*. A physician of enlightened views, he was involved in philanthropic activities such as providing free medicine for the poor. He was also the inventor of the Bureau d'Adresse et de Rencontre, an advertising center for people wishing to buy or sell things, offer or secure employment, or obtain information.

64 *"Zeno's doom"*: See Yourcenar's novel *The Abyss*. Zeno, the fictional central character, is a philosopher, alchemist, and physician living in sixteenth-century Flanders. The Angels are a group of monks and novices who are executed for their heretical practices. Zeno, though not a member of the group, is falsely implicated.

64 *"seventeenth-century Holland"*: The French text reads "la Hollande du XVIIIᵉ siècle," but this appears to be a typographical error, since Vermeer lived from 1632 to 1675.

65 *"Monsieur Jourdain's father"*: The allusion is to Molière's play *Le Bourgeois Gentilhomme* (1670), in which the valet Covielle facetiously tells M. Jourdain that Jourdain *père* was not a merchant but a gentleman: he had fine fabrics brought to his house and "gave them to his friends in exchange for money" (IV.5.31–33).

65 *"born in Cologne"*: Rubens was actually born in Siegen, Westphalia (today in western Germany), a small town in which his parents lived during their exile from Cologne.

66 *"famous straw hat"*: Yourcenar seems to be alluding to Rubens' well-known painting *Le Chapeau de Paille* (*The Straw Hat*). Yet this is generally taken to be a portrait not of Isabella Brant but of Susanna Fourment, Daniel's daughter.

66 *"sed aliqua esse quae potius sunt extra vitia quam cum virtutibus"*: "But there are some things which are free from faults, rather than possessing virtues" (Tacitus, *Historiae*, I.49).

69 *"all is order, luxury, calm, and sensual delight"*: The allusion is to Baudelaire's poem "Invitation au voyage": "Là, tout n'est qu'ordre et beauté, / Luxe, calme et volupté."

71 *"King Candaules"*: Greek name for King Sadyattes of Lydia (now northwest Turkey), who reigned ca. 700 B.C. According to legend, Candaules was so proud of his wife's beauty that he insisted on displaying her, nude, to his friend Gyges. He hid Gyges in a spot close to where his wife would undress, but she caught sight of the spy. In revenge, she gave Gyges the choice of either murdering her husband and becoming king or being put to death himself. Whether or not the legend is true, it is known that Gyges slew Candaules and reigned as king until about 652 B.C.

73 *"great-great-aunt"*: Yourcenar uses the term "arrière-grand-tante," but Helena Fourment was a good deal more distant than a great-great-aunt. They were separated by seven generations.

73 *"to whom none of our troubles or fears were alien"*: Yourcenar is alluding to the famous statement by Terence: "Homo sum; humani nil a me alienum puto" ("I am a man; I consider nothing human to be alien to me").

75 *"purchaser of Crayencour"*: Although the Crayencour estate was acquired by the Cleenewercks around 1700, and although Yourcenar refers to her eighteenth-century forebears as Crayencours, the name "de Crayencour" was not used officially until 1858. I am grateful to M. Georges de Crayencour for this information.

77 *"Bernis"*: François Joachim de Bernis (1715–94), cardinal and statesman. He served as minister of foreign affairs and as French ambassador to Venice and, later, to Rome.

78 *"Santerre"*: Antoine-Joseph Santerre, commander of the Paris National Guard during the French Revolution. When Louis XVI was about to be guillotined, Santerre ordered a drumroll to drown out the king's last words.

81 *"seventeenth of Nivôse, Year VIII"*: According to the French Revolutionary calendar (which was reckoned from September 22, 1792), this is the designation for January 8, 1800.

81 *"Year V"*: The year of the French Revolutionary calendar that ran from September 22, 1796, to September 22, 1797.

82 *"citoyenne"*: This French term and its masculine form *citoyen* (which mean "citizen") were much in vogue during the Revolutionary era. They served as democratic, politically correct forms of address, supplanting all aristocratic titles.

83 *"a marked Louis XIII–Charles X style"*: That is, built of brick, light-colored stone, and slate (thus having a striking red, white, and black façade), with lofty windows and a high, steeply pitched roof. The ornamentation is limited to quoins at the corners and

stone trim around the doors and windows. See the photographs of Mont-Noir in this volume.

89 *"Meditations"*: Lamartine's *Méditations poétiques* (1820), a collection of twenty-four odes and elegies, was immensely popular in its day. The poems are plaintive and melodious, and inaugurated a fashion for melancholy lyricism.

89 *"The Orientals"*: *Les Orientales* (1829) was Victor Hugo's fourth collection of poems; *Les Chants du crépuscule* (1835) was his sixth. Both volumes display the exoticism, sensuality, emotional intensity, and sympathy with nature that were the hallmarks of Romanticism.

89 *"Auguste Barbier"*: 1805–82; minor poet and satirist who enjoyed brief popularity in the 1830s for such verse collections as *Iambes* (on contemporary evils), *Il Pianto* (lamenting Italy's lost glory), and *Lazare* (impressions of England).

89 *"Casimir Delavigne"*: 1793–1843; French dramatist and poet whose works, especially his comedies, were widely admired in the 1820s and 1830s. His plays are transitional between the formal rigor of neoclassicism and the freedom of Romanticism.

89 *"Béranger"*: Pierre-Jean Béranger (1780–1857), author of lilting, witty, often satirical verses called *chansons*. Among his collections are *Chansons morales et autres* (1815) and *Chansons nouvelles* (1825). Though persecuted by the government for his political views, he was considered the national poet of France.

91 *"Frédéric Moreau"*: The hero of Gustave Flaubert's novel *L'Education sentimentale* (1869).

95 *"Citizen King"*: The name given to Louis-Philippe (1773–1850), who was crowned in 1830 as the elected king of a constitutional monarchy. His reign, which lasted until 1848 and which was known as the July Monarchy, marked the triumph of the wealthy bourgeoisie.

103 *"Illo tempore"*: Latin for "at that time" or "in those days." In the study of mythology and religion, *illo tempore* signifies the earliest days of the world—a time of purity and perfection in which the cosmos was created and in which the gods performed the archetypal acts on which human rituals would be based.

105 *"Paul de Kock"*: Charles-Paul de Kock (1794–1871), popular French novelist whose works were lively, amusing, often sentimental, and (more to the point here) risqué and even coarse. Among his many books were *Mon voisin Raymond* (1822) and *L'Amant de la lune* (1847).

108 *"Frohsdorf"*: That is, Charles-Augustin is a legitimist—a supporter of the senior branch of the Bourbon line, which included Charles X (reigned 1824–30) and Henri, comte de Chambord (his grandson). When Charles X was deposed in the July Revolution of 1830, he was succeeded by Louis-Philippe, a member of the cadet branch (descended from Louis XIV's brother), and the rule of the senior branch thus came to an end. But although Chambord never held the throne, he was known to legitimists as Henri V. He accompanied Charles X into exile and lived most of the rest of his life in Frohsdorf, Austria.

Translator's Notes

111 *"Diane de Cadignan"* and *"Esther"*: Beautiful courtesans, both characters in Balzac's *Comédie humaine*.

111 *"Guizot"*: François Guizot (1787–1874), historian and statesman. From 1812 to 1830 he was professor of modern history at the Sorbonne. During the July Monarchy (1830–48) he served as minister of education, ambassador to London, foreign minister, and prime minister. The conservative policies that he implemented under Louis-Philippe were largely responsible for the Revolution of 1848.

116 *"perhaps even their brother"*: Yourcenar is here alluding to Baudelaire's famous poem "Au Lecteur," which opens *Les Fleurs du mal* (1857). She is echoing its last line: "Hypocrite lecteur—mon semblable—mon frère!" ("Hypocrite reader—my double—my brother!")

119 *"Désaugiers"*: Marc-Antoine Désaugiers (1772–1827), author of popular comedies and vaudeville shows, as well as chansons and light verse similar in style to those of Béranger.

120 *"Prévert"*: Jacques Prévert (1900–77), popular French poet. His works range from the humorous to the satirical to the melancholy. Many of his poems and songs were sung in nightclubs before being collected and published, in volumes such as *Paroles* (1946) and *Spectacle* (1951). He also wrote important screenplays, including the one for Marcel Carné's film *Les Enfants du paradis* (1945).

121 *"Meta Sudans"*: Literally, "sweating milepost" or "sweating marker."

121 *"Belli"*: Giuseppe Gioacchino Belli (1791–1863), Italian poet whose realist works portrayed Roman life in colorful dialect. He composed more than two thousand humorous and satirical sonnets.

122 *"Dawn"* and *"Night"*: Two of the four allegorical figures (the others are *Day* and *Dusk*) that Michelangelo sculpted in the 1520s for the tombs of Giuliano and Lorenzo de' Medici. The tombs are located in the New Sacristy of the Church of San Lorenzo, Florence. The "tomb of the Grand Dukes" to which Yourcenar refers is the Princes Chapel of the same church, which contains the sarcophagi of six Medici Grand Dukes.

122 *"Faust, Part II"*: Goethe wrote the second part of his great philosophical drama *Faust* in 1832. Compared with the first part (1808), which he composed according to his notions of classical Greek regularity and perfection, it is more visionary and symbolic, and looser in form.

122 *"Hölderlin"*: Friedrich Hölderlin (1770–1843), German lyric poet considered a forerunner of Romanticism. His works are modeled on classical Greek literature, which he saw not as calm and restrained but as irrational and romantic. He went mad at the age of thirty-two.

122 *"Gérard de Nerval"*: Pseudonym of Gérard Labrunie (1808–55), an early French Romantic. Among his works are short stories, poems, essays, literary criticism, biographical sketches, travel narratives, and a translation of Goethe's *Faust*. His "Aurélia" is a hallucinatory record of the stages of his mental derangement, which began when he was thirty-three.

122 *"Maurice de Guérin"*: 1810–39; French author of poems, letters, journals, and prose fragments. His works are infused with Christian mysticism but are classical in form and full of sensuous evocations of pagan nature. His best-known work is the prose poem "Le Centaure."

123 *"Augustan History"*: In Latin, *Historia Augusta*—the name given to a late-fourth-century compendium containing the biographies of nine Roman emperors, from Hadrian to Caracalla, plus secondary *vitae* of a number of princes and pretenders. The document is a mixture of fact and fiction, and bears the names of six different authors, which may possibly be the pseudonyms of a single author. Its veracity, purpose, authorship, and precise date of composition have been the subject of much controversy.

125 *"Dying Gaul"*: Lifesize figure of a dying Celtic warrior, one of a number of statues made to commemorate the Greeks' defeat of the Gauls in Asia Minor in the late third century B.C. The version we know today is a Roman copy, in marble, of a Greek original that was executed in bronze around 225 B.C. The Gaul's wound may be self-inflicted, or he may simply have been mortally injured in battle. He is endowed with the dignity and heroic nudity of Greek warriors, indicating that the Greeks considered the Gauls worthy foes.

127 *"Winckelmann"*: Johann Joachim Winckelmann (1717–68), German classical archaeologist and art historian who lived much of his life in Italy. His major book was *Geschichte der Kunst des Altertums* (*History of Ancient Art*, 1764), which laid the foundations for modern scientific archaeology. He was murdered at a hotel in Trieste by a man named Arcangeli, who is said to have been trying to steal some valuable coins.

128 *"Lorenzaccio"*: Historical drama by Alfred de Musset, published in 1834. The play is set in Florence and concerns the assassination of the city's evil ruler by the virtuous young Lorenzo de' Medici, who becomes corrupted in the course of carrying out his plans.

129 *"war in Eritrea"*: In the latter part of the nineteenth century, Italy, Egypt, and Ethiopia fought for control of Eritrea. Italy gradually extended its territory and declared Eritrea a colony, but lost control of it in World War II. Today it is a province in northern Ethiopia.

129 *"Triple Alliance"*: In 1882 Italy signed a treaty of mutual defense with Germany and Austria-Hungary. This was followed, in 1887, by an agreement linking the three Mediterranean powers, Italy, Austria-Hungary, and Great Britain. Both accords were oriented against France and Russia.

129 *"Ardeantine mass graves"*: On March 24, 1944, in the caves of the Via Ardeantina near Rome, members of the German Army shot 335 political and Jewish prisoners in retaliation for an attack that the Italian Resistance had mounted the day before. The Resistance had fired on a German column in the Via Rasella and killed thirty-two soldiers. The Nazis' policy was to shoot ten Italians for every German killed.

129 *"Ciano"*: Nobile Galeazzo Ciano (1903–44), foreign minister of Italy and Benito Mussolini's son-in-law. Mussolini had him shot as a traitor.

132 *"Empedocles"*: Greek philosopher of the early fifth century B.C., born in Sicily. He taught that everything is composed of four essential substances (earth, air, fire, and water), believed in the transmigration of souls, and claimed to have worked miracles. It is said that he cast himself into the crater of Mount Etna (*mors ignea* = "fiery death"), to fool people into thinking he'd been taken up to heaven, but that the volcano spoiled the plan by spewing up one of his bronze sandals.

137 *"Luini"*: Bernardino Luini (c. 1480–1532), Italian painter of religious, mythological, and allegorical subjects whose style was heavily influenced by that of Leonardo da Vinci.

138 *"Canova"*: Antonio Canova (1757–1822), Italian sculptor of the neoclassical school. His large statues and bas-reliefs had great influence on the art of his day. Among his sculptures are portraits of Napoleon I and of George Washington which depict them as classical Romans.

138 *"Thorvaldsen"*: Albert Bertel Thorvaldsen (1770–1844), Danish sculptor. Along with Canova, he was one of the leading neoclassicists in Rome in the early 1800s; many American sculptors of the period studied with him. His works treat historical, religious, and mythological subjects.

141 *"Lido"*: A long, narrow, sandy island that separates the lagoon of Venice from the Adriatic. Today it is one of Europe's most popular beaches.

141 *"Clarens"*: A small town in the foothills of the Swiss Alps that is the setting for Jean-Jacques Rousseau's epistolary novel *Julie, ou la Nouvelle Héloïse* (1761), which tells of the love between Julie d'Etanges and her tutor Saint-Preux.

141 *"Klopstock"*: Friedrich Gottlieb Klopstock (1724–1803), German lyric poet and dramatist whose work had an important influence on Goethe. Many of his odes have been set to music by Beethoven, Schubert, Mahler, and others.

141 *"Hégésippe Moreau"*: 1810–38; minor Romantic poet whose best poems are descriptions of country life and who is remembered chiefly for his collection *Le Myosotis* (1838).

146 *"Henri V"*: See note to page 108, s. v. "Frohsdorf."

156 *"had guts"*: The idiom Michel-Charles uses here is "avait du poil au bon endroit" ("had hair in the right place").

158 *"Cavaignac"*: Louis-Eugène Cavaignac (1802–57), French general. After the Revolution of 1848, he became minister of war and harshly suppressed the workers' uprising in June of that year.

158 *"Changarnier"*: Nicolas Changarnier (1793–1877), French general and politician. After the Revolution of 1848, he was elected to the National Assembly, but resigned after the June uprising to become head of the Paris national guard. He later assumed command of all the regular army troops in Paris.

158 *"Louis-Napoleon"*: Louis-Napoleon Bonaparte (1808–73), nephew of Napoleon I. In 1848 he was elected president of the Second Republic and in 1852 was crowned head of the Second Empire as Napoleon III. He was forced to liberalize his regime in 1860 and was deposed in 1870 during the Franco-Prussian War.

173 *"Farmers General"*: A private tax company that, under the ancien régime, contracted with the crown to advance a specific sum to the Treasury in return for the right to "farm" certain indirect taxes (e.g., on salt, tobacco, leather, soap) and customs duties (especially on wine). It was also involved in the production, pricing, distribution, and marketing of many of the commodities it taxed. The company was brutal and larcenous, and became a focus of hatred during the Revolution. The members of the Farmers General amassed huge fortunes, which they sometimes used to promote literature and the arts. The book referred to here would have been a deluxe edition of Jean de la Fontaine's *Fables*, first published in 1668.

175 *"had real bacchic spirit"*: The cousin uses the word *évohé*—a term derived from classical Latin. The Romans supposedly cried *"Euhoe!"* during their orgies, to invoke Bacchus.

176 *"Bugeaud"*: Thomas Robert Bugeaud de la Piconnerie (1784–1849), French general and politician. In Algeria in the early 1840s he defeated the resistance and served as governor-general, but his repressive policies led to his resignation.

177 *"Condillac"*: Etienne de Condillac (1715–80), French philosopher. He extended Locke's ideas on the relationship between human faculties and sensations, and held that logical reasoning could be rigorously and precisely applied to problems of metaphysics, morals, and language.

177 *"La Fille Elisa"*: Naturalist novel, written by Edmond de Goncourt in 1877, about a girl who becomes a prostitute, murders her soldier-lover, and goes mad in prison. The book contains a grim critique of the French prison system.

178 *"Orleanism"*: After the revolution of February 1848, the Monarchist Party was divided into legitimists and Orleanists. The latter were supporters of the younger (Orléans) branch of the royal family, descended from Louis XIV's brother. The legitimists were supporters of the senior (Bourbon) branch, which included Charles X and Henri, comte de Chambord.

179 *"Doña Sol"*: Heroine of *Hernani* (1830), a verse drama by Victor Hugo.

182 *"Compiègne"*: Town in northern France; ancient site of royal gatherings and, from the seventeenth century to the nineteenth, the summer residence of the French kings.

182 *"Sedan"*: Town in northeastern France; site of Napoleon III's defeat and capture in 1870, during the Franco-Prussian War.

188 *"Fouquet"*: Jean Fouquet (c. 1420–c. 1480), French painter and illuminator, court painter to Charles VII and Louis XI.

188 *"Roger van der Weyden"*: c. 1400–64; known in French as Roger de la Pasture. Flemish painter famed for his ability to portray subtle emotions. He did a number of portraits (Philip the Good, Charles the Bold) and many religious paintings, the best known of which is his *Descent from the Cross* (c. 1435).

209 *"the grieving mother in Hugo's poem"*: The reference is to Victor Hugo's poem "Le Revenant," in his collection *Les Contemplations*, Vol. 1: *Autrefois, 1830–1843* (Book 3, poem 23). The poem tells of a mother who believes that her newborn son is the reincarnation of her firstborn, who died when he was three.

212 *"Fermina Marquez"*: Short novel written by Valery Larbaud in 1910. The setting is a boys' school just outside Paris, and the story describes how the students are affected when two girls from Bogotá, Colombia, the sisters of a new pupil, arrive in the neighborhood.

212 *"The Land Whose King Is a Child"*: Play written by Henry de Montherlant in 1951 (in French, *La Ville dont le prince est un enfant*). It is a study of sacred and profane love, involving two teenage students and a priest, at a Catholic boys' school in Paris. The title comes from Ecclesiastes 10:16: "Woe to thee, O land, when thy king is a child."

219 *"game of goose"*: Game played with tokens in the form of geese, on a box containing sixty-three compartments. The players roll dice to move their tokens through the box. The last compartment is the Goose's Garden, and the player who gets there first is the winner.

222 *"Terrible Year"*: The phrase refers to 1870, a year of disasters for France. The nation was soundly defeated in the Franco-Prussian War. Napoleon III himself was captured at the battle of Sedan on September 1, his armies lost the will to fight, and the Parisians suffered great hardships during a four-month siege and bombardment of their city. Victor Hugo's *L'Année terrible* (1872) is a collection of poems inspired by those events.

223 *"Paul Cambon"*: Pierre Paul Cambon (1843–1924), French diplomat. He served as ambassador to Great Britain (1898–1920) and helped negotiate important international agreements.

225 *"Commune"*: Class antagonism, which had intensified in France under the repressive policies of the Second Empire, erupted after the country's defeat in the Franco-Prussian War. In March 1871 rebellious workers declared Paris an autonomous Commune. After seventy-three days the French Army brutally suppressed the uprising, with a loss of 25,000 lives.

225 *"Faubourg Saint-Antoine"*: Old working-class suburb of Paris. It was the scene of heavy fighting on makeshift barricades during the French Revolution and the workers' uprisings of the nineteenth century.

227 *"Loves of the Chevalier de Faublas"*: In French, *Les Amours du Chevalier de Faublas* (1790), a novel by Jean-Baptiste Louvet de Couvray that recounts the amorous exploits of an amiable young rake.

230 *"Badinguet"*: Nickname of Louis-Napoleon, who became Napoleon III. In 1846 he escaped from the fortress of Ham (north of Paris, near Amiens) disguised as a workman named Badinguet.

230 *"Pierre Leroux"*: Lived 1797–1871; philosopher, economist, and idealistic social reformer who helped found the *Revue Indépendante* (1841). Among his works are *De l'égalité* (1838) and *De l'humanité, de son principe et de son avenir* (1840).

230 *"Proudhon"*: Pierre-Joseph Proudhon (1809–65), French social theorist, writer, and reformer. His first important work was *Qu'est-ce que la propriété* (1840), which began with the famous statement "La propriété, c'est le vol" ("Property is theft").

232 *"La Trappe"*: Abbey founded in 1140 at Mortagne, west of Paris near Alençon. The

monastery, a branch of the Cistercian order, was reformed around 1664 by Armand de Rancé. Trappists, noted for their austerity, live in strict seclusion from the world and devote their days to worship, labor, and study.

239 *"MacMahon"*: Marie-Edmé-Patrice de MacMahon (1808–93), marshal of France and president of the Republic (1873–79). He aided in the bloody suppression of the Commune of Paris in 1871. When he was president his monarchist tendencies had to be curbed repeatedly by the Chamber of Deputies, and he eventually resigned as a result of the conflicts.

241 *"Théophile Gautier"*: 1811–72; poet, novelist, art critic, and journalist, an ardent exponent of Romanticism and of "art for art's sake." He was a leading member of the group of poets known as the Parnassians, who strove for painterly clarity and perfection in their verbal compositions.

241 *"Rolla"*: Long poem written by Alfred de Musset in 1833, heavily influenced by Byron. It is the lyrical description of a "child of the times" and was viewed as a landmark of Romantic sensibility.

242 *"Deux-Sèvres"*: The town of Niort, near La Rochelle in western France, is the capital of the *département* of Deux-Sèvres.

243 *"La Belle Hélène"*: Light, amusing operetta composed by Jacques Offenbach in 1864. In every way, it is the antithesis of Wagner's *Die Walküre* (1854–56).

243 *"Princes of Youth"*: Under the First Empire, the Princes de la Jeunesse were princes of the imperial family whom the emperor Napoleon I designated to lead all the senators' sons on ceremonial occasions.

248 *"Tobias"*: Central character of the book of Tobit in the Apocrypha. Tobias is a young man who, with the Archangel Raphael's help, exorcises a demon from a young woman and cures his father's blindness.

249 *"Venusberg"*: Mountain near Eisenach that in German legend was symbolic of sensual passion. Venus was reputed to hold court in its caverns, enticing and virtually imprisoning people (such as Tannhäuser) with music and revelry.

253 *"anywhere at all"*: An allusion to a prose poem by Baudelaire titled "Anywhere Out of the World (N'importe où hors du monde)."

263 *"Ouida"*: Pseudonym of Louise de la Ramée (1839–1908), English novelist. Her lively, romantic stories include *Under Two Flags* (1867) and *In Maremma* (1882).

264 *"Irving"*: Sir Henry Irving (1838–1905), English actor who specialized in realist melodramas. From 1878 to 1903 he was manager of the Lyceum Theatre, London, where Ellen Terry was his leading lady.

279 *"Fées"*: The actual name of the estate was Le Fay. "Fées" translates as "fairies."

279 *"Marie de S."*: The French edition here reads "Marie de P.," but in *Quoi? L'Eternité* Yourcenar gives Marie's married name as Marie de Sacy.

280 *"La Tour"*: Maurice Quentin de La Tour (1704–88), French portraitist who worked in pastel. His subjects included Louis XV, Madame de Pompadour, Voltaire, and Rousseau.

280 *"La Légende des siècles"*: Epic poems by Victor Hugo, composed in three series (1859, 1877, and 1883). The poems portray humankind's spiritual and historical development, beginning with the Creation.

283 *"De Dion–Bouton"*: The firm of De Dion–Bouton, founded in 1893 by Albert de Dion and Georges Bouton, played an important part in the emerging automobile industry. Its earliest car, actually a three-wheeled motorcycle, was the most popular low-priced motor vehicle in France and England at the turn of the century. In 1899 the company began to manufacture a four-wheeled vehicle, the first of many. Michel-Joseph's *voiture* may have been any of De Dion–Bouton's early models.

289 *"Murad"*: There were five Ottoman sultans named Murad, beginning in the fourteenth century. Murad V (1840–1904) reigned for only one year (1876) before being declared insane.

297 *"Bertha of the Big Foot"*: Bertrada (d. 783), Frankish queen, wife of Pepin the Short and mother of Charlemagne. As Bertha of the Big Foot or Queen Goosefoot, she is a figure in Carolingian legend.

298 *"the 48th de marche"*: In the French Army, during the Franco-Prussian War, *régiments de marche* were composite regiments formed in wartime and made up principally of new recruits, along with a few reservists, volunteers, and veterans.

298 *"Gravelotte"*: Town in eastern France, near Metz, where French forces under Marshal Bazaine were defeated by the Prussians on August 18, 1870.

299 *"Chamilly"*: Noël Bouton de Chamilly, comte de Saint-Léger (1635–1715), French officer who fought in the Portuguese war of independence against Spain. He is said to have been the lover of Mariana Alcoforado, a nun of the convent of Beja in the province of Alemtejo, Portugal. Her letters to him were published in French translation (*Lettres Portugaises*, 1669) and were immensely popular. It has since been shown that the "translator," Gabriel de Lavergne, vicomte de Guilleragues, was in fact the author.

301 *"Bouvines"*: Town in northern France where Philippe-Auguste (Philippe II) defeated Otto IV, Holy Roman Emperor and German king, in 1214.

302 *"Borda"*: The school for cadets in the French naval academy. It is named after Jean-Charles Borda (1733–99), French mathematician and engineer who contributed to the advancement of nautical science.

309 *"Felix Krull"*: Gambler and adventurer, hero of Thomas Mann's *Bekenntnisse des Hochstaplers Felix Krull*, or *Confessions of Felix Krull, Confidence Man* (1954).

311 *"La Belle Otero"*: Caroline Otero (1869–1965), Spanish dancer and actress, and one of the most flamboyant courtesans of the Belle Epoque. She achieved success at the Folies-Bergère in the 1890s, performed all over Europe and several times in New York, and amassed a fortune from her many lovers, who included Kaiser Wilhelm II, Alfonso XIII of Spain, Nicholas II of Russia, the Prince of Wales (later Edward VII), Leopold II of Belgium, and (in New York) William K. Vanderbilt and Joseph Kennedy, Sr. She gambled away her money and died in poverty at the age of ninety-seven. Her

rival, Emilienne d'Alençon, who likewise performed at the Folies-Bergère, was notorious for her many love affairs with women as well as men.

312 *"Mrs. Warren"*: Central character in George Bernard Shaw's play *Mrs. Warren's Profession*, a satirical treatment of society's views of prostitution.

318 *"isba"*: In Russia, a hut or lodge made of logs.

324 *"Retz"*: Paul de Gondi, cardinal de Retz (1614–79). His *Mémoires* give a clear and vivid account of the political events of his day, and are filled with incisive portraits and aphorisms.

324 *"Willy"*: In 1900–3 Colette wrote a series of popular novels with her husband Henri Gauthier-Villars; the novels were published under the pen name "Willy." From 1904 to 1916, Colette wrote under the name of "Colette Willy"; thereafter she used simply "Colette."

324 *"Lugné-Poë"*: Aurélien-François Lugné-Poë (1869–1940), actor and producer at the Théâtre Libre and the Théâtre d'Art (later the Théâtre de l'Oeuvre) in Paris.

330 *"Claude Frollo"*: Character in Victor Hugo's novel *Notre-Dame de Paris* (1831), which takes place in fifteenth-century Paris. Frollo, the Faustian archdeacon of Notre-Dame, is an austere and intransigent man who makes other people suffer for his inner torments. He dabbles in the black arts and believes in fatality and predestination.

336 *"Carlo Dolci"*: 1616–86; Florentine painter. His most famous works are studies in sorrow and suffering (Christ, Saint Cecilia, Saint Sebastian, Mary Magdalen, and the Mater Dolorosa).

336 *"Guido Reni"*: 1575–1642; Italian painter and engraver, a rival of Caravaggio. He did decorative frescoes for many palaces and churches, most notably the Cathedral of Ravenna.

346 *"Landseer"*: Sir Edwin Henry Landseer (1802–1873), English painter best known for his anthropomorphic portrayals of animals, especially dogs.

346 *"Bouguereau"*: Adolphe William Bouguereau (1825–1905), French academic painter of historical and religious subjects, known for his elegant nudes.

346 *"Moustiers"*: Type of faïence (earthenware colored with opaque glazes) made in Moustiers-Sainte-Marie, a town in the lower French Alps that was famous for this ware in the seventeenth and eighteenth centuries.

347 *"Drumont"*: Edouard Drumont (1844–1917), French journalist and anti-Semitic leader, influential during the Dreyfus affair.

356 *"Giralda"*: Tower adjoining the cathedral of Seville, Spain; built 1163–84 as a minaret to the mosque that originally occupied the site. It takes its name from the *giraldilla*, or weathervane, that adorned its peak.